ENVIRONMENTAL INSIGHT

Robert M. Chute *Bates College*

ENVIRONMENTAL INSIGHT
readings and comment on human and nonhuman nature

Harper & Row, Publishers
New York / Evanston / San Francisco / London

To teach I would build a trap such that,
to escape, my students must learn

CONTENTS

PREFACE

I am assuming that most people who read this book will be undergraduates who do not intend to be professional biologists. The articles and editorial comment may, I hope, be of interest and value to others as well, but it is to those students who are usually given the negative title of "nonmajors" that this book is directed.

To these students the biology instructor has a special responsibility. He is often their one chance to gain some biological insight—to see themselves from a biological point of view. All subjects in the curriculum, once their direct professional relevance is subtracted, are truly educational insofar as they enlarge man's perspective of himself and his relationships. The contribution of the science of biology to the general education of its students is not the demonstration of a unique method of study. Its contribution is a content of ideas, concepts, and observations which can forever change the way one looks at one's self and surroundings. The same holds for the other sciences and the subsciences, such as ecology, which make up Biology.

The authors of the articles which follow and the editors of the various periodicals in which the articles were originally published have my sincerest thanks. This book is built of their efforts. I hope the pattern into which I have arranged their contributions will not diminish the value of their work in either their opinion or yours.

ROBERT M. CHUTE

ENVIRONMENTAL INSIGHT

INTRODUCTION

These original papers in environmental science have been selected to fit
within a preconceived outline. The objective has been to present the
beginning student with a series of research reports and review papers
which lead to a greater insight into the relationship of man to nonhuman
nature. The collection thus has an unabashed bias and is not designed
to be an introduction to the broad field of ecology. The papers and the
integrated editorial comment support the position that the problems
arising from man's relationship with his environment cannot be solved
by science and technology alone. Biological insight is necessary to the
development of solutions but not sufficient in itself.

Major emphasis is placed on the fact that man, like other animals, is
part of a system, an ecosystem, and is a part of many interlocking cycles
for the utilization of energy, water, and elements. Man can understand
his relationship to his environment only if he realizes his role, and his
responsibilities, in the system and the cycles of which he is a part.

Over the past two decades an increasing number of environmental
scientists have been warning of an impending crisis. Man's proliferating
technology supports an exploding population. How long can it be before
these waves of expansion crash against the limits of a world of finite
resources and space? With few exceptions the various prophets of
environmental crisis differ only with respect to the time they expect the
situation to become critical. A minority presume that some natural control
mechanism will intervene to limit human reproduction and modify
human behavior in an appropriate manner. That such changes must occur
is evident. It is far from certain that they will occur soon enough or
that they will occur "automatically" without conscious individual effort
and concerted social action.

The area illuminated by these readings is no sterile, academic discipline.
The original authors may not have intended it to be so, but these papers
can be a guide to an understanding of a critical human problem. They
can serve as part of the basis for some of the most important social
decisions yet made by man. As such, the concepts they express should be
part of the working knowledge of all people.

The great social significance of the articles included in this book does
not distract from their value to the pre-professional student. Neither can
their discussion from a professional viewpoint do more than enhance
their human value. The papers selected are intended to be illustrative
rather than definitive treatments. They are presented, not because they
are all "classical" studies, but because they should be interesting and
provocative. The bibliographies included with most of the papers will

1

provide an introduction into a much wider area of the man–nature problem.

Editorial comments accompanying the papers may be different in intent from those of the original authors. For this reason I have presented the papers in their entirety, so the authors' words may occasionally refute my arguments. The comments, and the inclusion of some interpretive and "nonscientific" material, are designed to allow the readers to carry the discussion as far beyond the conventional limits of biology as they wish. As surely as biology can offer insight into the nature of the critical environmental problems facing man, so the solution of these problems must involve an approach in which the perspectives of the humanities, the social sciences, and the natural sciences are fully integrated.

PART ONE

MAN IN/AND/OR NATURE

> . . . For I have learned
> To look on nature, not as in the hour
> Of thoughtless youth; but hearing oftentimes
> The still, sad music of humanity,
> Nor harsh nor grating, though of ample power
> To chasten and subdue . . .
>
> *William Wordsworth*
> Lines Composed a Few Miles Above Tintern
> Abby, on Revisiting the Banks of the Wye Dur-
> ing a Tour, July 13, 1798

In The Tragedy of the Commons *Garrett Hardin gives us a metaphor to illuminate one of the major problems of man in nature. The finite resources of the world, the limited material basis for life, is the commons which all organisms, including man, must share. The tragedy is the seeming inability of man to administer limited resources in an equitable way. The problem is made critical, according to Hardin, by an unchecked growth in the human population. In fact, the growth of our population may be said to be the problem, because it is this growth which renders the existing restrictions and regulations on the use of the commons inadequate. As a further aggravation of the dilemma of freedom or restriction in the use of the commons, an exploding technology gives each member of the increasing population a greater power to consume, alter, or destroy.*

All this becomes the concern of a biologist because the problem must be assessed in terms of the biological potential of the species for reproduction and a determination of those natural resources which are needed for all life and thus must be shared by all who live. These assessments cannot be simple and anthropocentric because man's existence is related, with varying degrees of dependency, to the existence of a multitude of nonhuman organisms. Thus decisions regarding the administration of the commons must involve "justice" for many forms of life and not for man alone.

It is easy to assume that the problems arising from man's relationship to nature, once recognized, can be solved by the same powerful technology that helps to create the problems. It is a main theme of Hardin's article that the tragedy of the commons represents one of a class of problems for which there is no technological solution—if we define "technical" to involve only the techniques of the natural sciences.

Of course, the power of technology can be used to restore or to repair the environment, but the decision to use technology in this fashion and not in some other must first be motivated. And the directors of technology must be informed of limits of the natural world and about the ecology of man. Knowledge of man's physical and biological relationship to the environment must be coupled with moral and social determination of the "proper" relationship of man to his environment and of man to man.

THE TRAGEDY OF THE COMMONS

Garrett Hardin

At the end of a thoughtful article on the future of nuclear war, Jerome Wiesner and Herbert York[1] concluded that: "Both sides in the arms race are . . . confronted by the dilemma of steadily increasing military power and steadily decreasing national security. *It is our considered professional judgment that this dilemma has no technical solution.* If the great powers continue to look for solutions in the area of science and technology only, the result will be to worsen the situation."

I would like to focus your attention not on the subject of the article (national security in a nuclear world) but on the *kind* of conclusion they reached, namely that there is no "technical solution" to the problem. An implicit and almost universal assumption of discussions published in professional and semipopular scientific journals is that the problem under discussion has a "technical solution." A technical solution may be defined as one that requires a change only in the techniques of the natural sciences, demanding little or nothing in the way of change in human values or ideas of morality.

In our day (though not in earlier times) technical solutions are always welcome. Because of previous failures in prophecy it takes courage to assert that a desired technical solution is not possible. Wiesner and York exhibited this courage; publishing in a science journal they insisted that the solution to the problem was not to be found in the natural sciences. They cautiously qualified their statement with the phrase, "It is our considered professional judgment. . . ." Whether they were right or not is not the concern of the present article. Rather, the concern here is with the important concept of a class of human problems which can be called "no technical solution problems"; and more specifically, with the identification and discussion of one of these.

It is easy to show that the class is not a null class. Recall the game of tick-tack-toe. Consider the problem, "How can I win the game of tick-tack-toe?" It is well known that I cannot, if I assume (in keeping with the conventions of game theory) that my opponent understands the game perfectly. Put another way, there is no "technical solution" to the problem. I can win only by giving a radical meaning to the word "win." I can hit my opponent over the head; or I can drug him; or I can falsify the records. Every way in which I "win" involves, in some sense, an aban-

Reprinted with permission from *Science*, Vol. 162, 1968, pp. 1243–1248. Copyright 1968 by the American Association for the Advancement of Science. The author is Professor of Human Ecology at the University of California at Santa Barbara.

donment of the *game*, as we intuitively understand it. (I can also, of course, openly abandon the game—refuse to play it. This is what most adults do.)

The class of "No technical solution problems" has members. It is the thesis of the present article that the "population problem" as conventionally conceived, is a member of this class. How it is conventionally conceived needs some comment. I think it is fair to say that most people who anguish over the population problem are trying to find a way to avoid the evils of overpopulation without relinquishing any of the privileges they now enjoy. They think that farming the seas or developing new strains of wheat will solve the problem—technologically. I shall try to show here that the solution they seek cannot be found. The population problem cannot be solved in a technical way, any more than can the problem of winning the game of tick-tack-toe.

WHAT SHALL WE MAXIMIZE?

Population, as Malthus said, naturally tends to grow "geometrically"; or as we would say, exponentially. In a finite world this means that the per capita share of the world's goods must steadily decrease. Is ours a finite world?

A fair defense can be put forward for the view that the world is infinite; or that we don't know that it isn't. But, in terms of the practical problems we must face in the next few generations with the foreseeable technology, it is clear that we will greatly increase human misery if we do not, during the immediate future, assume that the world *available to the terrestrial human population is finite.* "Space" is no escape.[2]

A finite world can support only a finite population; therefore, population growth must eventually equal zero. (The case of perpetual wide fluctuations above and below zero is a trivial variant that need not be discussed.) When this condition is met, what will be the situation of mankind? Specifically, can Bentham's goal of "the greatest good for the greatest number" be realized?

No—for two reasons, each sufficient by itself. The first is a theoretical one. It is not mathematically possible to maximize for two (or more) variables at the same time. This was clearly stated by von Neumann and Morgenstern,[3] but the principle is implicit in the theory of partial differential equations, dating back at least to D'Alembert (1717–1783).

The second reason springs directly from biological facts. To live, any organism must have a source of energy (e.g., food). This enregy is utilized for two purposes: mere maintenance, and work. For man, maintenance of life requires about 1,600 kilocalories a day ("maintenance calories"). Anything that he does over and above merely staying alive will be defined as work, and is supported by "work calories," which he takes in. Work calories are used not only for what we call work in common speech; they are also required for all forms of enjoyment, from gormandizing and automobile racing to playing music and writing poetry. If our goal is to maximize population it is obvious what we must do: we must make the work calories per person approach as close to zero as possible. No gourmet meals, no vacations, no sports, no music, no literature, no art. . . . I think everyone will grant, without argument or proof, that maximizing population does not maximize goods. Bentham's goal is impossible.

In reaching this conclusion I have made the usual assumption that it is the acquisition of energy that is the problem. The appearance of atomic energy has led some to question this assumption. Given an infinite source of energy, however, population growth still produces an inescapable problem. The problem of the acquisition of energy is replaced by the problem of its dissipation, as J. H. Fremlin has so wittily shown.[4] The arithmetic signs in the analysis are, as it were, reversed; but Bentham's goal is still unattainable.

The optimum population is, then, less than the maximum. The difficulty of defining the optimum is enormous; so far as I know no one has seriously tackled this problem. Reaching an acceptable and stable solution will surely require more than one generation of hard analytical work; and much persuasion.

We want the maximum good per person; but what is "good"? To one person it is wilderness, to another it is ski lodges for thousands. To one it is estuaries to nourish ducks for hunters to shoot at; to another it is factory land. Comparing one good with another is, we usually say, impossible because goods are incommensurable. Incommensurables cannot be compared.

Theoretically this may be true; but in real life *incommensurables are commensurable*. All that is needed is a criterion of judgment and a system of weighting. In nature the criterion is survival. Is it better for a species to be small and hideable, or large and powerful? Natural selection commensurates the incommensurables. The compromise achieved depends on a natural weighting of the values of the variables.

Man must imitate this process. There is no doubt that in fact he already does, but unconsciously. It is when the hidden decisions are made explicit that the arguments begin. The problem for the years ahead is to work out an acceptable theory of weighting. Synergistic effects, nonlinear variation, and difficulties in discounting the future make the intellectual problem difficult, but not (in principle) insoluble.

Has any cultural group solved this practical problem at the present time, even on an intuitive level? One simple fact proves that none has: there is no prosperous population in the world today that has, and has had for some time, a growth rate of zero. Any people that has intuitively identified its optimum point will soon reach it, after which its growth rate becomes and remains zero.

Of course, a positive growth rate might be taken as evidence that a population is below its optimum. It is widely recognized, however, that, by any reasonable standards, the most rapidly growing populations on earth today are (in general) the most miserable. This association (which need not be invariable) casts doubt on the optimistic assumption that the positive growth rate of a population is evidence that it has yet to reach its optimum.

We can make little progress in working toward optimum population size until we explicitly exorcize the spirit of Adam Smith in the field of practical demography. In economic affairs, *The Wealth of Nations* (1776) popularized the "invisible hand," the idea that an individual who "intends only his own gain," is, as it were, "led by an invisible hand to promote . . . the public interest."[5] Adam Smith did not assert that this was invariably true, and perhaps neither did any of his followers. But he contributed to a dominant tendency of thought that has ever since interfered with positive action based on rational analysis, namely the tendency to assume that decisions reached individually will, in fact, be the best decisions for an entire society. If this assumption is correct it justifies the continuance of our present policy of *laissez-faire* in reproduction. If it is correct we can assume that men will control their individual fecundity so as to produce the optimal population. If the assumption is not correct, we need to re-examine our individual freedoms to see which ones are defensible.

TRAGEDY OF FREEDOM IN A COMMONS

The rebuttal to the "invisible hand" in population control is to be found in a "scenario" first sketched in a little known pamphlet[6] in 1833 by a mathematical amateur named William Forster Lloyd (1794–1852). We may well call it "The Tragedy of the Commons," using the word "tragedy" as the philosopher Whitehead used it:[7] "The essence of dramatic tragedy is not unhappiness. It resides in the solemnity of the remorseless working of things." He then goes on to say: "This inevitableness of destiny can only be illustrated in terms of human life by incidents which in fact involve unhappiness. For it is only by them that the futility of escape can be made evident in the drama."

The tragedy of the commons develops in this way. Picture a pasture open to all. It is to be expected that each herdsman will try to keep as many cattle as possible on the commons. Such an arrangement may work reasonably satisfactorily for centuries because tribal wars, poaching, and disease keep the numbers of both man and beast well below the "carrying capacity" of the land. Finally, however, comes the day of reckoning, i.e., the day when the long-desired social stability becomes a reality. At this point, the inherent logic of the commons remorselessly generates tragedy.

As a rational being each herdsman seeks to maximize his gain. Explicitly or implicitly, more or less consciously, he asks: "What is the utility *to me* of adding one more animal to my herd?" This utility has two components:

1. A positive component, which is a function of the increment of one animal. Since the herdsman receives all the proceeds from the sale of the additional animal, the positive utility is nearly +1.
2. A negative component, which is a function of the additional overgrazing created by one more animal. But since the effects of overgrazing are shared by all the herdsmen, the negative utility for any particular decision-making herdsman is only a fraction of −1.

Adding together the component partial utilities, the rational herdsman concludes that the only sensible course for him to pursue is to add another animal to his herd. And another; and another . . . But this is the conclusion reached by each and every rational herdsman sharing a commons. Therein is the tragedy. Each man is *locked in* to a system that compels him to increase his herd without limit—in a world that is limited. Ruin is the destination toward which all men rush, each pursuing his own best interest in a society that believes in the freedom of the commons. *Freedom in a commons brings ruin to all.*

Some would say that this is platitudinous, that is, a truth known to all. Would that it were! In a sense it was learned thousands of years ago, but natural selection favors the forces of psychological denial. The individual benefits *as an individual* from his ability to deny the truth even though society as a whole, of which he is a part, suffers. Education can counteract the natural tendency to do the wrong thing, but the inexorable succession of generations requires that the basis for this knowledge be constantly refreshed.

A simple incident that occurred a few years ago in Leominster, Massachusetts, shows how perishable the knowledge is. During the Christmas shopping season the parking meters downtown were covered with plastic bags that bore tags reading: "Do not open until after Christmas. Free parking courtesy of the mayor and city council." In other words, facing the prospect of an increased demand for already scarce space, the city fathers reinstituted the system of the commons. (Cynically, we suspect that they gained more votes than they lost by this retrogressive act.)

In an approximate way, the logic of the commons has been understood for a long time, perhaps since the discovery of agriculture or the invention of private property in real estate. But it is understood mostly only in special cases, which are not sufficiently generalized. Even at this late date, cattlemen leasing national land on the western ranges demonstrate no more than an ambivalent understanding, constantly pressuring federal authorities to increase the head-count to the point where overgrazing produces erosion and weed-dominance. Similarly, the oceans of the world continue to suffer from the survival of the philosophy of the commons. Maritime nations still respond automatically to the shibboleth of the "freedom of the seas." Professing to believe in the "inexhaustible resources of the oceans," they bring species after species of fish and whales closer to extinction.[8]

The National Parks present another instance of the working out of the tragedy of the commons. At present, they are open to all, without limit. The Parks themselves are limited in extent—there is only one Yosemite Valley—while population seems to grow without limit. The values that visitors seek in the Parks are steadily eroded. Plainly, we must soon cease to treat the Parks as commons or they will be of no value to anyone.

What shall we do? We have several options. We might sell them off as private property. We might keep them as public property, but allocate the right to enter them. The allocation might be on the basis of wealth, using an auction system. It might be on the basis of merit, as defined by some agreed-upon standards. It might be by lottery. Or it might be on a first-come, first-served basis, administered to long queues. These, I think, are all the reasonable possibilities. They are all objectionable. *But we must choose*—or acquiesce in the destruction of the commons that we call our National Parks.

POLLUTION

In a reverse way, the tragedy of the commons reappears in problems of pollution. Here it is not a question of taking something out of the commons, but of putting something in—sewage, or chemical, radioactive and heat wastes into water; noxious and dangerous fumes into the air; and distracting and unpleasant advertizing signs into the line of sight. The utility calculations are much the same as before. The rational man finds that his share of the cost of the wastes he discharges into the commons is less than the cost of purifying his wastes before releasing them. Since this is true for everyone, we are locked into a system of "fouling our own nest," so long as we behave only as independent, rational, free-enterprizers.

The tragedy of the commons as a foodbasket is averted by private property, or something formally like it. But the air and waters surrounding us cannot readily be fenced, and so the tragedy of the commons as a cesspool must be prevented by different means, by coercive laws or taxing devices that make it cheaper for the polluter to treat his pollutants than to discharge them untreated. We have not progressed as far with the solution of this problem as we have with the first. Indeed, our particular concept of private property, which deters us from exhausting the positive resources of the earth, favors pollution. The owner of a factory on the bank of a stream—whose "property" extends to the middle of the stream—often has difficulty seeing why it is not his natural "right" to muddy the waters flowing past his door. The law, always behind the times, requires elaborate stitching and fitting to mold it to his newly perceived aspect of the commons.

The pollution problem is a consequence of population. It did not much matter how a lonely American frontiersman disposed of his waste. "Flowing water purifies itself every ten miles," my grandfather used to say, and the myth was near enough to the truth when he was a boy, for there weren't too many people. But as population became denser the natural chemical and biological recycling processes became overloaded, calling for a redefinition of property rights.

HOW LEGISLATE TEMPERANCE?

Analysis of the pollution problem as a function of population density uncovers a not generally recognized principle of morality, namely: *the morality of an act is a function of the state of the system at the time it is performed.*[9] Using the commons as a cesspool does not harm the general public under frontier conditions, because there is no public; the same behavior in a metropolis is unbearable. A hundred and fifty years ago a plainsman could kill an American bison, cut out only the tongue for his dinner, and discard the rest of the animal. He was not in any important sense being wasteful. Today, with only a few thousand bison left, we would be appalled at such behavior.

In passing, it is worth noting that the morality of an act cannot be determined from a photograph. One does not know whether a man killing an elephant or setting fire to the grassland is harming others until one knows the total system in which he act appears. "One picture is worth a thousand words," said an ancient Chinese; but it may take 10,000 words to validate it. It is as tempting to ecologists as it is to reformers in general to try to persuade others via the photographic shortcut. But the guts of an argument can't be photographed: they must be presented rationally—in words.

That morality is system-sensitive escaped the attention of most codifiers of ethics in the past. "Thou shalt not . . ." is the form of traditional ethical directives, which make no allowance for particular circumstances. (Christ did; and his continued existence was unbearable to the Establishment.) The laws of our society follow the pattern of ancient ethics, and therefore are poorly suited to governing a complex, crowded, changeable world. Our epicyclic solution is to augment statutory law with adminstrative law. Since it is practically impossible to spell out all the conditions under which it is safe to burn trash in the back yard or run an automobile without smog-control, by law we delegate the details to bureaus. The result is administrative law, which is rightly feared for an ancient reason: *Quis custodiet ipsos custodes?*—"Who shall watch the watchers themselves?" John Adams said we must have "a government of laws and not men." Bureau administrators, trying to evaluate the morality of acts in the total system, are singularly liable to corruption, producing a government by men, not laws.

Prohibition is easy to legislate (though not necessarily to enforce!); but how do we legislate temperance? Experience indicates that it can be accomplished best through the mediation of administrative law. We limit possibilities unnecessarily if we suppose that the sentiment of *Quis custodiet* denies us the use of administrative law. We should rather retain the phrase as a perpetual reminded of fearful dangers we cannot avoid. The great challenge facing us now is to invent the corrective feedbacks that are needed to keep custodians honest. We must find ways to legitimate the needed authority of both the custodians and the corrective feedbacks.

FREEDOM TO BREED IS INTOLERABLE

The tragedy of the commons is involved in population problems in another way. In a world governed solely by the principle of "dog eat dog" —if indeed there ever was such a world—it would not be a matter of public concern how many children a family had. Parents who bred too exuberantly would leave fewer descendants, not more, because they would be unable to care adequately for their children. David Lack and others have found that such a negative feedback demonstrably controls the fecundity of birds.[10] But men are not birds, and have not acted like them for millennia, at least.

If each human family were dependent only on its own resources; *if* the children of improvident parents starved to death; *if*, thus overbreeding brought its own "punishment" to the germ line—*then* there would be no public interest in controlling the breeding of families. But our society is deeply committed to the welfare state,[11] and hence confronted with another aspect of the tragedy of the commons.

In a welfare state, how shall we deal with the family, the religion, the race, or the class (or indeed any distinguishable and cehesive group) that adopts overbreeding as a policy to secure its own aggrandizement?[12] To couple the concept of freedom to breed with the belief that everyone born has an equal right to the commons is to lock the world into a tragic course of action.

Unfortunately this is just the course of action that is being pursued by the United Nations. In late 1967 some thirty nations agreed to the following:

> The Universal Declaration of Human Rights describes the family as the natural and fundamental unit of society. It follows that any choice and decision with regard to the size of the family must irrevocably rest with the family itself, and cannot be made by anyone else.[13]

It is painful to have to deny categorically the validity of his "right"; denying it, one feels as uncomfortable as a resident of Salem who denied the reality of witches in the seventeenth century. At the present time, in liberal quarters, something like a taboo acts to inhibit criticism of the United Nations. There is a feeling that the U.N. is "our last and best hope," that we shouldn't find fault with it; we shouldn't play into the hands of the arch-conservatives. Let us not forget, however, what Robert Louis Stevenson said: "The truth that is suppressed by friends is the readiest weapon of the enemy." If we love the truth we must openly deny the validity of the Universal Declaration of Human Rights, even though it is promoted by the United Nations. We should also join with Kingsley Davis[14] in attempting to get Planned Parenthood to see the error of its ways in embracing the same tragic ideal.

CONSCIENCE IS SELF-ELIMINATING

It is a mistake to think that we can control the breeding of mankind *in the long run* by an appeal to conscience. Charles Galton Darwin made this point when he spoke on the centennial of the publication of his grandfather's great book. The argument is straightforward and Darwinian.

People vary. Confronted with appeals to limit breeding, some people will undoubtedly respond to the plea more than others. Those who have more children will produce a larger fraction of the next generation than those with more susceptible consciences. The difference will be accentuated, generation by generation. In C. G. Darwin's words:

> It may well be that it would take hundreds of generations for the progenitive instinct to develop in this way, but if it should do so, nature would have taken her revenge, and the variety *Homo contracipiens* would become extinct and would be replaced by the variety *Homo progenitivus*.[15]

The argument assumes that conscience or the desire for children (no matter which) is hereditary—but hereditary *only in the most general formal sense*. The result will be the same whether the attitude is transmitted via germ cells, or exosomatically, to use A. J. Lotka's term. (If one denies the latter possibility as well as the former, then what's the point of education?) The argument has here been stated in the context of the population problem, *but it applies equally well to any instance in which society appeals to an individual exploiting a commons to restrain himself for the general good—by means of his conscience. To make such an appeal is to set up a selective system that works toward the elimination of conscience from the race.* [My italics.]

PATHOGENIC EFFECTS OF CONSCIENCE

The long-term disadvantage of an appeal to conscience should be enough to condemn it; but it has serious short-term disadvantages as well.

If we ask a man who is exploiting a commons to desist "in the name of conscience," what are we saying to him? What does he hear—not only at the moment but also in the wee small hours of the night when, half asleep, he remembers not merely the words we used but also the non-verbal communication cues we gave him unawares? Sooner or later, consciously or subconsciously he senses that he has received two communications, and that they are contradictory:

1. (Intended communication) "If you don't do as we ask, we will openly condemn you for not acting like a responsible citizen."
2. (The unintended communication) "If you *do* behave as we ask, we will secretly condemn you for a schlemiel, a sucker, a sap, who can be shamed into standing aside while the rest of us exploit the commons."

In a word, he is damned if he does and damned if he doesn't. He is caught in what Gregory Bateson has called a "double bind." Bateson and his co-workers have made a plausible case for viewing the double bind as an important causative factor in the genesis of schizophrenia.[16] The double bind may not always be so damaging, but it always endangers the mental health of anyone to whom it is applied. "A bad conscience," said Nietzsche, "is a kind of illness."

To conjure up a conscience in others is tempting to anyone who wishes to extend his control beyond the legal limits. Leaders at the highest level succumb to his temptation. Has any President during the past generation failed to call upon labor unions to moderate "voluntarily" their demands for higher wages, or to steel companies to honor "voluntary" guide-lines on prices? I can recall none. The rhetoric used on such occasions is designed to produce feelings of guilt in noncooperators.

For centuries it was assumed without proof that guilt was a valuable, perhaps even an indispensable, ingredient of the civilized life. Now, in this post-Freudian world, we doubt it. Paul Goodman speaks from the modern point of view when he says:

No good has ever come from feeling guilty, neither intelligence, policy, nor compassion. The guilty do not pay attention to the object but only to themselves, and not even to their own interests, which might make sense, but to their anxieties.[17]

One does not have to be a professional psychiatrist to see the consequences of anxiety. We in the western world are just emerging from a dreadful two-centuries-long Dark Ages of Eros, which was sustained partly by prohibition laws, but perhaps more effectively by the anxiety-generating mechanisms of education. Alex Comfort has told the story well in *The Anxiety Makers;*[18] it is not a pretty one.

Since proof is difficult, we may even conceded that the results of anxiety may sometimes, from certain points of view, be desirable. The larger question we should ask is whether, as a matter of policy, we should ever encourage the use of a technique the tendency of which (if not the intention) is psychologically pathogenic. We hear much talk these days of "responsible parenthood"; the coupled words are incorporated into the titles of some organizations devoted to birth control. Some people have proposed massive propaganda campaigns to instill responsibility into the nation's (or the world's) breeders. But what is the meaning of the word "responsibility" in this context? Is it not merely a synonym for the word "conscience"? When we used the word "responsibility" in the absence of substantial sanctions are we not trying to browbeat a free man in a commons into acting against his own interest? "Responsibility" is a verbal counterfeit for a substantial *quid pro quo*. It is an attempt to get something for nothing.

If the word "responsibility" is to be used at all, I suggest that it be in the sense Charles Frankel uses it.[19] "Responsibility," says this philosopher, "is the product of definite social arrangements." Notice that Frankel calls for social arrangements—not propaganda.

MUTUAL COERCION, MUTUALLY AGREED UPON

The social arrangements that produce responsibility are arrangements that create coercion, of some sort. Consider bank-robbing. The man who takes money from a bank acts as if the bank were a commons. How do we prevent such action? Certainly not by trying to control his behavior solely by a verbal appeal to his sense of responsibility. Rather than rely on propaganda we follow Frankel's lead and insist that a bank is not a commons; we seek the definite social arrangements that will keep it from becoming a commons. That we thereby infringe on the freedom of would-be robbers we neither deny nor regret.

The morality of bank-robbing is particularly easy to understand because we accept complete prohibition of this activity. We are willing to say "Thou shalt not rob banks," without providing for exceptions. But temperance also can be created by coercion. Taxing is a good coercive device. To keep downtown shoppers temperate in their use of parking space we introduce parking meters for short periods, and traffic fine for longer ones. We need not actually forbid a citizen to park as long as he wants to; we need merely make it increasingly expensive for him to do so. Not prohibition, but carefully biased options are what we offer him. A Madison Avenue man might call this "persuasion"; I prefer the greater candor of the word "coercion."

Coercion is a dirty word to most liberals now, but it need not forever be so. As with the four-letter words, its dirtiness can be cleansed away by exposure to the light, by saying it over and over without apology or embarrassment. To many, the word coercion implies arbitrary decisions of distant and irresponsible bureaucrats; but this is not a necessary part of its meaning. The only kind of coercion I recommend is mutual coercion, mutually agreed upon by the majority of the people affected.

To say that we mutually agree to coercion is not to say that we are required to enjoy it, or even to pretend we enjoy it. Who enjoys taxes? We all grumble about them. But we accept compulsory taxes because we recognize that voluntary taxes would favor the conscienceless. We institute and (grumblingly) support taxes and other coercive devices to escape the horror of the commons.

An alternative to the commons need not be perfectly just to be preferable. With real estate and other material goods, the alternative we have chosen is the institution of private property coupled with legal inheritance. Is this system perfectly *just?* As a genetically trained biologist I deny that it is. It seems to me that, if there are to be differences in individual inheritance, legal possession should be perfectly correlated with biological inheritance—that those who are biologically more fit to be the custodians of property and power should legally inherit more. But genetic recombination continually makes a mockery of the doctrine of "like father, like son" implicit in our laws of legal inheritance. An idiot can inherit millions, and a trust fund can keep his estate intact. We must admit that our legal system of private property plus inheritance *is* unjust —but we put up with it because we are not convinced, at the moment, that anyone has invented a better system. The alternative of the commons is too horrifying to contemplate. Injustice is preferable to total ruin.

One of the peculiarities of the warfare between reform and the status quo is that it is thoughtlessly governed by a double standard. Whenever a reform measure is proposed it is often defeated when its opponents triumphantly discover a flaw in it. As Kingsley Davis has pointed out,[20] worshippers of the status quo sometimes imply that no reform is possible without unanimous agreement, an implication contrary to historical fact. As nearly as I can make out, automatic rejection of proposed reforms is based on one of two unconscious assumptions:

1. That the status quo is perfect; or
2. That the choice we face is between reform and no action; if the pro-

posed reform is imperfect, we presumably should take no action at all, while we wait for a perfect proposal.

But we can never do nothing. That which we have done for thousands of years is also action. It also produces evils. Once we are aware that the status quo *is* action, we can then compare its discoverable advantages and disadvantages with the predicted advantages and disadvantages of the proposed reform, discounting as best we can for our lack of experience. On the basis of such a comparison, we can make a rational decision, which will not involve the unworkable assumption that only perfect systems are tolerable.

THE RECOGNITION OF NECESSITY

Perhaps the simplest summary of this analysis of man's population problems is this: the commons, if justifiable at all, is justifiable only under conditions of low population density. As the human population has increased, the commons has had to be abandoned in one aspect after another.

First we abandoned the commons in food gathering, enclosing farm land and restricting pastures and hunting and fishing areas. These restrictions are still not complete throughout the world.

Somewhat later we saw that the commons as a place for waste disposal would also have to be abandoned. Restrictions on the disposal of domestic sewage are widely accepted in the western world; we are still struggling to close the commons to pollution by automobiles, factories, insecticide sprayers, fertilizing operations, and atomic energy installations.

In a still more embryonic state is our recognition of the evils of the commons in matters of pleasure. There is almost no restriction on the propagation of sound waves in the public medium. The shopping public is assaulted with "mindless music," without its consent. Our government is paying out billions of dollars to create the SST plane, which will disturb fifty thousand people for every one person who is whisked from coast to coast three hours faster. Advertizers muddy the airwaves of radio and TV and pollute the view of travellers. We are a long way from outlawing the commons in matters of pleasure. Is this because our puritan inheritance makes us view pleasure as something of a sin, and pain (i.e., the pollution of advertizing) as the sign of virtue?

Every new enclosure of the commons involves the infringement of somebody's personal liberty. Infringements made in the distant past are accepted because no contemporary complains of a loss. It is the newly proposed infringements that we vigorously oppose: cries of "rights" and "freedom" fill the air. But what does "freedom" mean? When men mutually agreed to pass laws against robbing, mankind became more free, not less so. Individuals locked into the logic of the commons are free only to bring on universal ruin; once they see the necessity of mutual coercion, they become free to pursue other goals. I believe it was Hegel who said, *"Freedom is the recognition of necessity."*

The most important aspect of necessity that we must now recognize, is the necessity of abandoning the commons in breeding. No technical solution can rescue us from the misery of overpopulation. Freedom to breed will bring ruin to all. At the moment, to avoid hard decisions many of us are tempted to propagandize for conscience and "responsible parenthood." The temptation must be resisted, because an appeal to independently acting consciences selects for the disappearance of all conscience in the long run, and an increase in anxiety in the short.

The only way we can preserve and nurture other and more precious freedoms is by relinquishing the freedom to breed, and that very soon. "Freedom is the recognition of necessity"—and it is the role of education to reveal to all the necessity of abandoning the freedom to breed. Only so, can we put an end to this aspect of the tragedy of the commons.

1. J. B. Wiesner and H. F. York, *Scientific American,* **211** (April 1964):27.
2. G. Hardin, *J. Heredity,* **50** (1959):68; S. von Hoernor, *Science,* **137** (1962): 18.
3. J. von Neumann and O. Morgenstern, *Theory of Games and Economic Behavior,* Princeton: Princeton Univ. Press, 1947, p. 11.
4. J. H. Fremlin, *New Scientist,* no. 415 (1964):285.
5. Adam Smith, *The Wealth of Nations,* New York: Modern Library, 1937, p. 423.
6. W. F. Lloyd, *Two Lectuers on the Checks to Population,* Oxford, 1833.
7. A. N. Whitehead, *Science and the Modern World,* New York: Mentor, 1948, p. 17.
8. S. McVay, *Scientific American,* **216** (August 1966):13.
9. J. Fletcher, *Situation Ethics,* Philadelphia: Westminster Press, 1966.
10. D. Lack, *The Natural Regulation of Animal Numbers,* Oxford: Clarendon Press, 1954.
11. H. Girvetz, *From Wealth to Welfare,* Stanford: Stanford Press, 1950.
12. G. Hardin, *Persp. Biol. Med.,* **6** (1963):366.
13. U Thant, *Intern. Planned Parenthood News,* no. 168, February 1968, p. 3.
14. K. Davis, *Science,* **158** (1967):730.
15. S. Tax (ed), *Evolution After Darwin,* Chicago: Univ. of Chicago Press, 1960, vol. 2, p. 469.
16. G. Bateson, D. D. Jackson, J. Haley, and J. Weakland, *Behav. Sci.,* **1** (1956): 251.
17. P. Goodman, *New York Review of Books,* **10** (23 May 1968):22.
18. A. Comfort, *The Anxiety Makers,* London: Nelson, 1967.
19. C. Frankel, *The Case for Modern Man,* New York: Harper, 1955, p. 203.
20. J. D. Roslansky, *Genetics and the Future of Man,* New York: Appleton-Century-Crofts, 1966, p. 177.

As you read the papers in this collection it will be helpful to make a summary in your own words. One possible summary of Hardin's paper is presented below. (Of course, this only proves that you have read the author's words, and real understanding will come when you question the author's words, draw inferences from his conclusions, and relate the individual articles to one another.) Hardin concludes that recognition of the necessities of man's position can, or should, free man from the tragedy of the commons. By "mutual coercion, mutually agreed upon," the commons can be managed to provide some good for all—provided the population is limited to a manageable size. Coercion, regulation, and restraint are made necessary by the failure of any appeal to conscience and failure of voluntary control. Coercion, as opposed to conscience, must operate with regard to the use of food and energy sources, space, rates of consumption, use of wildlands and recreation facilities, and the disposal of domestic and industrial wastes. "Freedom in a commons," says Hardin, "brings ruin to all."

Like any logical argument, Hardin's brings us to valid conclusions because of the argument's internal structure. Only if the premises upon which the argument is based are in true correspondence to natural events will the conclusions be useful in guiding our actions in the natural world. A good study of sources no more technical than the daily paper or the weekly news magazines will reveal repeated examples of conflict over "the commons" which can be fitted to Hardin's model. It is, after all, the age-old conflict between man as an individual and man as a member of society.

The growing concern over environmental problems has revived interest and speculation regarding man's origin, the "nature" of human nature, and ethical and moral aspects of man's relationship to nonhuman nature. To what extent are man's difficulties the consequence of his innate characteristics or the denial of the expression of such characteristics? To what extent have religion and other cultural institutions conditioned our concepts of nonhuman nature in a manner which leads us in nonadaptive directions?

Richard L. Means, in his brief article, Why Worry About Nature, *states in his subtitle: "The press, religion—all our institutions—have led us into wrong relationships with the natural world. . . ." These "wrong relationships" arise, it is implied, from the insistence of our Western religious tradition on the dominion (translated into action as "domination") of man over nonhuman nature. At fault is the concept that it is man's destiny to overcome nature—that nature, in fact, is to be defined as that which man must overcome in order to exist.*

WHY WORRY ABOUT NATURE?

The press, religion—all our institutions—have led us into wrong relationships with the natural world, a sociologist maintains. Is this a key to our moral crisis?

Richard L. Means

Albert Schweitzer once wrote, "The great fault of all ethics hitherto has been that they believed themselves to have to deal only with the relation of man to man." Modern ethical discussion does not seem to have removed itself very far from this fallacy. Joseph Fletcher's *Situation Ethics: The New Morality*, for instance, deals piecemeal with man's relations to his fellows without even suggesting that man's relation to nature—to the physical and biological world—raises questions of moral behavior. Perhaps this oversight is due to the general psychological and subjective tone of much current social criticism. Or, even more likely, it represents the "revolt against formalism," the eschewing of the abstract and sweeping interpretations of man and nature once the passion of American social scientists.

It is true that the Thoreau-like comments of Joseph Wood Krutch or the aggressive naturalistic interpretations of the Austrian scientist, Konrad Lorenz, find a grudging response among some social scientists. But contemporary social scientists have so completely separated considerations of culture from nature that it will take some intellectual effort to overcome this dichotomy. Moreover, although the relations of man and nature may be envisioned in various ways—all the way from control to passive obedience—the notion that man's relation to nature is a moral one finds very few articulate champions, even among contemporary religious writers. Harvey Cox's book, *The Secular City*, for example, is set in an urban world in rather extreme isolation from the surrounding problems of resources, food, disease, etc. The city is taken for granted and the moral dimensions of Cox's analysis are limited to man's relations to man within this urban world, and not with the animals, the plants, the trees, the air—that is, the natural habitat.

Eric Hoffer, one of the few contemporary social critics who have met head-on the issue of man's relationship to nature, has warned in these pages of the danger of romanticizing nature. ["A Strategy for the War with Nature," *SR*, Feb. 5, 1966]. Longshoreman, dishwasher, student of human tragedy, and exposer of the corruptions and perversions of power, Mr. Hoffer says that the great accomplishment of man is to transcend nature, to separate one's self from the demands of instinct. Thus, according to Hoffer, a fundamental characteristic of man is to be found in his capacity to free himself from the restrictions of the physical and biological.

In a way, Hoffer is correct. Surely the effects on man of flood, famine, fire, and earthquake have been great and hardly indicate a beneficence in nature which is ready and willing to rush headlong to the succor of man. But Hoffer's attack is basically political. It is an attack on "romantic individualism"—a special interpretation of man's relation to nature. Hoffer knows full well that romantic individualism leads easily to a kind of egoism and antirationalism which can pervert and destroy democratic institutions.

One is reminded of Hitler's call to neglect reason and to "think with one's blood." Values—tradition, home soil, nationalism, and race—have often been legitimized on the basis of a vague nature mysticism. Such a nature mysticism is the very essence of romantic individualism (though, of course, there may be other types of nature romanticism which do not advocate egotist striving). Perhaps the problem lies in the focus on the "individual" as delineated by Hoffer. He assumes that the response to nature couched in the terms of a naïve faith in nature's bountiful, miracle-working properties is an individual response. And, of course, it always is, to a degree, but, by failure to consider the collective or social side of man's relation to nature, the true moral dimensions of the problem are obscured.

It may be that *man* is at war with nature, but *men* are not (or, at least, cannot be). The reason is that certain individual attitudes and actions, when taken collectively, have consequences for nature, and these consequences may be most clearly understood under the stark realities of social survival itself. Take the problems of radioactive wastes, Strontium 90 contamination, etc. Man does not just do battle with the natural world; he may, in the act of cooperating with it, also shape and change it. Men join in a chain of decisions which facilitate the emergence of a new symbiotic relationship to nature—that is, we create civilization and culture. This crucial assumption strikes at the very roots of romantic individualism. One man, totally alone, acting before nature and using nature to satisfy needs of warmth, comfort, and creativity, is very difficult to imagine. Even Robinson Crusoe had his man Friday!

Hoffer seems to neglect the possibility that man's cooperation in the subjection of nature need not be conceptualized simply on the basis of brute force. Physical work, mechanical and otherwise—from the labor of the Chinese masses to the works of a sophisticated high-tower steeplejack—depends on the intrusion of human ideas into the natural world.

Aided by machines, cranes, bulldozers, factories, transportation systems, computers, and laboratories, man does force nature's hand. This does not, however, force us to an acceptance of metaphysical materialism, the naïve belief that matter and physical force are the only realities. The power of ideas, of values, provides the presuppositions which in the first place create a particular web of human interaction between nature and man. The power of the contemplative idea, the chain of speculative reason, the mathematician's art, and the philosopher's dreams must also be considered. If this point of view is accepted, then the question of man's relation to nature is a much more crucial moral issue than Eric Hoffer seems to suggest.

What, then, is the moral crisis? It is, I think, a pragmatic problem —that is, it involves the actual social consequences of myriad and unconnected acts. The crisis comes from the combined results of a mistreatment of our environment. It involves the negligence of a small businessman on the Kalamazoo River, the irresponsibility of a large corporation on Lake Erie, the impatient use of insecticides by a farmer in California, the stripping of land by Kentucky mine operators. Unfortunately, there is a long history of unnecessary and tragic destruction of animal and natural resources on the face of this continent.

One might begin the indictment with the classical case of the passenger pigeon which once flew across America in tremendous numbers, and then end with the destruction of the seal industry. The trouble is, however, we do not seem to learn very much from these sad happenings, for (to the anguish of men who have thrilled to the images created by Herman Melville and the great white whale) such marine scientists as Scott McVay believe that commercial fishing is endangering the whale, the last abundant species in the world. For those more inclined toward a cash nexus, there goes a profitable industry. For those of us who have a respect for nature—in particular, for our mammalian kinsmen—the death of these great creatures will leave a void in God's creation and in the imagination of men for generations to come.

Another case in point is the attempt to dam and flood mile after mile of the Grand Canyon in order to produce more electricity—a commodity we seem to have in great abundance. The Grand Canyon, of course, is not a commodity; it is truly, in popular parlance, a "happening." Uncontrolled by man, created by nature, it cannot be duplicated. Any assault on its natural state is an equal attack on man's capacity to wonder, to contemplate his environment and nature's work. In short, such activities seem to belittle and diminish man himself. Thus the activities of those who suggest such destruction assume a restricted view of man and his capacity for joy in nature. In this sense, such activities are immoral. We could lengthen the list, but it should be clear that destruction of nature by man's gratuitous "busyness" and technological arrogance is the result of a thoughtless and mindless human activity.

A second basic issue is the growing, biological pollution of the environment. Discussions of the pollution in just one river, the mighty Hudson, in financial terms stagger the imagination. The economic costs just to keep the river in its present undesirable state are immense—and to make any progress back toward a less polluted river will cost billions of dollars. The same is true of other great bodies of water.

And consider the state of the air we breathe. Air pollution has demonstrable ill effects on man, as many reports confirm. But in addition, for the economically-minded, A. J. Haagen-Smit, a leading expert on air pollution, notes that a largely ignored breakdown in standards of efficiency and technology also is involved:

> From all the emissions of an automobile, the total loss of fuel energy is about 15 per cent; in the U.S. that represents a loss of about $3 billion annually. It is remarkable that the automobile industry, which has a reputation for efficiency, allows such fuel waste.

Perhaps an issue becomes most moral when it is personal, existential —appeals to our own experience. Scientists vary in estimates of the time when the Great Lakes will be largely polluted, but the day of reckoning may be much too near. When I was a boy in Toledo, Ohio, summer after summer many of my neighbors and playmates went to cottages along the shores of Lake Erie. Today, visiting these cottages is anything but a happy event, and some owners are attempting desperately to sell their properties to any bidder. An analysis by Charles F. Powers and Andrew Robertson on "The Aging Great Lakes" [*Scientific American*, November, 1966] is not at all comforting for those of us who love the miles of sandy beach of Lake Michigan or the rugged, cold, wind-whipped shores of Lake Superior. Although Lake Michigan will not immediately turn into a polluted wasteland like Lake Erie, with dark spots of water without aeration where only worms can live, pollution is growing in the southern end of Lake Michigan. And these problems, as Powers and Robertson point out, are beginning to touch even relatively unspoiled Lake Superior.

Why is man's relation to nature a moral crisis? It is a moral crisis because it is a historical one involving man's history and culture, expressed at its roots by our religious and ethical views of nature—which have been relatively unquestioned in this context. The historian of medieval culture, Lynn White, Jr., brilliantly traced the origin and consequences of this expression in an insightful article in *Science* last March: "The Historical Roots of Our Ecological Crisis." He argues that the Christian notion of a transcendent God, removed from nature and breaking into nature only through revelation, removed spirit from nature and allows, in the ideological sense, for an easy exploitation of nature.

On the American scene, the Calvinistic and the deistic concepts of God were peculiarly alike at this point. Both envisioned God as absolutely transcendent, apart from the world, isolated from nature and organic life. As to the contemporary implications of this dichotomy between spirit and nature, Professor White says:

The newly elected Governor of California, like myself a churchman but less troubled than I, spoke for the Christian tradition when he said (as is alleged), "when you've seen one redwood tree, you've seen them all." To a Christian a tree can be no more than a physical fact. The whole concept of the sacred grove is alien to Christianity and to the ethos of the West. For nearly two millennia Christian missionaries have been chopping down sacred groves, which are idolatrous because they assume spirit in nature.

Perhaps, as Lynn White suggests, the persistence of this as a moral problem is illustrated in the protest of the contemporary generation of beats and hippies. Although the kind of "cool cat" aloofness expressed by this generation grates on the nerves of many of us, and more than a few "squares" find difficulty in "digging" the new hair styles (not to mention Twiggy), there may be a "sound instinct" involved in the fact that some of these so-called beats have turned to Zen Buddhism. It may represent an overdue perception of the fact that we need to appreciate more fully the religious and moral dimensions of the relation between nature and the human spirit.

Why do almost all of our wisest and most exciting social critics meticulously avoid the moral implications of this issue? Perhaps, in the name of political realism, it is too easy to fear the charge that one anthropomorphizes or spiritualizes nature. On the other hand, the refusal to connect the human spirit to nature may reflect the traditional thought pattern of Western society wherein nature is conceived to be a separate substance—a material—mechanical, and, in a metaphysical sense, irrelevant to man.

It seems to me much more fruitful to think of nature as part of a system of human organization—as a variable, a changing condition—which interacts with man and culture. If nature is so perceived, then a love, a sense of awe, and a feeling of empathy with nature need not degenerate into a subjective, emotional bid for romantic individualism. On the contrary, such a view should help destroy egoistic, status politics, for it helps unmask the fact that other men's activities are not just private, inconsequential, and limited in themselves; their acts, mediated through changes in nature, affect my life, my children, and the generations to come. In this sense, justification of a technological arrogance toward nature on the basis of dividends and profits is not just bad economics—it is basically an immoral act. And our contemporary moral crisis, then, goes much deeper than questions of political power and law, of urban riots and slums. It may, at least in part, reflect American society's almost utter disregard for the value of nature.

There are several common cultural concepts which could contribute to a feeling that man is separate from, and thus at war with, nature. Despite warnings in the legends of Daedalus and Faustus, we live in a culture in which the technician, artificer, and engineer have been much admired. Our history and literature hail the colonist and the frontiersman, building and spreading civilization in spite of the forces of nature. We indulge in the rationalization, through a misapplication of Darwinism, of "rugged individualism," proving its rightness through suppression of opposition, both human and nonhuman.

It is possible, as Means suggests, that these cultural inclinations are linked to the Judaic-Christian tradition. It may also be true that the rapid shift of population to urban as opposed to rural habitats may be creating a real, geographically based, separation of man from nonhuman nature. This latter point may assume increasing significance, because an increasingly broad application of the "one man, one vote" principle places more and more of the decision-making and planning power in the hands of urban residents.

There are opposing forces. The Romantic movement, insofar as it is still influential, promotes an awe of Nature as a spiritually uplifting force. Through the writing of Thoreau and others we can learn it is possible to admire wildness as opposed to civilization. The pressures of increasing population and technological power make a position of anthropocentric individualism increasingly difficult to maintain, especially because the position is simultaneously undermined by accumulating ecological knowledge.

After all these and other possible cultural influences are identified and classified, the question reamins: What effect do these concepts really have upon the course of events? Is the pattern of action of a culture really determined by such concepts, however real, or by other, more material matters? This is the question considered by Yi-Fu Tuan in Our Treatment of the Environment in Ideal and Actuality.

It is very difficult to offer final proof that cultural influences have been a root cause of man's environmental problems. In theory it should be more difficult to prove that they have not been. When Yi-Fu Tuan brings this possibility to our attention, however, it seems reasonable that short-term, materialistic decisions would precede cultural justification. We perhaps should hope that this is the case, because mistaken decisions based on self-interest should be correctable when the nature of the mistake is revealed. I am not sure we even know how to begin to change basic cultural determinants.

OUR TREATMENT OF THE ENVIRONMENT IN IDEAL AND ACTUALITY

Yi-Fu Tuan

Ethnocentrism is characteristic of peoples all over the world. It is difficult for any viable culture to avoid seeing itself as the center of light
shading into darkness. In Europe, to be sure, in the late seventeenth and
early eighteenth centuries, this glorification of self was temporarily reversed. *Là-bas on était bien.* In the spirit of that age Europe was viewed
as a portion of the earth afflicted with the blight of tyranny and superstition; beyond lay unspoiled Nature, unspoiled and rational peoples still
appareled in celestial light (1). This romantic spirit has continued to
affect the thinking of the West to the present day. Sensitive Westerners
are wont to contrast their own aggressive, exploitative attitude to nature
with the harmonious relationships of other times and other places. This
view should be commended for generosity, but it lacks realism and fails
to recognize inconsistency and paradox as characteristic of human existence.

In recent years two ideas that have bearing on our relationships to our
environment are receiving greater recognition. One is that the balances
of nature can be upset by people with the most primitive tools, the other
that a wide gap may exist between a culture's ideals and their expression
in the real world.

A current debate of interest in connection with the first point is the
role of man in the extinction of Pleistocene mammals. Although the issue
is far from resolution, I think we must admit that Paul Martin has made
a good case for what he calls "prehistoric overkill" (2). We are readily
persuaded that the disappearance of the bison was brought about by
masterful and predatory white men, but find the thought that primitive
hunters could cause the wholesale destruction of fauna somewhat un-
palatable.

The second point is a commonplace of experience in daily life; that a
high-minded philosopher should actually live his philosophy is a matter
for surprise, and we take it for granted that few of a politician's pro-
fessed ideals are convertible into substance. But in the study of the ideas
and ideals of cultures, especially non-Western cultures, there remains a
tendency to assume that they have force and correspond to reality. It
seems to go against the grain for a scientist to seek for polarities, di-

Reprinted with permission from the *American Scientist*, Vol. 58, 1970, pp. 214–249.
The author is Professor of Geography at the University of Minnesota, Minneapolis.

chotomies, and paradoxes; he would rather see unity and harmony. Contrarieties exist, however, in cultures as in individuals. A nonliterate, stable people such as the Zuñis of New Mexico do indeed make much of their aspiration to achieve harmonious order in the affairs of nature and of men, but their community is nonetheless wracked from time to time by bitter factionalism (3).

If small and stable societies do not often work as harmonious wholes, it is not surprising that large and complex civilizations like those of Europe and China should contain numerous dysfunctions. One of these is ecological imbalance. This is a theme I wish to take up—but indirectly; my primary concern is with the gaps that exist between an expressed attitude toward environment and actual practice. Such gaps may be taken as one of the signs of maladjustment in society.

To the question, what is the basic difference between European and Chinese attitudes to nature, many people might answer that whereas the European sees nature as subordinate to man the Chinese sees himself as part of nature. Although there is some truth in this generalization, it cannot be pressed too far. A culture's publicized ethos about its environment seldom covers more than a fraction of the total range of its attitudes and practices pertaining to that environment. In the play of forces that govern the world, esthetic and religious ideals rarely have a major role.

Christianity has often been blamed for Western man's presumption of power over nature. Professor Lynn White (4), for example, speaks of the Christian religion as the most anthropocentric the world has seen: it not only established a dualism between man and nature but insisted that it is God's will that man should exploit nature for proper ends. Christianity, White says, has destroyed antiquity's feeling for the sacredness of places and of natural things, and has made it possible for man to exploit his environment indifferent to the spirits that once guarded the trees, hills, and brooks. The Christian religion he further credits with Western man's prideful faith in perpetual progress, an idea that was unknown to Greco-Roman antiquity and to the Orient.

Opinions such as these reenforce the view that Christianity constituted a great divide. But the official triumph of Christ over the pagan deities brought no revolutionary change to the organization either of society or of nature. At the level of the actual impress of man on environment, both constructive and destructive, the pagan world had as much to show as Christianized Europe did, until the beginning of the modern period. Contrary to the commonly accepted opinion of twentieth-century scholars, classical antiquity knew progressivism. As Ludwig Edelstein has recently noted, the pre-Socratic philosopher Xenophanes believed in progress; and his faith could well have been buoyed up by the engineering achievements of this time (5). Lines in Sophocles' *Antigone* refer to the power of man to tear the soil with his plow. Plato in

Critias described the negative side of that power—deforestation and soil erosion (6). By the early Hellenistic period, technical ingenuity was performing feats that justified Aristotle's boast: "Vanquished by nature, we become masters by technique" (7).

But the Romans did far more than the Greeks to impose their will on the natural environment. "Public roads," as Gibbons wrote in admiration, "ran in a direct line from one city to another, with very little respect for the obstacles either of nature or of private property. Mountains were perforated, and bold arches thrown over the broadest and most rapid streams" (8). An even more overriding example of the triumph of the human will over the lineaments of nature is the Roman grid method of dividing up the land into *centuria quadrata*, each containing a hundred *heredia*. As John Bradford puts it (9), centuriation well displayed the arbitrary but methodical qualities in Roman government. With absolute self-assurance and great technical competence the Romans imposed the same formal pattern of land division on the well-watered alluvium of the Po Valley as on the near-desert of Tunisia. Even today the forceful imprint of centuriation can be traced across thousands of square miles on both sides of the central Mediterranean, and it can still stir the imagination by its scale and boldness.

Against this background of the vast transformations of nature in the pagan world, the inroads made in the early centuries of the Christian era appear relatively modest. Christianity teaches that man has dominion over nature—but for a long time this new dignity was more a tenet of faith than a fact of experience: for man's undisputed power over nature to become a realized fact Europe had to await the growth of human numbers, the achievement of greater administrative centralization, and the development and application of new technological skills. Farmsteads and arable fields multiplied at the expense of forests and marshes through the Middle Ages, but these lacked the permanence, the geometric order, and the prideful assertion of the human will that one can more readily read into the Roman road systems, aqueducts, and centuriated landholdings.

When we turn to China, we again find discrepancies between esthetic ideals and performance, as well as unforeseen conflicts and dysfunctions that are inevitable in a complex civilization. Western intellectuals who look at Chinese culture tend to be overgenerous, following the example of the eighteenth-century *philosophes* rather than the chauvinism of nineteenth-century European scholars.

Seduced by China's Taoist and Buddhist traditions, they like to compare the Oriental's quiescent and adaptive approach toward nature with the aggressive masculinity of Western man.

An adaptive attitude toward nature does indeed have ancient roots in China. Evidence of it occurs in diverse sources. Well known to the West is the concept of *feng-shui* or geomancy, aptly defined as "the art of adapting the residences of the living and the dead so as to co-operate and harmonize with the local currents of the cosmic breath" (*10*). A general effect of the belief in feng-shui has been to encourage a preference for natural curves—for winding paths and structures that seem to fit into the landscape rather than to dominate it—and at the same time to promote a distaste for straight lines and layouts.

Ancient Chinese literature contains scattered evidence that the need to regulate the use of resources was recognized. Even as early as the Eastern Chou period (8th–3rd century B.C.) the deforestation resulting from the expansion of agriculture and the building of cities seems to have led to an appreciation of the value of trees. In the *Chou Li*—a work which was probably compiled in the third century B.C. but may well include earlier material—two classes of conservation officials are mentioned: the inspectors of mountains and of forests. They were charged with protecting certain species, and with seeing to it that the common people cut trees at the proper season, except when emergencies required making coffins or strengthening dykes (*11*). Another ancient literary reference to conservation practice is Mencius' advice to King Huai of Liang that he would not lack for wood if he allowed the people to cut trees only at the proper time (*12*).

Throughout Chinese history perspicacious officials have on various occasions warned against the dire consequences of deforestation. They deplored the indiscriminate cutting of trees in the mountains not only because of its harmful effect on stream flow and on the quality of soil in the lowland but also because they believed that forested mountain ridges slowed down the horse-riding barbarians. As one scholar of the Ming dynasty put it, "I saw the fact that what the country relies on as strategically important is the mountain, and what the mountain relies on as a screen to prevent advance are the trees" (*13*). The scholar-officials also recognized the esthetic value of forested mountains. The Wu-tai mountains in northern Shan-hsi, for example, were famous, but shorn of their trees can they retain their fame?

These references suggest that an old tradition of forest care existed in China. On the other hand it is clear that the concern arose in response to damages that had already occurred, even in antiquity. Animistic belief and Taoist nature philosophy lie at the back of an adaptive attitude to environment; alone these might have produced a sequestered utopia. But China, with her gardens and temple compounds, was also a vast bureaucracy, a civilization, and an empire. Opposed to the attitude of passivity was the "male" principle of dominance. One of the greatest culture heroes of China was the semilegendary Yu, whose fame lay not in his precepts but in his acts—his feats of engineering.

An idea that lent support to the dominance side in Chinese culture was one which discerned a model of the cosmos in the earthly environment. It held that the regular motions of the stars could be expressed architecturally and ritually in space and time on earth. The walled city was given a rectilinear pattern, an orientation, and a grandeur that reflected the order and dimension of heaven (*14*). The earth's surface itself lacks paradigms of geometric order. Mountains and water are irregularly disposed. Experience of them has led to such unaggressive precepts as the need to observe and placate the spirits of the earth, the need for man to contemplate terrestrial harmony and adapt himself to it. By contrast observation of the stars has encouraged the aggressive side of Chinese culture, nurturing its predilections for order, hierarchy, and control.

Visitors to China in the nineteenth and early part of the twentieth centuries have often commented on the treelessness of the North, and the acute problems of soil erosion on the loess-covered plateaus. These areas were once well wooded. Deforestation on a vast scale took place as population increased and more and more land was taken over by farmers. But this alone does not account for the extent of the clearing. Other factors militated against prudence. One was the ancient custom, first recorded in the fourth century B.C., of burning trees in order to deprive dangerous animals of their hiding places (*15*). Even in contemporary China farmers are known to start fires for no evident purpose.

Asked why, they may say it is to clear land for cultivation—although the extent of burning far exceeds the needs for this purpose—or it is to leave fewer places in which bandits may hide, or to encourage the growth of small-sized sprouts in the burnt-over area and avoid the labor of splitting wood (*16*). The real reason for the burning is difficult to pin down.

Forests in North China were also depleted to make charcoal for industrial fuel. From the tenth century on, the expanding metallic industries swallowed up many hundred of thousands of tons of charcoal each year, as did the manufacture of salt, alum, bricks, tiles, and liquor. By the Sung dynasty (960–1279 A.D) the demand for wood and charcoal as both household and industrial fuels had exceeded the timber resources of the country; the result was the increasing substitution of coal for wood and charcoal (*17*).

An enormous amount of timber was needed for construction in the old Chinese cities, probably more than was required in European cities of comparable size. One reason for this is the dependence of traditional Chinese architecture on wood as the basic structural material. Great cities like Ch'ang-an, Lo-yang, and Hang-chou made severe demands on the resources of the surrounding country. The rapid expansion of Hang-chou in the thirteenth century to a metropolis of some one and a half million people led to the denuding of the neighboring hills. Despite the demand of the swelling urban population for food, some farmers found it more profitable to give up rice cultivation and grow trees (*18*). Rebuilding the wooden houses after fires put a further strain on timber resources; but of greater consequence was the deliberate devastation of whole cities in times of upheaval, when rebels or nomadic invaders toppled a dynasty. The succeeding phase of reconstruction was normally achieved in haste by armies of men who made ruthless inroads on the forest.

In a complex society benign institutions can introduce effects that were no part of their original purpose. The indirect results of any major action or event are largely unpredictable, and we tend to see the irony only in retrospect. For example, Buddhism in China is at least partly responsible for the preservation of trees around temple compounds, islands of green in an otherwise denuded landscape. On the other hand Buddhism introduced into China the idea of cremation of the dead; and from the tenth to the fourteenth centuries cremation was common enough in the southeastern coastal provinces to create a timber shortage there (19). Large parts of Mongolia have been overgrazed by sheep and goats. The most abused land appeared as sterile rings around the lamaseries, whose princely domains pastured large herds though the monks were not supposed to consume meat. In Japan, the seventeenth-century official and conservationist Kumazawa Banzan was inclined to put most of the blame for the deforestation of his country on Buddhism; the Buddhists, he contended, were responsible for seven-tenths of the nation's timber consumption. One reason for this grossly disproportionate consumption was that instead of living in "grass hermitages" they built themselves huge halls and temples (20).

Another example of fine irony concerns that most civilized of the arts: writing. Soot was needed to make black ink, and soot came from burnt pine. As E. H. Schafer has put it, "Even before T'ang times, the ancient pines of the mountains of Shan-tung had been reduced to carbon, and now the busy brushes of the vast T'ang bureaucracy were rapidly bringing baldness to the T'a-hang Mountains between Shansi and Hopei" (21).

Although ancient pines may already have disappeared from Shan-tung by the T'ang dynasty, from the testimony of the Japanese monk Ennin we know that large parts of the peninsula were still well wooded in the ninth century (22). The landscapes described by Ennin provide sharp contrast to the dry, bare scenes that characterize so much of Shan-tung in modern times. Shan-tung has many holy places; the province includes the sacred mountain T'ai-shan and the ancient state of Lu, which was the birthplace of Confucius. The numerous shrines and temples have managed to preserve only tiny spots of green amid the brown. Around Chiao-chou Bay in eastern Shan-tung a conspicuous strip of forest lies behind the port of Ch'ing-tao. It is ironic that this patch of green should owe its existence not to native piety but to the conservation-minded Germans.

The unplanned and often careless use of land in China belongs, one hopes, to the past. The Communist government has made an immense effort to control erosion and to reforest. Besides such large projects as shelterbelts along the semiarid edges of the North, forest brigades of the individual communes have planted billions of trees around villages, in cities, along roads and river banks, and on the hillsides. A visitor from New Zealand reported in 1960 that as seen from the air the new growths spread "a mist of green" over the once bare hills of South China (23). For those who admire the old culture, it must again seem ironic that the "mist of green" is no reflection of the traditional virtues of Taoism and Buddhism; on the contrary, it rests on their explicit denial (24).

Problems of despoliation of the environment must be attacked along several fronts. Engineers offer technical solutions. Social scientists need to examine those societal dysfunctions that leave strains and scars on our habitats. One symptom of maladjustment lies in the conflicts between an ideal of nature or environment and our practice. Such conflicts are embarrassing to observe for they expose our intellectual failure to make the connection, and perhaps also our hypocrisy; moreover, they cannot always be resolved. Contradictions of a certain kind may be inherent in the human condition, and not even stable and simple cultures are exempt. Ideals and necessities are frequently opposed as, for example, on the most fundamental level, keeping one's cake and eating it are incompatible. Some consume beauty for gain; but all of us must consume it to live.

REFERENCES

1. Willey, B. 1962. *The eighteenth-century background* (Penguin Books), pp. 19–21.
2. Martin, P. S. 1963. *The last 10,000 years* (Tucson: Univ. of Arizona Press), pp. 64–65, 70; P. S. Martin and H. E. Wright, Jr., eds., *Pleistocene extinctions*, Proc. of the 7th Congress of the Internat. Assoc. for Quaternary Research, vol. 6, New Haven: Yale Univ. Press, 1967.
3. Vogt, E., and E. M. Albert, eds. 1966. *People of Rimrock: A study of value in five cultures* (Cambridge: Harvard Univ. Press), pp. 201–2.
4. White, L., 1967. The historical roots of our ecologic crisis, *Science* 155: 1205.
5. Edelstein, L. 1967. *The idea of progress in classical antiquity* (Baltimore, Md.: The Johns Hopkins Press), pp. 3, 11–13.
6. Sophocles, *Antigone*, trans. by Gilbert Murray, quoted in Arnold Toynbee, *Greek historical thought* (New York: New American Library, 1952), p. 128; Plato, *Critias*, ibid., pp. 146–47. On the theme of man-nature relationships in Western thought, see Clarence Glacken's monumental *Traces on the Rhodian shore*, Berkeley, Cal.: Univ. of California Press, 1967.
7. Aristotle, *Mechanics* **847**, a 20.
8. Gibbons, E. *The decline and fall of the Roman Empire*, chap. 2.
9. Bradford, J. 1957. *Ancient landscapes* (London), p. 145.

10. Chatley, H. 1917. "Feng Shui," in *Encyclopaedia Sinica,* ed. by S. Couling (Shanghai), p. 175.
11. *Chou Li,* trans. by E. Biot as *Le Techeou-li* (Paris: 1851) 1:371–74.
12. Mencius, Bk. 1, pt. 1, 3:3.
13. Chen Teng. (1596). Gazetteer. Quoted by W. C. Lowdermilk and D. R. Wickes, *History of soil use in the Wu T'ai Shan area,* Monograph, Royal Asiatic Soc., North China Branch, 1938, p. 8.
14. Wright, A. F. 1965. Symbolism and function: reflections on Changan and other great cities, *J. Asian Studies* 24:670.
15. Mencius, Bk. 3, pt. 1, 4:7.
16. Steward, A. N., and Y. Cheo. 1935. Geographical and ecological notes on botanical exploration in Kwangsi province, China, *Nanking Journal* 5:174.
17. Hartwell, R. 1962. A revolution in Chinese iron and coal industries during the Northern Sung, 960–1126 A.D., *J. Asian Studies* 21:159.
18. Gernet, J. 1962. *Daily life in China on the eve of the Mongol invasion 1250–1276* (London: Allen & Unwin), p. 114.
19. Moule, A. C. 1957. *Quinsai* (Cambridge Univ. Press), p. 51.
20. McMullen, J. 1967. "Confucianism and forestry in seventeenth-century Japan." Unpublished paper, Toronto. I am grateful to Professor McMullen for allowing me to read this.
21. Schafer, E. H. 1962. The conservation of nature under the T'ang dynasty, *J. Econ. and Soc. Hist. of the Orient* 5:299–300.
22. Reischauer, E. O. 1955. *Ennin's travels in T'ang China* (New York: Ronald Press), pp. 153–56.
23. Buchanan, K., 1960. The changing face of rural China, *Pacific Viewpoint,* 1:19.
24. Murphey, R. 1967. Man and nature in China, *Modern Asian Studies 1,* no. 4:313–33.

PART TWO

SYSTEMS AND CYCLES

> All the rivers run into the sea; yet the sea is not full; unto the place from whence the rivers come, thither they return again.
>
> *Ecclesiastes 1:7*

To avoid overgeneralization concerning cultural differences we can adopt an attitude similar to that of the geneticist regarding racial differences. Just as races differ in the frequency with which certain gene alleles occur, so certain cultural influences may be more prevalent in one culture than another. A reserve of heterogeneous concepts provides a basis for change, and for the inconsistency and paradox which Yi-Fu Tuan marks as a characteristic of human nature. The particular set of responses which a culture makes to its environment may well depend upon a series of historical, material events, and not upon a binding cultural tradition.

When ideals and necessities come into conflict, no one is surprised if necessities are satisfied and ideals are deferred or altered. There are, however, two general classes of "necessities." We can call these vital needs and created needs. Vital needs are the requirements of life: air, food, space, water, etc. Created needs are those without which life is clearly possible, but which are nonetheless strongly desired. It is obvious that some accommodation between ideals and vital needs must be reached if a population is to survive. Conflict between ideals and created needs, or between created needs and vital needs, provides grounds for argument. This is the area of discussion and debate which has followed recognition of our environmental crisis.

Identification of man as an animal, similar to other animals in regard to vital needs, provides a basic list of such needs. The realization that all animals, simple or complex, are both similar and unique defines an important area of research: the determination of those needs, if any, which are uniquely human.

The identification of man as an animal also implies a place for man in the interwoven relationships which constitute the ecosystem. In his survey of man's ecological position, The Ecology of Man, the Animal, S. Charles Kendeigh emphasizes that most characteristics considered to be uniquely human can be explained as specializations based on structures or functions found in nonhuman organisms. Evolution serves as a bridge between nonhuman and human nature and provides a biological perspective for man. This biological perspective is a valuable addition to the discussion concerning the relationship of man to nonhuman nature. If man is a product of nonhuman nature, an extension of that "otherness," then he cannot separate himself from it or place himself above it. He can only try to determine his place within it.

THE ECOLOGY OF MAN, THE ANIMAL

S. Charles Kendeigh

The fundamental and basic concepts of animal ecology are also the fundamental and basic concepts of human ecology. Primitive man had few, if any, characteristics not also found in animals. Modern man is certainly more highly developed and specialized psychologically than any animal, but specialization of one sort or another is found in every animal species. Specialization is a product of evolution, and those characteristics or traits of man often considered to be unique can all be traced back to primitive characteristics, traits, or potentialities found also in animals. Many analogous traits not in direct line of descent to man have been evolved in other organisms. Let us enumerate a few.

Erect bipedal locomotion occurs in birds. A squirrel will use its hands to manipulate a nut, or a monkey a banana, as expertly as man. Laughter in man appears as an exaggeration of facial expressions and specific behavior indicating pleasure found among mammals at play. Sticks are used as a tool by a Galapagos finch to pry insect larvae out of holes in dead wood; spiders set a web net to capture food from the air as a fisherman does from the water; and hermit crabs use empty shells as homes and shields against predation by enemies. Many tropical species maintain sexual and reproductive activities throughout the year as does man who comes from tropical ancestors. Parental care of young is perhaps more complex and highly developed in birds than in any other animal, including man. Intercommunication between individuals is well evolved within animal species, not by use of a vocabulary or the written word it is true but by a great variety of scent stimuli—color displays, sounds, call-notes, and songs—each conveying a special meaning. It may not be entirely coincidental that the songs of birds have an esthetic appeal to man; perhaps they have also to birds themselves who have evolved specific song patterns, melodies, and qualities of tone through a long period of natural and sexual selection. Social hierarchies exist among many gregarious species of animals and territorial behavior is evidenced among solitary nesting ones, equivalent to similar behavior in the human species. The leaf-cutting ants of the tropics practice agriculture when they bring leaves into their nest-mounds on which they cultivate a mold used as food. They likewise practice sanitation by systematically removing and depositing feces and wastes at some distance from their nests. The organized

Reprinted with permission from *BioScience*, Vol. 15, No. 8, 1965, pp. 521–523. The author is Senior Staff Member of the Center for Zoonoses Research at the University of Illinois, Urbana.

industry of ants, termites, and some birds is well shown in the construction of colonial nests. Division of labor is expressed at various levels in the animal kingdom, beginning with separation of reproductive and somatic cells in the colonial protozoans and the differentiation of tissues and organs in the lower invertebrates and attaining complex dimensions among the social insects where different individuals are adapted for special functions. Division of labor is also evident in the biotic community where various species play special roles in the cycling of nutrients, the capture and transmission of energy, the regulation of population balances, the creation of microclimates, etc., analogous to the role of different trades or vocations in the human community. Animals may even have a primitive type of culture and ethics, if we mean a mores or behavior that is beneficial and traditional for the species and which is handed down to succeeding generations in large part by learning of the young.

Man's chief claim to uniqueness lies in the highly specialized development and functioning of his brain. His morphological and physiological capacities to do things are very limited, likewise his innate tolerance of even moderately rugged climatic conditions. However, his highly evolved intelligence has enabled him to circumvent many of his limitations: he has invented complex tools to do his tasks, he uses fire and air-conditioning to keep his shelter comfortable, his manufactured clothing allows him to invade microclimates for which otherwise he is not physiologically adapted, and his industrial skill has enabled him more completely to exploit natural resources. Conceptual thought, capacity for abstraction and synthesis, the use of symbols in speech and writing, ability to reason and anticipate events, self-consciousness, and the spiritual and esthetic values seen in religion and art were doubtless latent in primitive man and had to be developed through effort and practice to reach the fruition seen in modern man. This cultural evolution has gone on mostly independently of biological evolution, and the mind of modern civilized man is the latest step in an evolutionary process that began only about 40,000 to 50,000 years ago and reached explosive proportions only within the last 5000 years. This specialization, although unique to man, is actually no more unique in evolution than specializations of other sorts found in many other animals. Man still requires food, water, and space; a favorable microclimate; protection from enemies; and reproduction. To obtain these requirements for life he must fit into an ecosystem as do other animal species, even through the ecosystem is a highly modified one of his own creation.

If one looks at the geological time table, one sees that during the last billion or so years life has evolved from single celled plants and animals living in the sea to more comple invertebrates and primitive fish, invasion of fresh-water and land habitats, and evolution of insects, amphibians, reptiles, birds, and mammals. Man did not come physically into this succession until a million or so years ago. There can be no prediction nor certainty but that in the next million years—or billion years—many new types of animal life will appear; and man, as we know him today, will either be exterminated or greatly altered in appearance, form, and function.

Man probably originated, as did most groups of vertebrate animals, in the Old World tropics and dispersed as shifting climates, vegetation, and land bridges permitted, into Europe, northern Asia, North and South America, Australia, and southern Africa. In these different areas, populations of man became isolated for many thousands of years and were prevented from interbreeding with other populations by physiographic, climatic, or biotic barriers. As is common with animals, this geographic isolation allowed genetic variations to occur and become established, involving color of skin, texture of hair, and other characteristics. Variations in tribal customs evolved. Occupany of new environments and contacts with different biota exposed populations in different areas to different selection pressures and they came to occupy somewhat different ecological niches. If this geographic isolation had persisted a few more thousand years, doubtlessly reproductive isolating mechanisms, already partially formed, would have become fully established, and *Homo sapiens* would have differentiated into a number of new species. The evolution of civilization, however, interrupted this process of speciation. Artificial means of transportation encouraged world-wide travel, and this brought the bypassing of geographical barriers, the breaking down of ecological and ethological evolving reproductive isolating mechanisms, and the fusing of the races and their cultures again into one, so that the species was preserved in its biological unity.

The population density and distribution of primitive man varied in relation to natural conditions according to the normal or Gaussian curve, reaching a peak under optimum conditions and tailing off toward both maximum and minimum limits of physiological tolerance for environmental extremes. Shelford's law of tolerance is a generalization of these relations between abundance, physiological comfort, and environmental factors applicable to all organisms. Modern man has skewed the curve somewhat by this fabrication of artificial home and working environments but the law still applies.

Liebig's law of the minimum and Blackman's limiting factors state that the growth, activity, or even existence of an organism is determined or regulated by that essential factor or condition in shortest supply. Modern man has developed methods of distributing essential elements or products to alleviate local deficiencies, but when his transport system breaks down or in areas where it has not been perfected, the working of this law is apparent.

Primitive man was certainly a constituent member of the biotic community. He was dependent upon the vegetation for shelter from the weather, as protection against enemies, as a source of food, and for use in other ways. His niche in the community has been compared with that of one of the larger carnivores. He had to compete with other carnivores and the larger herbivores for the essentials of life, and his role in the community was determined by his successes and failures in establishing favorable interrelations. When primitive man changed into modern man with the perfection of his intelligence and his invention of new tools, he changed from an ordinary member of the community to an ecological dominant. By building a home of his own that gave shelter from both weather and enemy and the development of agriculture, he was no longer dependent on the community as it was originally constituted. He modified the community to suit his own needs, determined to a large extent what other species he would permit to associate with him, and established the rules and conditions for their doing so. During geological time there have been a long series of organisms that have assumed dominance for periods of time, and often by no less drastic changes in the habitat and community. Man, in fact, has not yet obtained complete dominance in the arctic tundra, the desert, the tropical rain forest, or the ocean. Even in temperate regions, whenever man relaxes his dominance or mismanages the habitat, there is reversion of the region to dominance by other native species.

Civilized man, as primitive man, is still dependent on plants for nutrition and energy. Civilized man, however, has created an ecosystem where the kinds of nutrients that he likes and the energy that he needs can be obtained more efficiently than in ecosystems which he does not dominate. Crops have been developed through selective breeding and have been cultivated by special methods to give high yields. Competition for food from other species has been greatly reduced by use of fences, guns, pesticides, and the hoe. Plant crops are either consumed directly or fed to domesticated animals in a higher trophic level, so that meat as well as vegetables are eaten. In removing this harvest from his ecosystem he removes nutrient elements that in natural ecosystems circulate continuously, first through plants, then animals, then to the transformers in the soil that render them available for reabsorption by plants. Man acknowledges the important role of nutrient cycles in the ecosystem when he returns the nutrients that he has taken for food in the form of fertilizers unsuitable for his direct assimilation.

In natural ecosystems, food chains start with green plants because of their unique ability to capture solar energy and to synthesize nutrients from raw materials. With each additional link in the food chain through which energy and nutrients are transmitted there is a loss of some 80 or 90%. Each trophic level uses energy for maintaining its own existence and activities and there is wastage through prey not eaten, nonpredatory deaths, excreta, and heat. Consequently, with addition of links in the food chain, there is decrease in number of individuals or biomass that can be supported and in variety of species. The biomass of herbivores is always greater than the biomass of carnivores. In densely populated parts of the human world, man has largely given up the luxury of eating beef, pork, fowl, and lamb and depends instead on wheat, rice, or corn, thereby eliminating one trophic level and taking fuller advantage of the productivity of the land. If man could reduce the length of the food chain still further through bypassing plants and using solar radiation directly for the manufacture of food and for other uses, he would have a supply of energy several hundred times greater than is now captured by plants.

The sigmoid growth curve represents approximately the manner and rate by which cells, organs, individuals, populations, and communities increase in size and complexity. In the lower part of the curve, conditions for growth are very favorable and growth proceeds at an ever accelerating pace. However, inhibiting factors come to exert an increasingly important role and beyond the point of inflection they gradually bring the growth curve to an asymptote. With animals, the size of the asymptotic population is determined by available space, suitable food, and favorable climate. Factors that may ultimately stabilize the population at the asymptote are density-dependent, that is, they vary in intensity of their action with the density of the population. These factors consist of predation, disease, emigration, competition, and fecundity. Some species, certain insects and perhaps Arctic rodents and grouse among others, never attain stabilized populations. Their populations continue to increase to the limit of space or food supply or until unfavorable weather occurs. Then there is a crash and the few scattered survivors start the growth process over again.

Modern man has largely eliminated predation as a mortality factor, he has conquered many diseases and may conceivably subdue the rest, and he has emigrated to all favorable parts of the world even though he has not settled in large numbers as yet in some parts of it. With the harnessing of solar energy and intelligent use of minerals, man may be able to produce a superabundance of food through a sort of artificial photosynthesis as well as apply this energy industrially. Likewise, he may obtain control over the weather. Space is limited, however, at least on earth, and it is difficult to see what he can do about it aside from building megalopoli, skyscrapers, underground burrows, sea platforms, or vast air chambers underwater. Space may be the limiting factor ultimately setting the limit to the size of the human population on earth. The amount of space reduction that the human animal will tolerate may not be just space to stand on but space in which he can carry on a comfortable existence. Competition will continue to be a potent factor, as it is in regulating all animal populations. War may someday be eliminated and the world someday may function as a single economic unit, but it is difficult to conceive how competition between individuals can be significantly reduced as the limits of space are approached; more likely it will become accentuated in the final struggles for existence.

With the advent of civilization and modern industrialization, all efforts to date have been to reduce mortality rates and expand available resources. This has thrown the stabilized populations of primitive man out of balance and brought on a new accelerating phase in the growth curve. Populations will not again be brought into stabilization until birth rate and mortality rates again balance. This means that the birth rate must be reduced in proportion to the reduction of mortality rate. This occurs in populations of wild animals more or less automatically through changes in physiology and behavior. Man's biggest challenge in the present age is whether his great intellect will give him the self-discipline and skill to regulate his own population growth to the level best suited for the perpetuation of the culture that he has evolved as well as for his physical existence.

The laws of Nature apply to man as they do to animals. There are no exceptions. If he can come to understand what they are and how they work, he will know better what to anticipate concerning their effects on himself. He cannot ignore the dynamic forces of the environment with impunity, but being blessed with an intelligence far above that of other animals, he can guard against them or alleviate their effects to his own advantage.

ECOLOGY

Robert M. Chute

Ecology is more than a study of an organism *in* its environment. It is the integrated study of organisms *and* their environment. Individual ecologists may work on only one problem at a time and their working view of ecology may be quite limited in scope. The ideas, the concepts, that are the consequence of their individual work fit together, hopefully without contradiction, to build an intellectual construct of great dimensions and significance. What ecologists are about is no less than building an understanding of the role of living things in the structure and function of the universe. Ecology, as an integrative discipline, can provide a framework within which man's seemingly disparate activities can be seen in relationship to each other and, perhaps dimly, in relation to a whole. Ecology is not the only integrative discipline, but it is a useful one, and the practical reasons for its study are compelling. Dealing with the essential physical and chemical factors, food, and energy, it involves us in consideration of the prerequisites of existence. Life may not be sufficient to ensure the successful pursuit of happiness but it is surely necessary.

Of fundamental importance in contemporary ecology is the concept of the ecosystem. This concept is the recognition that living things interact with, and exchange energy and materials with, their nonliving environment. The system of relationships between the organism and its environment is an ecosystem. All the substance of an organism has its origin outside the body of the organism, in the environment. All the energy we see expressed as work, growth, movement, and reproduction has its origin in the environment. The organism is the means of its expression, not its source.

The activity of organisms in their environment is subject to the same physical laws which describe the interactions of nonliving matter and the transformation of energy in nonliving systems. Two such descriptive physical laws of special significance to students of ecology are the first and second laws of thermodynamics, dealing with the conservation of matter and energy and the efficiency of energy transformations. In the most general terms the first law tells us that energy and matter cannot be created or destroyed but only changed from one form to another. Thus the origin, the evolution, the growth and development, the nutrition, and the excretion of organisms represent the transformations of existent matter and its redistribution in space. The second law informs us that every transformation of matter and energy is less than 100 percent efficient and that organisms, to continue to function, must continue to receive new supplies of matter and energy. These laws tell us some of the limits of the possible. Their recognition helps to dispel the "wishful thinking" that so often confounds man in his study of himself in relation to the environment.

The study of the necessary relationships between different types of organisms and between organisms and their environment has resulted in the description of various biogeochemical cycles. These cycles, represented in Figure 1 by the carbon cycle, provide a convenient way of summarizing a very complex situation. Similar cycles can be constructed for all the chemical elements used by organisms.

The occurrence of organisms in the environment is discontinued: They are found here but not there. The limited region of the total environment where a species lives defines its habitat. The analysis of habitats, with an attempt to understand the discontinuous distribution of organisms, has been a major aspect of ecological study. This study has led to the recognition of an upper and a lower limit of tolerance of any species to

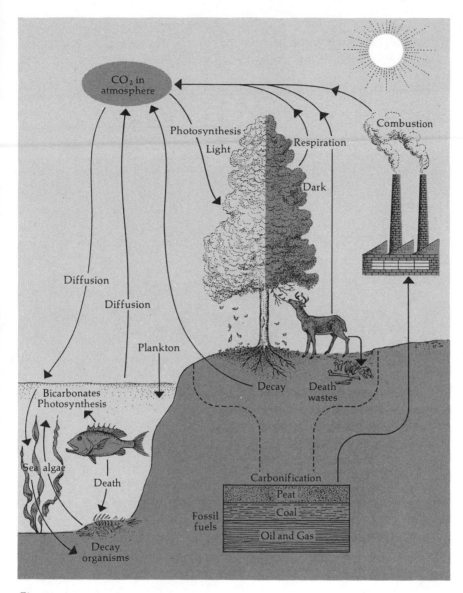

Fig. 1
The carbon cycle in the ecosystem.

physical and chemical factors (heat, pressure, salt concentration, acidity). This law of tolerance helps to define the range of possible habitats for a species.

Within the possible habitats for a species the population density may be quite uniform or may vary widely from one possible habitat to another. The whole complex of factors which define the habitat can limit the population, depending upon the level or availability of the factors. Usually one factor, the limiting factor, can be found which, if changed, will allow population to increase until some other substance or condition assumes the limiting role.

Habitat analysis determines the conditions under which a species can and does exist. An examination of the ecological niche of the species begins to reveal the processes by which the organism carries out its role in the exchange and transformation of material and energy within the ecosystem. Niche is a word with physical and spatial connotations as a result of its use in other contexts. Here niche is used to refer to the spe-

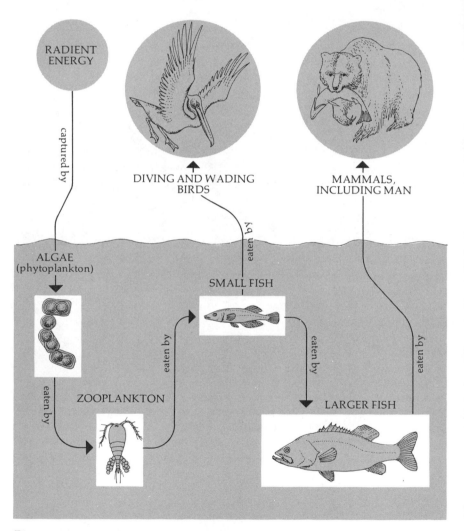

Fig. 2
Food chain for an aquatic community.

cific set of processes or activities by which the organism satisfies its vital needs through interaction with its environment. In a sense an organism's niche is its *function* in the environment, whereas habitat is its *location*.

There are two ways in which these functions can be schematized. Different species occupying the same habitat can be arranged in a food chain or food web expressing the dependency of each species upon other species or upon its environment for food and energy. An example of such

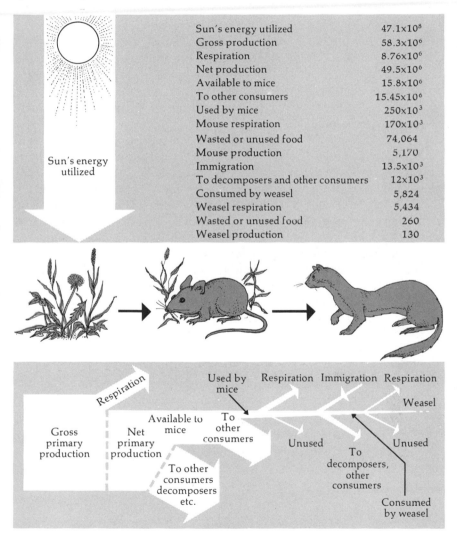

Sun's energy utilized	47.1×10^8
Gross production	58.3×10^6
Respiration	8.76×10^6
Net production	49.5×10^6
Available to mice	15.8×10^6
To other consumers	15.45×10^6
Used by mice	250×10^3
Mouse respiration	170×10^3
Wasted or unused food	74,064
Mouse production	5,170
Immigration	13.5×10^3
To decomposers and other consumers	12×10^3
Consumed by weasel	5,824
Weasel respiration	5,434
Wasted or unused food	260
Weasel production	130

Fig. 3
Energy flow through a food chain in an old-field community in southern Michigan. The relative sizes of the blocks suggest the quantity of energy flowing through each channel. (Values are in cal per ha/per year.) (Based on data from Golley, 1960.)

a food chain is shown in Figure 2. The food chain illustrated quickly becomes a network or food web when we include more and more species and more and more cross-connections.

A second way to illustrate functional relationships in an ecosystem is to deal with types of organisms rather than with species. Following this approach the plants and animals in Figure 2 becomes representatives of functional types. The algae are primary producers, the zooplankton primary consumers, the small fish secondary consumers, and so on. All photosynthetic organism within the ecosystem would be classed together as primary producers and all herbivorus species grouped together as primary consumers. These general categories are frequently referred to as *trophic levels.* Use of the concept of trophic level greatly simplifies the process of thinking about the diverse collection of organisms which may occupy a single habitat and provides a basis for comparison between habitats. Figure 3 illustrates one way in which the energy relationships between producers, consumers, and decomposers can be simplified and displayed. It is important to note the small fraction of the primary production energy used by the weasel. A human population, if dependent upon animals as a major source of food, is in a position analogous to the weasel population in this example. The trophic level or trophic structure approach is specifically useful when we study a biotic community. In ecological terms a biotic community is the assemblage of species populations coexisting in an area. By analysis of a community in terms of trophic levels, by recognizing the direction and magnitude of flow of energy and material between trophic levels, we can gain new insight into the interdependence between organisms and into the operation of the community as a whole.

This approach also lends itself to the quantitative treatment of environmental events. In their report, Nutrient Cycling, *F. H. Bormann and G. E. Likens redefine and demonstrate the usefulness of the concepts of the biogeochemical cycle and trophic levels. They also expose some of the difficulties in obtaining quantitative data for even a relatively small and well-defined biotic community.*

NUTRIENT CYCLING

F. H. Bormann and G. E. Likens

Life on our planet is dependent upon the cycle of elements in the biosphere. Atmospheric carbon dioxide would be exhausted in a year or so by green plants were not the atmosphere continually recharged by CO_2 generated by respiration and fire (1). Also, it is well known that life requires a constant cycling of nitrogen, oxygen, and water. These cycles include a gaseous phase and have self-regulating feedback mechanisms that make them relatively perfect (2). Any increase in movement along one path is quickly compensated for by adjustments along other paths. Recently, however, concern has been expressed over the possible disruption of the carbon cycle by the burning of fossil fuel (3) and of the nitrogen cycle by the thoughtless introduction of pesticides and other substances into the biosphere (4).

Of no less importance to life are the elements with sedimentary cycles, such as phosphorus, calcium, and magnesium. With these cycles, there is a continual loss from biological systems in response to erosion, with ultimate deposition in the sea. Replacement or return of an element with a sedimentary cycle to terrestrial biological systems is dependent upon such processes as weathering of rocks, additions from volcanic gases, or the biological movement from the sea to the land. Sedimentary cycles are less perfect and more easily disrupted by man than carbon and nitrogen cycles (2). Acceleration of losses or, more specifically, the disruption of local cycling patterns by the activities of man could reduce existing "pools" of an element in local ecosystems, restrict productivity, and consequently limit human population. For example, many agriculturalists, food scientists, and ecologists believe that man is accelerating losses of phosphorus and that this element will be a critical limiting resource for the functioning of the biosphere (1, 5).

Recognition of the importance of these biogeochemical processes to the welfare of mankind has generated intensive study of such cycles. Among ecologists and foresters working with natural terrestrial ecosystems, this interest has focused on those aspects of biogeochemical cycles that occur *within* particular ecosystems. Thus, information on the distribution of chemical elements and on rates of uptake, retention, and release in vari-

Reprinted with permission from *Science*, Vol. 155, 1967, pp. 424–429. Copyright 1967 by the American Association for the Advancement of Science. Dr. Bormann is Dostler Professor of Forest Ecology, Yale University School of Forestry, New Haven, Conn. Dr. Likens is an Associate Professor at Cornell University, Ithaca, N.Y.

ous ecosystems has been accumulating (6). Little has been done to establish the role that weathering and erosion play in these systems.

Yet, the rate of release of nutrients from minerals by weathering, the addition of nutrients by erosion, and the loss of nutrients by erosion are three primary determinants of structure and function in terrestrial ecosystem. Further, with this information it is possible to develop total chemical budgets for ecosystems and to relate these data to the larger biogeochemical cycles.

It is largely because of the complex natural interaction of the hydrologic cycle and nutrient cycles that it has not been possible to establish these relationships. In many ecosystems this interaction almost hopelessly complicates the measurements of weathering or erosion. Under certain conditions, however, these apparent hindrances can be turned to good advantage in an integrated study of biogeochemical cycling in small watershed ecosystems.

It is the function of this article (i) to develop the idea that small watersheds can be used to measure weathering and erosion, (ii) to describe the parameters of watersheds particularly suited for this type of study, and (iii) to discuss the types of nutrient-cycling problems that this model renders susceptible to attack. Finally, (iv) the argument is developed that the watershed ecosystem provides an ideal setting for studies of ecosystem dynamics in general.

ECOSYSTEM DEFINED

Communities such as fields and forests may be considered as ecological systems (7) in which living organisms and their physical and biological environments constitute a single interacting unit. These ecosystems occupy an arbitrarily defined volume of the biosphere at the earth-atmosphere interface.

Lateral boundaries of an ecosystem may be chosen to coincide with those of a biological community, such as the edges of a forest, or with the boundary of some pronounced characteristic of the physical environment, such as the shoreline of a small island. Most often, however, the continuous nature of vegetation and of the physical environment makes it difficult to establish exact lateral boundaries on the basis of "community" or "environmental discontinuity" (8). Often the investigator arbitrarily selects an area that may be conveniently studied.

From a functional point of view it is meaningless to include within the vertical limits of an ecosystem *all* of the column of air above and of soil and rock below the laterally defined ecosystem. For a working model of an ecosystem, it seems reasonable to include *only* that part of the column where atoms and molecules may participate in the chemical cycling that occurs within the system (see the "intrasystem cycle" of Fig. 1). When

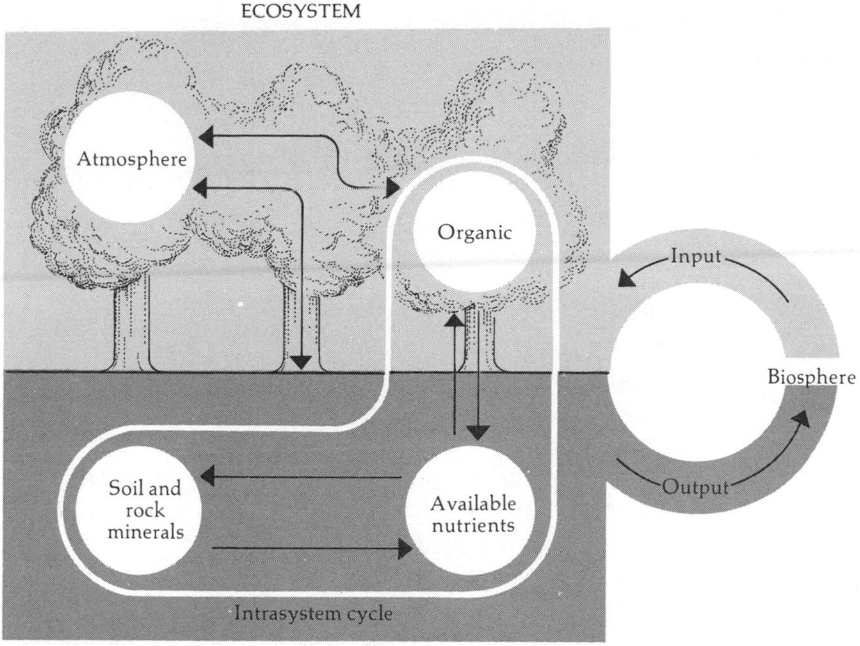

ECOSYSTEM

Atmosphere

Organic

Input

Biosphere

Soil and
rock
minerals

Available
nutrients

Output

Intrasystem cycle

Fig. 1
*Nutrient relationships of a terrestrial ecosystem, showing sites of accumulation
and major pathways. Input and output may be composed of geologic, meteorologic, and biologic components, as described in the text.*

the biological community is taken as a determinant, the vertical extensions of the terrestrial ecosystem will be delimited by the top of the vegetation and the depth to which roots and other organisms penetrate into
the regolith (9). Vertical dimensions, defined in this manner, can expand
or contract depending on the growth potential of present or succeeding
communities. Thus, volumetric changes with time can be considered—
for example, those associated with primary and secondary succession or
with cliseral changes.

THE ECOSYSTEM AND BIOGEOCHEMICAL CYCLING

The terrestrial ecosystem participates in the various larger biogeochemical
cycles of the earth through a system of inputs and outputs. Biogeochemical input in forest or field ecosystems may be derived from three major
sources: geologic, meteorologic, and biologic. Geologic input is here defined as dissolved or particulate matter carried into the system by moving
water or colluvial action, or both. Depositions of the products of erosion
or mass wasting and ions dissolved in incoming seepage water are exam-

ples of geologic input. Meteorologic input enters the ecosystem through the atmosphere and is composed of additions of gaseous materials and of dissolved or particulate matter in precipitation, dust, and other wind-borne materials. Chemicals in gaseous form fixed by biologic activity within the ecosystem are considered to be meteorologic input. Biological input results from animal activity and is made up of depositions of materials originally gathered elsewhere; examples are fecal material of animals whose food was gathered outside the system, or fertilizers intentionally added by man.

Chemical may leave the ecosystem in the form of dissolved or particulate matter in moving water or colluvium, or both (geologic output); through the diffusion or transport of gases or particulate matter by wind (meteorologic output); or as a result of the activity of animals, including man (biologic output).

Nutrients are found in four compartments within the terrestrial ecosystem: in the atmosphere, in the pool of available nutrients in the soil, in organic materials (biota and organic debris), and in soil and rock minerals (Fig. 1). The atmospheric compartment includes all atoms or molecules in gaseous form in both the below-ground and the above-ground portions of the ecosystem. The pool of available nutrients in the soil consists of all ions adsorbed on the clay-humus complex or dissolved in the soil solution. The organic compartment includes all atoms incorporated in living organisms and in their dead remains. (The distinction between living and dead is sometimes hard to make, particularly in the case of woody perennial plants.) The soil-rock compartment is comprised of elements incorporated in primary and secondary minerals, including the more readily decomposable minerals that enter into equilibrium reactions with the available nutrients.

The degree to which a nutrient circulates within a terrestrial ecosystem is determined, in part, by its physical state. Gases are easily moved by random forces of diffusion and air circulation; consequently, nutrients with a prominent gaseous phase tend not to cycle within the boundaries of a particular ecosystem but, rather, to be continually lost and replaced from outside. On the other hand, elements without a prominent gaseous phase may show considerable intrasystem cycling between the available-nutrient, organic, and soil-rock compartments (Fig. 1). This internal cycle results from (i) the uptake of nutrients by plants, (ii) the release of nutrients from plants by direct leaching, (iii) the release of nutrients from organic matter by biological decomposition, and (iv) equilibrium reactions that convert insoluble chemical forms in the soil-rock compartment to soluble forms in the available-nutrient compartment, and vice versa.

Available nutrients not only enter the ecosystem from outside but are added by the action of physical, chemical, and biological weathering of rock and soil minerals already within the system. Although some ions are continually withdrawn from the available-nutrient compartment, forming secondary minerals in the soil and rocks, for most nutrient elements there is a net movement out of the soil-rock compartment. As the ecosystem is gradually lowered in place by erosion or by the downward growth of roots, new supplies of residual rock or other parent material are included; in some systems these materials may also be added as geologic input.

HYDROLOGIC-CYCLE, NUTRIENT-CYCLE INTERACTION

At many points, nutrient cycles may be strongly geared to the hydrologic cycle. Nutrient input and output are directly related to the amounts of water that move into and out of an ecosystem, as emphasized by the "leaching" and "flushing" concepts of Pearsall (10), Dahl (11), and Ratcliffe (12), while temporal and absolute limits of biogeochemical activities within the system are markedly influenced by the hydrologic regime. Biologic uptake of nutrients by plants and release of nutrients by biological decomposition are closely related to the pattern of water availability. Potential levels of biomass within the system are determined in large measure by precipitation characteristics. Similarly, the nature and rate of weathering and soil formation are influenced by the hydrologic regime, since water is essential to the major chemical weathering processes [ion exchange, hydrolysis, solution, diffusion, and oxidation-reduction, and adsorption and swelling (13)].

BIOGEOCHEMICAL STUDIES OF ECOSYSTEMS

Although study of nutrient input, nutrient output, and weathering is necessary for an understanding of field and forest ecosystem (6), ecologists, foresters, and pedologists have generally focused attention on the internal characteristics alone. Thus, considerable information has been accumulated on uptake, retention, and release of nutrients by the biota of ecosystems, and on soil-nutrient relationships (see, for example, 6, 14). Rarely are these internal characteristics of the ecosystem correlated with input and output data, yet all these parameters are necessary for the construction of nutrient budgets of particular ecosystems, and for establishing the relationship of the smaller system to the biosphere.

Quantitative data on input-output relationships are at best spotty. There are many data on nutrient output due to harvesting of vegetation, but for particular natural ecosystems there are only sporadic data on nutrient input in precipitation, or on nutrient output in drainage waters (6). Recently, small lysimeters have been used successfully in the measurement of nutrient dynamics within the soil profile and in the measurement of nutrient losses in drainage water (*15*). The lysimeter technique seems to be well suited for studying ecosystems characterized by coarse-textured soils with a relatively low field capacity (*16*), high porosity, and no surface runoff. For most ecosystems, however, lysimeters are probably of limited value for measuring *total* nutrient output because (i) they are of questionable accuracy when used in rocky or markedly uneven ground, (ii) they cannot evaluate nutrient losses in surface waters, and (iii) their installation requires considerable disturbance of the soil profile.

The lack of information on the nutrient-input, nutrient-output relationships of ecosystems is apparently related to two considerations: (i) integrated studies of ecosystems tend to fall into an intellectual "no man's land" between traditional concepts of ecology, geology, and pedology; (ii) more important, the measurement of nutrient input and output requires measurement of hydrologic input and output. Unquestionably this lack of quantitative information is related to the difficulties encountered in measuring nutrients entering or leaving an ecosystem in seepage water or in sheet or rill flow, and to the high cost, in time and money, of obtaining continuous measurements of the more conventional hydrologic parameters of precipitation and stream flow. In many systems the problem is further complicated by the fact that much water may leave by way of deep seepage, eventually appearing in another drainage system; direct measurement of loss of water and nutrients by this route is virtually impossible.

SMALL-WATERSHED APPROACH
TO BIOGEOCHEMICAL CYCLING

In some ecosystems the nutrient-cycle, hydrologic-cycle interaction can be turned to good advantage in the study of nutrient budgets, erosion, and weathering. This is particularly so if an ecosystem meets two specifications: (i) if the ecosystem is a watershed, and (ii) if the watershed is underlain by a tight bedrock or other impermeable base, such as permafrost. Given these conditions, for chemical elements without a gaseous form at biological temperatures, it is possible to construct nutrient budgets showing input, output, and net loss or gain from the system. These data provide estimates of weathering and erosion.

If the ecosystem were a small watershed, input would be limited to meteorologic and biologic origins. Geologic input, as defined above, need not be considered because there would be no transfer of alluvial or colluvial material between adjacent watersheds. Although materials might be moved within the ecosystem by alluvial or colluvial forces, these materials would originate within the ecosystem.

When the input and output of dust or windblown materials is negligible (this is certainly not the case in some systems), meteorologic input can

be measured from a combination of hydrologic and precipitation-chem-
istry parameters. From periodic measurements of the elements contained
in precipitation and from continuous measurements of precipitation
entering a watershed of known area, one may calculate the temporal
input of an element in terms of grams per hectare. Noncoincidence of the
topographic divide of the watershed and the phreatic divide may introduce a small error (17).

Losses from this watershed ecosystem would be limited to geologic and
biologic output. Given an impermeable base, geologic output (losses due
to erosion) would consist of dissolved and particulate matter in either
stream water or seepage water moving downhill above the impermeable
base. Although downhill mass movement may occur within the system,
the products of this movement are delivered to the stream bed, whence
they are removed by erosion and stream transportation.

Geologic output can be estimated from hydrologic and chemical measurements. A weir, anchored to the bedrock, will force all drainage water
from the watershed to flow over the notch, where the volume and rate of
flow can be measured. These data, in combination with periodic measures
of dissolved and particulate matter in the outflowing water, provide an
estimate of geologic output which may be expressed as grams of an element lost per hectare of watershed.

The nutrient budget for a single element in the watershed ecosystem
may be expressed as follows: (meteorologic input + biologic output) −
(geologic output + biologic output) = net loss or gain. This equation
may be further simplified if the ecosystem meets a third specification—
if it is part of a much larger, more or less homogeneous, vegetation unit.
Biological output would tend to balance biological input if the ecosystem
contained no special attraction or deterrent for animal populations moving at random through the larger vegetation system, randomly acquiring
or discharging nutrients. On this assumption, the nutrient budget for a
single system would become: (meteorologic input per hectare) − (geologic output per hectare) = net gain or loss per hectare. This fundamental
relationship provides basic data for an integrated study of ecosystem
dynamics.

SMALL WATERSHEDS FOR ECOSYSTEM RESEARCH

The relationship of the individual terrestrial ecosystem to biogeochemical
cycles of the biosphere can be established by the small-watershed approach. Data on input and output of nutrients provide direct measurements of this relationship, while data or net loss provide, as explained
below, an indirect measure of weathering rates for soil and rock minerals
in relatively undisturbed ecosystems.

The small watershed may be used for experiments at the ecosystem level. This has been shown by numerous experiments concerned with hydrologic relationships (see, for example, 18). Thus, it is possible to test the effects of various experimental treatments on the relationship of the individual ecosystem to the biospheric nutrient cycles. Experiments can be designed to determine whether logging, burning, or use of pesticides or herbicides have an appreciable effect on net nutrient losses from the system. This information is not generally available at the ecosystem level.

The small watershed, with its measured parameters of hydrologic and chemical input, output, and net change, is an excellent vehicle for the study of interrelationships within a single ecosystem. Nutrient output may be related to hydrologic parameters such as seasonal and diurnal variations in stream flow, seasonal patterns of precipitation, individual rainstorms, and variations in evapotranspiration. Characteristics of the nutrient cycle may also be related to phenological events occurring within the ecosystem, such as leaf development, initiation of root growth, leaf fall, and litter turnover. In combination with current methods of biomass and nutrient analysis (see, for example, 6), the small-watershed approach provides a comprehensive view of the status and behavior of individual elements within an individual ecosystem.

Weathering, or the rate at which an element bound in soil and rock minerals is made available, can be estimated from net losses of that element as calculated by the nutrient-budget method. Within the ecosystem (watershed), atoms of an element (one that lacks a gaseous form at ecosystem temperatures) may be located in (i) soil and rock minerals, (ii) the biota and organic debris, and (iii) the pool of available nutrients (Fig. 1). There is an intense intrasystem cycling between categories (ii) and (iii) as large quantities of ions are taken up by the vegetation each year and released by direct leaching or stepwise decomposition in the food chain. Ions are continually released to the intrasystem cycle by weathering of soil and rock material. Some of these ions, however, are reconstituted as secondary minerals. If an ecosystem is in a state of dynamic equilibrium, as the presence of climax forest would suggest (19), ionic levels in the intrasystem cycle must remain about the same for many years. Thus, in the climax ecosystem, net ion losses (output minus input) must be balanced by equivalent additions derived from weathering of soil and rock materials. Thus, net ionic losses from an undisturbed, relatively stable terrestrial ecosystem are a measure of weathering within the system. In a successional ecosystem (in which nutrients are accumulating in biomass and organic debris over the course of years), the rate at which an ion is released by weathering must equal its rate of net loss from the ecosystem plus its rate of net accumulation in the biota and organic debris (Fig. 1).

The watershed model allows comparison in relative importance of solution and suspended bed load in removing nutrients from an ecosystem. Nutrient matter can be removed from an ecosystem by three forms of transportation in streams: in solution in the stream water, as inorganic and organic suspended load kept in motion by turbulent flow, and as inorganic and organic bed load slid or rolled along the stream bottom (20). Solution losses may be measured, as described above, from stream-flow data and periodic measurements of dissolved substances in the stream. Part of the losses of suspended matter may be estimated from stream-flow data and periodic measurements of particulate matter obtained by straining or filtering stream water as it comes over the weir. The remaining suspended matter and all of the bed load may be measured above the weir, where these materials collect in the ponding basin. These comparative measurements should be of interest not only to the ecologist concerned with ecosystem dynamics but also, since stream transportation is one of the important aspects of fluvial denudation, to geologists.

The small-watershed approach provides invaluable baseline information for the investigation of stream biology. Life-history studies of stream organisms, population studies, and shifts in community structure and diversity might be correlated with the measured physical and chemical parameters of drainage streams. Analyses of uptake, release, and transport of various nutrients by stream organisms could be made. Moreover, the vegetation of a watershed and the stream draining it are an inseparable unit functionally, and it would be of great interest to obtain information on the biological interaction between them.

SITES FOR WATERSHED STUDIES

Small watersheds meeting the conditions outlined above are probably common. However, even if the desired conditions are met, the investigator studying nutrient cycling is faced with the task of initiating a hydrologic study before he can attack his major problem. This is a time-consuming and expensive procedure, involving construction and maintenance of weirs, establishment of a precipitation network, and continuous collection of records, as well as land rental fees and possible road construction costs. A practical solution to this problem is inauguration of nutrient cycling studies at established hydrologic laboratories, where the required conditions exist and where hydrologic parameters are being measured and data are available.

The feasibility of this approach is demonstrated by our study at the Hubbard Brook Experimental Forest in West Thornton, New Hampshire. There, with the support of the National Science Foundation and the excellent cooperation of the Northeastern Forest Experiment Station, we are studying nutrient cycling and ecosystem dynamics on six small monitored watersheds. We have accumulated data on weathering rates, input, output, and the annual budget of several ions in this northern hardwood

Table 1
Budgets for dissolved cations in watershed No. 3 (42.4 hectares) for the period
June 1963 to June 1964

Cation	Input (kg/hectare)	Output (kg/hectare)	Net change (kg/hectare)
Calcium	3.0	7.7	—4.7
Sodium	1.0	6.3	—5.3
Magnesium	0.7	2.5	—1.8

ecosystem. Also, studies of biomass, phenology, productivity, annual
rates of nutrient turnover, and other factors are being made in one undisturbed watershed and in one in which conditions are being experimentally
modified.

Preliminary data on input, output, and net change for three cations are
presented in Table 1. These results allow us to add some numerical
values to our ecosystem model (Fig. 2). For the calcium cycle, for example, input would be about 3 kilograms per hectare, while output (erosion)

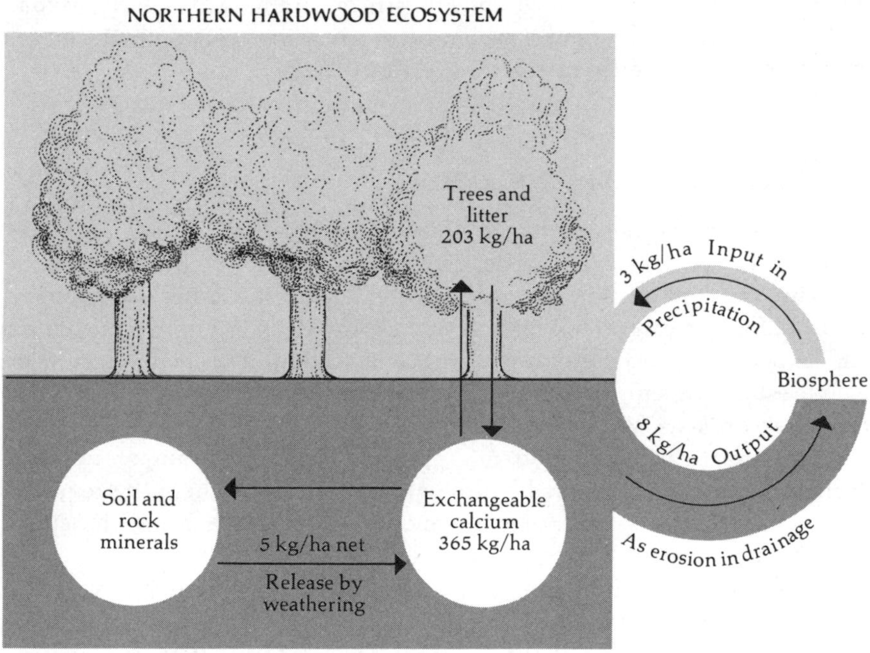

NORTHERN HARDWOOD ECOSYSTEM

Fig. 2
Estimated parameters for the calcium cycle in an undisturbed northern hardwood ecosystem in central New Hampshire. [Data on trees, litter, and exchangeable calcium from Ovington (6)]

is estimated to be about 7.9 kilograms per hectare. Of this latter amount, 98 percent (7.7 kilograms per hectare) is lost in the form of dissolved substances in the stream water, while first approximations indicate that 2 percent is lost as calcium incorporated in organic matter flushed out of the ecosystem. On the basis of assumptions discussed above, it is estimated that the net amount of calcium lost, approximately 5 kilograms per hectare, is replaced by calcium released from soil and rock minerals by weathering. Hence 5 kilograms of calcium per hectare is added to the system each year by weathering.

As yet we have not measured the calcium content of the soil and vegetation or the annual uptake and release of calcium by the biota. From Ovington's data (6), for a beech forest in West England, which must be of about the same magnitude as values for our forest in New Hampshire, we see that 203 kilograms of calcium per hectare are localized in the trees and litter, while 365 kilograms per hectare represent exchangeable calcium in the soil. This gives a total of 568 kilograms of calcium per hectare in organic matter or as available nutrient. Assuming that our forest (Fig. 2) contains a similar amount of calcium, we estimate that a net annual loss of 5 kilograms per hectare would represent only nine-tenths of 1 percent of the total. This suggests a remarkable ability of these undisturbed systems to entrap and hold nutrients. However, if these calculations were based on actual amounts of calcium circulated each year rather than on the total, the percentage losses would be higher.

On its completion, the Hubbard Brook study will have yielded estimates, for individual elements, of many of the parameters and flux rates represented in the nutrient cycle shown in Fig. 1. These data will increase our understanding of fundamental nutrient relationships of undisturbed northern hardwood forests, and they will provide baseline information from which we can judge the effects on nutrient cycling of such practices as cutting, burning, and the application of pesticides.

Studies similar to these at Hubbard Brook could be established elsewhere in the United States. There are thousands of gaged watersheds operated by private and public interests (17), and some of these must meet the proposed requirements. On selected watersheds, cooperative studies could be made by the agencies or organizations controlling the watershed and university-based investigators interested in biogeochemical cycling. Just such cooperation, between federal agencies and universities, has been urged by the Task Group on Coordinated Water Resources Research (21).

Cooperative studies of this type have the advantage of providing a useful exchange of ideas between scientists in diverse fields who are working on the same ecosystem. The studies would provide a larger yield of information on a single system, the prospect of new concepts arising from the available information, and a greater scientific yield per dollar invested. Finally, cooperative studies would make available, for interpretation from the standpoint of nutrient cycling, an invaluable record of past hydrologic performance and, in some cases, of the responses of watersheds to experimental manipulation.

CONCLUSION

The small-watershed approach to problems of nutrient cycling has these advantages. (i) The small watershed is a natural unit of suitable size for intensive study of nutrient cycling at the ecosystem level. (ii) It provides a means of reducing to a minimum, or virtually eliminating, the effect of the difficult-to-measure variables of geologic input and nutrient losses in deep seepage. Control of these variables makes possible accurate measurement of nutrient input and output (erosion) and therefore establishes the relationship of the smaller ecosystem to the larger biospheric cycles. (iii) The small-watershed approach provides a method whereby such important parameters as nutrient release from minerals (weathering) and annual nutrient budgets may be calculated. (iv) It provides a means of studying the interrelationships between the biota and the hydrologic cycle, various nutrient cycles, and energy flow in a single system. (v) Finally, with the small-watershed system we can test the effect of various land-management practices or environmental pollutants on nutrient cycling in natural systems.

REFERENCES AND NOTES

1. L. C. Cole, *Sci. Amer.* **198**, 83 (Apr. 1958).
2. E. P. Odum, *Ecology* (Holt, Rinehart and Winston, New York, 1963).
3. R. Revelle, W. Broecker, H. Craig, C. D. Keeling, J. Smagorinsky, in *Restoring the Quality of Our Environment* (Government Printing Office, Washington, D.C., 1965), pp. 111–133.
4. L. C. Cole, *Saturday Rev.* (7 May 1966).
5. E. P. Odum, *Fundamentals of Ecology* (Saunders, Philadelphia, 1959).
6. J. D. Ovington, in *Advances in Ecological Research*, J. B. Cragg, Ed. (Academic Press, New York, 1962), vol. 1.
7. A. G. Tansley, *Ecology* **16**, 284 (1935).
8. L. B. Slobodkin, *Growth and Regulation of Animal Populations* (Holt, Rinehart and Winston, New York, 1961).
9. H. O. Buckman and N. C. Brady, *The Nature and Properties of Soils* (Macmillan, New York, 1960).
10. W. H. Pearsall, *Mountains and Moorlands* (Collins, London, 1960).
11. E. Dahl, "Rondane. Mountain vegetation in South Norway and its relation to the environment," *Skrifter Norske Videnskaps-Akad. Oslo 1, Mat. Naturv. Kl. 1956* (1956).
12. D. A. Ratcliffe, *J. Ecol.* **47**, 371 (1959).

13. C. Bould, in *Plant Physiology, A Treatise*, F. C. Steward, Ed. (Academic Press, New York, 1963), vol. 3.
14. J. R. Bray and E. Gorham, in *Advances in Ecological Research*, J. B. Cragg, Ed. (Academic Press, New York, 1964), vol. 2; K. J. Mustanoja and A. L. Leaf, *Botan, Rev.* **31**, 151 (1965).
15. D. W. Cole and S. P. Gessel, *Soil Sci. Soc. Amer. Proc*, **25**, 321 (1961); ———, in *Forest-Soil Relationships in North America*, C. T. Youngberg, Ed. (Oregon State Univ. Press, Corvallis, 1965).
16. D. W. Cole, *Soil Sci.* **85**, 293 (1958).
17. C. O. Wisler and E. F. Brater, *Hydrology* (Wiley, New York, 1959).
18. R. E. Dils. *A Guide to the Coweeta Hydrologic Laboratory* (Southeastern Forest Experimental Station, Asheville, N.C., 1957).
19. R. H. Whittaker, *Ecol. Monographs* **23**, 41 (1953).
20. A. N. Strahler, *The Earth Sciences* (Harper & Row, New York, 1963).
21. R. Revelle, *Science* **142**, 1027 (1963).
22. Financial support was provided by National Science Foundation grants GB 1144 and GB 4169. We thank J. Cantlon, N. M. Johnson, R. C. Reynolds, R. H. Whittaker, and G. W. Woodwell for critical comments and suggestions during preparation of the manuscript.

PART THREE

THE MONKEYWRENCH IN THE WATCHWORKS

The Ground Knows Its Place

Now celery. Now carrots. First root crops
then vines. Perennials planted in blocks
and at edges. Berries in rows. Berries
in patches. Military order in corn.
Sprawling map shaped blotches
of pumpkin and squash. Order makes gardens.
Weeds are only flowers growing
where they're not wanted. Order makes cities.
Order makes towns. Weeds are growing
where they're not wanted. The ground,
the black silent ground, usually knows its place.
To maintain order the farmer must plow.
Cultivation means ripping the weeds up.
Weed. Harvest. Keep everything in its place.

Robert M. Chute

Reprinted from *The Wormwood Review*, Vol. 9, No. 1, 1969, p. 27.

In discussions of the role of mutation in evolutionary process, biologists frequently try to reconcile two points: one, that much of the constantly shifting adaptation which occurs in evolution is the consequence of the accumulation of adaptive mutations; two, that the majority of observed mutations are harmful to the organism being observed. The reconcilation comes about by recognizing the very long time over which the evolution of a species takes place and the repetition of individual mutations over this long period. The organism at any specific point in time carries an accumulation of those mutations which have been adaptive. The probability that additional random mutations will improve the adaptiveness of the species becomes progressively less. A common analogy is the probability that a randomly selected new wheel would improve the function of a fine watch.

Each of the species making up a biotic community has been subject to a process of evolutionary adaptation in which the capacity to reproduce its kind under the conditions which exist in its ecosystem has been the measure of success. These conditions include the other species in the community as well as the physical and chemical, or abiotic, factors. As a consequence each species is, both by necessity and by definition, adapted to its ecological niche and to both the biotic and abiotic factors of its habitat.

The adaptation of an organism within the ecosystem has still another dimension. Not only must each species be able to satisfy its own vital needs, its impact upon the environment must not prevent the existence of other species upon which its own existence depends. No member species in the community can continue to exist if it ties up chemical elements in a molecular form which resists degradation and recycling. No producer which does not have the potential to be consumed can persist. No decomposer organism whose biochemical activities do not support the life of the organism whose bodies it decomposes can persist.

These are not to be considered as examples of "the wisdom of nature." It is best, perhaps, not even to consider them examples of something called "the balance of nature." They are merely the conditions necessary for the maintenance of an ecosystem, conditions which are the result of the nature of the physical world and of organisms.

The analogy of the random part added to a watch can be extended to the addition of a new ecological factor, a new selective pressure, to an existing ecosystem. The insertion of a new physical or chemical factor, or of the removal or addition of a species, is more apt to be disruptive than stabilizing. When such changes are supported by the power of man's technology and multiplied by his ever increasing numbers, the effect on the "watch" is more like dropping a monkeywrench than just adding a new wheel.

The use of chlorinated hydrocarbon pesticides such as DDT and DDD has provided an exceptionally well-documented example of the unanticipated effects of the creation of a new ecological factor. Some of the unexpected and undesirable consequences of the widespread use of persistent pesticides is due to the chemical properties of the compounds themselves, not to their function as pesticides. Other consequences arise from the failure to realize that it is impossible to control or eliminate one species or group of species in a biotic community without doing many other things as well. One can say, cleanly and exclusively, "I am going to control the gnats at Clear Lake, California." But one cannot do only that. Any control program will set in motion a chain of consequences, the net effect of which will be measured by the response of the ecosystem and not just the response of the target organism.

The decline in grebe populations following insecticide applications at Clear Lake was one of the earlier indications of the consequences of the introduction of persistent hydrocarbons into the environment. In their 1960 paper, Hunt and Bischoff review the first ten years of study of the impact of DDD on the Clear Lake biotic community.

INIMICAL EFFECTS ON WILDLIFE OF PERIODIC DDD APPLICATION TO CLEAR LAKE

Eldridge G. Hunt and A. I. Bischoff

INTRODUCTION

The indirect effects of pesticides on widllife are of growing concern to conservationists. These effects are insidious and are often entirely unnoticed or are not discernible for a long period after initial contact with a toxic material. The materials involved in this type of poisoning are usually of low acute toxicity; many are accumulative in action and are

Reprinted from *California Fish and Game*, Vol. 46, 1960, pp. 91–106. By permission of the California Department of Fish and Game. The work reported here was supported in part by Federal Aid in Wildlife Restoration, California Project W-52-R.

stored in animal flesh. These properties are found especially in certain members of the chlorinated hydrocarbon family of insecticides. The amount of toxic material accumulated in animal tissue may be increased over a period of years as a result of multiple contacts. Clinical symptoms or deleterious effects may appear at any time during this period. The level of accumulation of toxic material that can be tolerated before clinical symptoms occur may be different for the various animal species or individuals of the same species. Some animals are able to store large amounts of certain toxic materials in tissue with no apparent ill effects. However, continued accumulation of these materials usually affects vital functions and may eventually result in death (Wallace, 1959; Rudd, 1958).

The literature provides examples of the effects of this type of poisoning on animal populations. A few are decreased fecundity, interference with normal food chain activities, and upset of interdependent relationships of one animal species with another (Rudd, 1958; DeWitt, 1957; Genelly and Rudd, 1956; Springer, 1956).

The use of a chlorinated hydrocarbon insecticide DDD (dichloro diphenyl dichloroethane) in gnat control programs at Clear Lake, Lake County, California, resulted in a wildlife-pesticide problem. Involved were the effects of this insecticide on mammal, amphibian, and fish populations at the lake. A study of the effects of the gnat control programs on wildlife at Clear Lake was begun in March, 1958, by the California Department of Fish and Game and is scheduled to continue while present hazards to wildlife exist. This paper presents the results of chemical analyses from specimens collected at Clear Lake and information obtained from investigations in the area.

ACKNOWLEDGMENTS

The effects of the control programs on wildlife could not be determined conclusively without analyses of animal tissues for the presence and amount of DDD. These analyses were made by chemists of the Food and Drug Laboratory, California Department of Public Health; and the Bureau of Chemistry, California Department of Agriculture. We wish to thank the personnel from these laboratories not only for the actual chemical analyses, but also for their assistance in assessing the significance of the analyses. Guidance was provided by staff members of the Department of Fish and Game, Department of Public Health, and Department of Agriculture in planning various phases of the study. The collection of specimens was made by Game Management, Inland Fisheries, and Wildlife Protection personnel of the Department of Fish and Game. Assistance with these collections was also provided by employees of the Lake County Mosquito Abatement District. The study was enhanced by the co-operative attitude of the agencies concerned with this problem. Critical review of this manuscript was made by Dr. Robert L. Rudd.

PHYSICAL DESCRIPTION OF CLEAR LAKE

Clear Lake is an irregularly shaped body of fresh water approximately 19 miles long and seven miles wide (Fig. 1–1). The lake is about 1,325 feet above sea level and has a surface area of approximately 41,600 acres. It has an upper and lower portion connected by a narrows that is less than one mile wide. Clear Lake is relatively shallow with maximum depths of 30 feet in the upper portion and 50 feet in the lower portions. The marginal slope of the lake bottom is gradual in most places, espe-

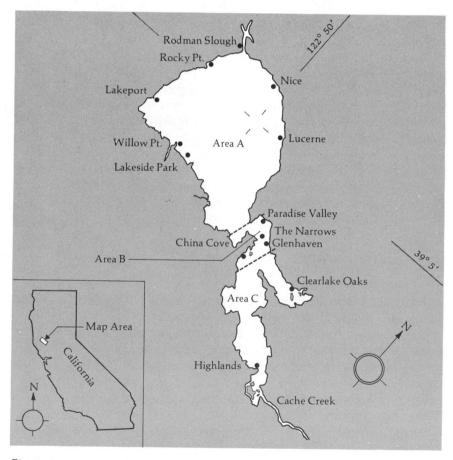

Fig. 1–1
Map of Clear Lake showing locations of animal collections. (Adapted from a drawing by Cliffa Corson)

cially in the larger upper portion where it is saucer shaped. The deposits on the bottom are predominately soft, deep, black ooze except for a few beaches and a portion of Konocti Bay, which are largely volcanic gravel.

Mountains of the Coast Range surround the lake and slope to the water's edge along most of the shoreline. The peaks of some of the highest mountains in the area are over 4,000 feet in elevation. Several alluvial plains fan out into the lake on the west side.

An estimate of the average amount of water during late summer is 300 billion gallons or 850,000 acre feet. The lake level fluctuates with seasonal precipitation and the demands for water from agricultural and domestic interests. Occasionally the level ranges from 8 or 10 feet above to one to two feet below the zero reading on a scale indicator used to measure variation in surface level (Lindquist and Deonier, 1943).

The annual bottom temperatures range from 45 to 78 degrees F. Compared with other mountain lakes, Clear Lake is rather turbid most of the time. The distance at which Secchi Disks can be seen may vary from 5 to 75 inches (Walker, 1949).

HISTORY OF GNAT CONTROL AT CLEAR LAKE

The periodic appearance of large numbers of gnats, *Chaoborus asticto- pus*, during the summer has presented a problem to Clear Lake residents for many years and has had an adverse effect on the large resort business. The annoyance caused by these insects is due wholly to their extreme abundance and attraction to light. These gnats are closely related to mosquitoes but are not bloodsuckers and probably do not feed as adults (Herms, 1937). Concern over the outbreaks of gnat popula- tions led to occasional studies over a period of years to determine meth- ods of control. The study of the biology and methods of controlling this insect has been extensive. Adverse effects on fish life have been con- sidered in the planning of chemical control programs. The following is a brief chronological account of activities relating to gnat control at Clear Lake from 1916 until the initiation of this study in 1958.

Between 1916 and 1941 several studies were made on the biology of the gnat. Experiments were conducted to determine the effectivness of several larvicides and ovicides. No large scale control program developed from these experiments. The possibility of using native fish to control the gnat also was explored and examinations made to determine the food habits of 10 fish species. This food habit study indicated that nine of the species examined consumed gnat larvae or pupae and/or adults at some time during the year. Although fish were found to consume great quan- tities of gnats, it was apparent that some other method of control was required.

During the war years all work was suspended, but in 1946 research to develop a satisfactory control program was resumed. Laboratory experiments with newly-developed chlorinated hydrocarbon insecticides indicated that these materials could be used to control the gnat. Two chemicals, DDT and DDD, were found to have desirable properties and were selected for further study.

Studies made on the toxicity and effect of these chemicals on fish and gnat larvae in aquaria and in smaller bodies of water in the Clear Lake area indicated that DDD would provide the satisfactory gnat control with less hazard to the aquatic environment and its inhabitants than DDT. The final selection of DDD as the larvicide to be used in Clear Lake was made after test applications of this material to nearby Blue Lake in 1947 and Detert Reservoir in 1948. DDD was reported as causing relatively low fish mortality when used at a dilution of one part of insecticide to 70 million parts of water (Lindquist and Roth, 1950). The effects of the DDD treatment of Blue Lake on bottom organisms were reported by Lindquist and Roth (1950), and on insects, fish, and plankton by Murphy and Chandler (1948). A hydrographic survey of Clear Lake was made in the winter of 1948 and 1949 by the U.S. Geological Survey to provide necessary information on the volume of water and the physical properties of the lake. Results of this survey were used in computing desired insecticide dosages and in planning the actual DDD application.

The first large scale DDD treatment of Clear Lake was made in September, 1949; 14,000 gallons of chemical concentrate were used. The insecticide was prepared by a chemical company according to the following formula: DDD (TDE) 30 grams, emulsifier 30 ml. and xylene 72 ml. (Lindquist *et al.* 1951). The material was applied from six barges towed by tug boats. Final dilution in the lake water was estimated at one part of active insecticide to 70 million parts of water. Additional treatment of 20 small lakes and reservoirs within 15 miles of Clear Lake was made. It was determined that a 99 percent kill of gnat larvae resulted from this treatment. As a result very few gnats were observed for two years.

In July, 1951, gnat larvae were found by a night plankton tow, for the first time since the 1949 treatment. The numbers of gnat larvae and adults increased; and a second DDD treatment of the lake was made in September, 1954. The concentration of active insecticide in the lake water shortly after this treatment was greater than the first treatment and was estimated to have been one part of active insecticide to 50 million parts of water. Rate of larval kill was again estimated at 99 percent. All mud samples taken later that year were negative for *Chaoborus* (Brydon, 1955).

In December, 1954, 100 western grebes, *Aechmophorus occidentalis*, were reported dead, and specimens were sent to the Department of Fish and Game Disease Laboratory. (Any mention of grebes in the text unless otherwise designated refers to western grebes.) Infectious disease was not detected in these specimens. In March, 1955, more dead grebes were reported, and results of autopsies on specimens submitted to the disease laboratory were also negative for infectious disease.

Gnat populations increased during 1955–56; and a third treatment of Clear Lake was made in September, 1957. DDD was again applied at the rate of one part of active insecticide to 50 million parts of water. Gnat control was considered not to be as successful as after previous treatments. The lower rate of success was attributed by some observers to inimical weather conditions during application and by others to a buildup of resistance to DDD by the gnats. During December, 1957, approximately 75 grebes were reported dead on the shores of Clear Lake. A few weeks after this report two sick grebes were submitted to the disease laboratory. No infectious disease was found. Two sections of fat from these birds were submitted to the Bureau of Chemistry, California Department of Agriculture, for toxicological examination. Results of chemical analysis of the fatty tissue indicated DDD was present at the unusually high concentration of 1,600 p.p.m. (parts per million). Contaminated food was suspected to be the cause of death.

Accordingly in March, 1958, a fish collection was made by personnel of the Lake County Mosquito Abatement District. Samples were submitted for toxicological examination. They included single specimens of carp, *Cyprinus carpio*, white catfish, *Ictalurus catus*, black crappie, *Pomoxis nigromaculatus*, brown bullhead, *Ictalurus nebulous*, largemouth bass, *Micropterus salmoides*, and Sacramento blackfish, *Orthodon microlepidotus*. Visceral fat was analyzed by Department of Agriculture chemists. The amount of DDD found in the fat ranged from 40 p.p.m. in the carp to 2,500 p.p.m. in the brown bullhead. After the results of these analyses were received by the Department of Fish and Game the present study was initiated and is being continued.

METHODS

Animals collected for chemical analyses were taken by conventional methods. Fish were either netted in gill nets, seines, or fyke nets, or were taken by hook and line. Birds collected for testing were shot; and bullfrogs, *Rana catesbeiana*, were provided by the local warden. Samples of fish for chemical analysis were usually skinned and filleted. Some fish samples were submitted whole except for being eviscerated, but they proved difficult to grind in preparation for chemical analysis. Visceral fat was dissected from the internal organs of certain fish. Fish from two of the three collections made were classified according to brood year and age groups by accepted methods (Marzolf, 1955; Lagler, 1952). No fish in the second collection were aged. However, an attempt was made to collect older fish of similar size.

The quantitative analysis for DDD in grebe flesh was made from composite samples of visceral and subcutaneous fat. Samples of frog tissues were analyzed from visceral fat only. Flesh samples that could not be analyzed in a fresh condition were frozen and stored until analysis could be made.

The analytical procedure used for detection of DDD was a modification of the Schechter-Haller Method for color development (Pontoriero and Ginsburg, 1953). Removal of interfering substances such as fat was accomplished by use of the Davidow exchange column following extraction of the sample with solvent (Davidow, 1950), or with the use of dimethylformamide (Burchfield and Sterrs, 1953). The presence of DDD was determined by specific color development. The only commonly encountered compounds that give the same color reactions are nontoxic isomers and metabolites of DDT and DDD. To be sure that isomers or metabolites were not involved in the color determination, bio-assays using house flies, *Musca domestica*, were done on the first fish samples. Results of these bio-assays established the presence of a toxic substance, and no additional bio-assays were made. Since no appreciable amount of DDT had been used in the area, the toxic substance in all analyses was assumed to be DDD.

PROCEDURE AND RESULTS

Samples of flesh tissue for chemical analyses were limited to specimens collected in the Clear Lake area. Some life history data on bird and fish species were also obtained. The original selection of species to be sampled was based on both availability and suspected DDD contamination. Animals believed to have come in contact with DDD and which were readily available were collected first. Information derived from analyses of samples of the first two collections indicated that certain species could be used as indicators of maximum DDD concentrations. Subsequent collections were planned to include primarily these species.

The number of animals taken during each collection was determined by one or more of the following: (1) the total number of samples that could be readily analyzed by co-operative agencies, (2) the availability of the animal to be sampled, and (3) the number needed to provide an adequate sample. The number of analyses varied with each collection but was always less than 25. Analyses were made of composite as well as single samples. Samples were considered adequate when the data obtained satisfactorily clarified specific problems. All fish collected were apparently healthy and exhibited no symptoms of being affected by the insecticide. Symptoms of fish poisoned by chlorinated hydrocarbons were described by Henderson *et al.* (1958).

First Collection

Samples obtained during the first collection, May, 1958, were composed entirely of fish taken from two locations, one at each end of the lake. The basic information desired from these samples included: (1) the distribution and comparative levels of contamination of DDD in fish, (2) the effect of cooking on breakdown of this chemical, (3) the amount of DDD in different fish species, and (4) the percentage of the fish population that was contaminated with DDD. The results of chemical analysis of this collection are given in Table 1–1. For purposes of simplification only common names will be used in the tables.

Table 1–1
Analysis of fish flesh from collection made in May, 1958

| Species | Year class | Age group | Visceral fat | Parts per million of DDD | | | |
| | | | | Edible flesh | | Fat of edible flesh† | |
				Raw	Cooked	Raw	Cooked
Bluegill	1955	III	—	9.52	—	255	—
	1956	II	—	5.27	—	293	—
	1957	I*	175	6.75	—	278	—
	1957	I*	254	7.14	—	350	—
Black crappie	1956	II*	2,690	115.00	—	2,840	—
Brown bullhead	1954	IV	548	79.90	60.3	1,110	1,010
	1955	III	342	11.80	—	218	—
	1955	III	650	24.60	—	912	—
Largemouth bass	1954	IV	1,550	115.00	133.0	1,360	1,310
Sacramento blackfish	1956	II	983	10.90	—	773	—
	1956	II	—	17.60	—	475	—
Hitch	1956	II	—	10.90	—	106	—
	1957	I	—	28.10	—	763	—

* Composite of two fish; all other samples of individual fish.
† Fat between the muscle tissues.

Results of these analyses regarding the distribution and comparative levels of contamination of DDD in fish flesh agreed with findings of other investigations that most of the insecticide is accumulated in fatty tissue (U.S. Dept. Pub. Health, Educ. and Welfare, 1955; Bann *et al.* 1956; Metcalf, 1957). The amount of chemical in visceral and flesh fat from the same samples was similar. Two samples of edible flesh were wrapped in aluminum foil and baked at 400 degrees F. for one hour prior to analysis. There was very little breakdown of DDD, and the major change due to cooking was loss of water and transfer of some fat containing DDD from the flesh to the cooking container. Those species

Table 1–2
Analysis of fish flesh from collection made in July, 1958

Species	Area	Number fish in sample	PPM of DDD edible fish
Black crappie	A	6	5.4
	B	5	61.0
	C	1	5.8
Brown bullhead	A	25	15.5
	B	1	32.2
	C	32	24.8
Bluegill	A	24	7.3
	B	49	10.0
	C	20	6.6
Carp	A	10	51.3
	B	35	62.3
	C	4	63.8
Sacramento blackfish	A	1*	—
	B	16	20.4
	C	—	—
Hitch	A	—	—
	B	52	18.5
	C	—	—
Largemouth bass	A	1*	5.0
	B	1	97.3
	C	2	19.7
White catfish	A	11	30.4
	B	50	81.6
	C	6	129.0
Tagged catfish 10-year-old	B	1	133.0
Total	A	79	—
	B	210	—
	C	65	—

* These fish were of insufficient size to constitute a satisfactory sample for analysis.

containing the highest concentration of DDD in edible flesh were brown bullhead, largemouth bass, and black crappie. It was apparent that larger samples taken from additional locations would be necessary to obtain more precise information regarding the extent of DDD contamination of the fish at Clear Lake.

Consideration was also given to possible contamination of amphibians with DDD. Visceral fat from nine bullfrogs was analyzed and found to contain 5 p.p.m. of DDD. This level of accumulation was considered low, and no further examinations of frog tissue were made.

Second Collection

The second collection, July, 1958, was also composed entirely of fish. An attempt was made to obtain a representative sample of the more numerous fish species from several key areas along the lake shore. Because of the large number collected, fish were segregated into groups of similar size and appearance instead of aging them by conventional methods. This proved unfortunate because data collected from other samples regarding age and DDD accumulation were not directly comparable. One tagged white catfish 10 years old was collected and was the only sample of known age in this collection. Results of analysis of the second collection are given in Table 1–2. The area designation used in this table of A, B, and C was established arbitrarily. Area A corresponds to the upper section of the lake, Area B to the central section of the lake, and Area C to the lower sections of the lake. All three areas of the lake contained DDD contaminated fish.

Of the nine fish species in the second collection the highest concentration of DDD was found in white catfish and largemouth bass. These species were chosen for sampling on all subsequent collections. Sampling of any other fish species was to be intermittent.

Third Collection

The third collection was made in October, 1958, and included samples of largemouth bass, white catfish, Sacramento blackfish, grebes, and plankton. Results of the analysis of these samples are presented in Table 1–3. The year-old group of Sacramento blackfish and largemouth bass included in this sample was hatched seven to nine months after the last DDD treatment. Flesh samples of both species, one a plankton eater (Sacramento blackfish), the other a carnivore (largemouth bass), contained significant amounts of DDD. Grebes collected were believed to be from a large population of winter visitors. At the time of the grebe collection several thousand grebes were on the lake. In the same general area four weeks prior to the collection fewer than 50 grebes were seen.

The plankton samples were too small for accurate chemical analysis. Due to the inadequacy of the sample the presence or absence of DDD in plankton at Clear Lake could not be established.

Table 1–3
Analysis of animal flesh from collection made in October, 1958

Species	Year class	Age group	Percent fat in edible flesh	Parts per million DDD	
				Edible flesh	Visceral fat
White catfish	1956	II	—	22	—
	1955	III	—	26	—
	1953	V	—	64	—
	1953	V	3.0	109	—
	1953	V	—	113	—
	1953	V	4.0	142	—
	1953	V	—	178	2,110
	1953	V	9.5	196	2,375
	1950	VIII	2.0	106	—
	1950	VIII	—	111	—
	1950	VIII	—	221	—
	1949	IX	—	162	—
	1949	IX	2.1	175	—
Largemouth bass	1958	0	6.0	22*	—
	1958	0	—	24*	—
	1958	0	—	25*	—
	1957	I	—	30	—
	1957	I	—	42	—
	1951	VII	2.0	138	—
Sacramento blackfish	1958	0	1.5	7*	—
	1958	0	—	9*	—
Western grebe	Mature	—	†	—	723

* Composite samples not filleted; all other samples were fillets.
† Composite sample of subcutaneous and visceral fat.

Table 1–4 (pages 78–79) presents data on the amount or range of DDD found in all samples of animal flesh analyzed. The amount of DDD found in all flesh samples exceeded by many times the specified rate of dilution of active insecticide in the lake on a p.p.m. basis. All fish, bird, and frog samples contained DDD. Because of a difference in food habits it was believed that carnivorous fish accumulated a greater amount of DDD than did plankton eating fish of similar size and age.

Two additional collections have been made at Clear Lake, and the results of analysis have not been received at the time of this writing. Present plans call for the contamination of sampling at four-month intervals until the DDD continuation in animal flesh is considered by the investigators to be insignificant.

Several observations indicate a decrease in the nesting grebe population at Clear Lake since the first DDD treatment. Prior to this treatment the nesting population of grebes was in excess of 1,000 pairs (A. H. Miller, pers. com., 1959). During the nesting seasons of 1958 and 1959 less than 25 pairs were seen during surveys made by Spruill (pers. com., 1959) and the authors. Separate surveys in 1959 by Miller and Spruill each reported that nests of grebes were not found in areas where they had been in previous years. As many as 15 pairs of grebes were reported on the lake during this past nesting season but no nests or young have been found. It is not known whether these birds constructed nests that were not found or they made no attempt to nest. A collection of five adult grebes was made in August, 1959. There were an estimated 60 grebes on the lake at that time, and although the normal nesting season had been completed no immature birds of this species were seen. These data, although fragmentary, indicate little or no nesting success of this species during 1959. However, nests of several pied billed grebes, *Podilymbus podiceps*, and coots, *Fulica americana*, were found; and mallards, *Anas platyrhynchos platyrhynchos*, and cinnamon teal, *Anas cyanoptera* nested successfully in the area. Reasons for this reported difference in nesting success are not known.

After the 1954 and 1957 applications of DDD dead grebes were reported. Based on examination of specimens submitted to the laboratory, disease was not believed to have caused the death of these birds. Toxicological examination was not made on dead grebes in 1954. Two grebes were submitted for toxicological examination in January, 1958. Fat samples from these birds contained 1,600 p.p.m. of DDD. According to chemists of the Department of Agriculture the probable cause of death of these birds was chronic DDD poisoning. As further indication that they were poisoned, both birds exhibited nervous tremors comparable to those characterizing chlorinated hydrocarbon poisoning as described by Radeleff and Woodward (1955). Several other grebes observed on Clear Lake showed similar symptoms (Speth and Taylor, pers. com., 1958).

No attempt was made to determine acute or chronic toxicity of DDD to grebes, and no reference to toxicity of any chlorinated hydrocarbon to this or related species was found in literature. However, strong circumstantial evidence indicates that grebe losses occurring after DDD treatments were caused by chronic poisoning from DDD. Differences in DDD concentrations in the fat from fish and grebes may also be interpreted to suggest that grebes show a higher susceptibility to DDD than do many fishes.

Table 1–4
Range of DDD contamination of all specimens collected at Clear Lake

	Number of		Visceral fat				Edible flesh					
					P.P.M. of DDD				Parts per million DDD			
Species	Specimens analyzed	analyses	Analyses	Specimens	Single samples	Composite samples	Analyses	Specimens	Single samples	Composite samples	Cooked samples	Fat of cooked samples
White catfish	82	20	3	1*	1,700-2,375	—	14	14	22.0-221.0	—	—	—
							3	67	—	30.4-129.0	—	—
Largemouth bass	19	12	2	1*	1,550-1,700	—	6	6	5.0-138.0	—	133.0†	1,310†
							4	12	—	19.7-25.0	—	—
Brown bullhead	62	10	4	1*	342-2,500	—	4	4	11.8-79.9	—	60.3†	1,010†
							2	57	—	15.5-224.8	—	—
Black crappie	15	6	1	1	1,600	—	1	1	5.8	—	—	—
			1	2	—	2,690	3	11*	—	5.4-115.0	—	—
Bluegill	100	9	2	2	175-254	—	3	3	5.3-8.5	—	—	—
							4	95	—	6.6-10.0	—	—

Hitch	54	3	—	—	—	—	2 1	2 52	10.9– 28.1	—	— 18.5-	—	—
Sunfish	1	1	—	—	—	—	1	1	5.4	—	—	—	—
Sacramento blackfish	32	7	2	1*	700–983	—	2 3	2 29*	10.9– 17.6	—	7.0– 20.4	—	—
Carp	50	4	1	1	40 —	—	3	49	—	—	51.3– 62.3	—	—
Total fish	415	72	—	—	—	—	—	—	—	—	—	—	—
Frogs	9	1	1	9	—	5	—	—	—	—	—	—	—
Grebe	7	2	2	7	—	723	—	—	—	—	—	—	—
Total	431	75	—	—	—	—	—	—	—	—	—	—	—

* Includes specimens used in other analyses.
† Single analysis of one fish.

DISCUSSION

The use of DDD has affected certain wildlife species in the Clear Lake area. Dead grebes were observed following each DDD application. Various amounts of the toxic material were found in all animals examined. From what source the animals accumulated DDD and to what extent animal populations were affected by this chemical is not fully known.

At present there is no significant public health hazard involved in consumption of Clear Lake fish according to toxicologists of the State Department of Public Health. However, to assure that safe levels for human consumption of Clear Lake fish are not exceeded and to prevent the possibility of increasing the present hazard of DDD poisoning of wildlife, no further treatment of Clear Lake with DDD will be made. It is probable, therefore, that a complete understanding of this particular pesticide–wildlife problem will never be obtained. However, some of the data presented in this paper may be applicable to other problems resulting from similar pesticide applications.

Conclusive results based on chemical analyses showed that all organisms contained DDD. These results established which types of tissue had the greatest concentration of DDD, the amount of chemical found in tissues of various species, and the extent of DDD contamination of fish in the lake.

Results based on circumstantial evidence are believed to be correct. The information collected pertaining to the chronic poisoning of grebes is not complete. It is known that these birds are subject to periodic die-offs, and such an occurrence could have reduced the nesting population at Clear Lake. Additional information will be required to relate accurately the results of chemical analyses of tissues and the cause of death of the grebes. The use of fat analysis to establish a diagnosis of poisoning can be misleading. Apparently, high levels of insecticides can be built up without harm by certain animals (Radeleff and Woodward, 1955).

Although the data are in part circumstantial, the following items indicate poisoning rather than other causes of mortality: (1) the decline in the grebe population corresponded with the period in which pesticide applications were made, (2) the absence of any known infectious disease in autopsied grebes picked up after two of the chemical treatments of the lake, (3) clinical symptoms common to poison victims were exhibited by some grebes from the lake, and (4) an abnormally high concentration of DDD was found in fatty tissues of dead grebes. Observations of dead grebes were made following each DDD application. These die-offs began one or two months after pesticide application and usually lasted several weeks. The fact that die-offs were noted during these periods only, indicates the possibility of chronic poisoning of grebes.

Assuming that grebes were poisoned by DDD, it is important to know how they obtained the toxicant. It is believed that most of the toxic materials was assimilated from ingested contaminated fish and insects. The food of grebes at Clear Lake has been reported to consist primarily of fish, with some insects included (Lawrence, 1950). The chemical could also have been absorbed through the skin or picked up from contaminated feathers consumed by the birds or from other less conspicuous sources. A more logical assumption is that the control programs resulted in the creation of "poisonous fish." The toxicant accumulated in the grebes as a result of ingesting these "poisonous fish" and other contaminated food and resulted in the death of grebes.

The accumulation of DDD in fish could be correlated with food habits exhibited in normal food chain relationships. Generally speaking smaller fish accumulated less DDD on a p.p.m. basis than did larger fish. Plankton eaters accumulated less of the toxic material than carnivorous fish species of the same size. For example, flesh samples of one-year-old largemouth bass contained more than twice the amount of DDD than flesh samples of a one-year-old Sacramento blackfish. Flesh samples from three- to seven-year-old bass contained up to five times as much DDD as a one-year-old bass and 20 times as much as a one-year-old Sacramento blackfish. The theory of DDD transmission through a food chain would be more acceptable if the presence of DDD in plankton organisms could have been established.

It is assumed that certain species of Clear Lake fish such as white catfish and largemouth bass possess a greater tolerance for DDD than do grebes. This is based on results of analysis of fatty tissue. Analysis of visceral fat from apparently healthy largemouth bass and white catfish indicated accumulation of DDD at levels as high as 2,275 p.p.m. and 1,700 p.p.m., respectively. The highest concentration of DDD found in grebe tissue—1,600 p.p.m.—was from birds believed killed by chronic DDD poisoning.

Several theories may be offered regarding further aspects of the Clear Lake problem. Two of these theories pertain to possible consequences of further DDD treatments. The first relates to the establishment of resistance to DDD by various animals. After animals build up a resistance to DDD, or other chlorinated hydrocarbon insecticides, a relatively greater degree of exposure may be endured without perceptible adverse effects. Examples of resistance to chlorinated hydrocarbons in insects is well documented by Hammerstrom (1958) and Shepard (1958), but this phenomenon has not been reported in warmblooded animals. Fish might accumulate DDD in small increments and might not be affected by small additional dosages beyond the normal toxic threshold. Presumably these fish would not be affected by additional DDD treatments.

A second theory expresses an opposing idea. This is based on the fact that certain species have already accumulated and stored large amounts of the toxic chemical, and one or more additional treatments would result in the loss of many fish. DDD already accumulated might not break down and be eliminated, and that accumulation of DDD would continue until lethal dosages were reached. In experiments with DDT conducted by Tarzwell (1950), continued applications of sub-lethal dosages of this material resulted in fish losses.

There may be other effects of these insecticide programs that will become evident in the future, and there are probably some effects that will never be measured. An example of this pertains to the effect of insecticides on reproduction. The accumulation of sub-lethal dosages of DDD by various animal species might reduce fecundity. It has been shown by other investigators that feeding DDT to quail and pheasants resulted in lower than normal rate of hatch and a greater number of malformed progeny than was found in control birds (Genelly and Rudd, 1956; DeWitt, 1955).

If it were true that certain fish have at present accumulated DDD to a level slightly below the critical toxic level, then such fish could be endangered by further consumption of other contaminated fish. This would mean that a die-off of fish caused by DDD poisoning may yet occur without further treatment of the lake.

SUMMARY

1. A study is being made of the effects on wildlife of DDD used in gnat control programs at Clear Lake, Lake County, California. The study began in May, 1958, and is being continued at the date of this writing.
2. This paper is based on chemical analysis of animal tissue of specimens collected at Clear Lake and on information obtained during field investigations in that area.
3. Conclusive results obtained during the study were:
    (a)   All fish, bird, and frog samples analyzed contained DDD.
    (b)   The amount of DDD found in all flesh samples exceeded the specified rate of dilution of active insecticide in the lake water on a p.p.m. basis.
    (c)   Flesh samples of largemouth bass and Sacramento blackfish hatched between seven and nine months after the last DDD application contained 22 to 25 p.p.m. and 7 to 9 p.p.m. of DDD, respectively.
    (d)   All areas of the lake contained DDD contaminated fish.
4. Conclusions based in part on circumstantial evidence were:
    (a)   Grebe losses occurring after DDD applications were caused by chronic DDD poisoning.
    (b)   The nesting population of grebes at Clear Lake has declined as a result of DDD treatment of the lake.

(c) Certain species of fish possess a greater tolerance for DDD than do grebes.
(d) Because of a difference in food habits carnivorous fish accumulated a greater amount of DDD than did plankton eating fish of the same size.

LITERATURE CITED

Bann, J. M., T. J. DeCino, N. W. Earl, and Y. P. Sun. 1956. The fate of aldrin and dieldrin in the animal body. Agr. Food Chem., Vol. 4, No. 11, pp. 937–941.

Brydon, Harold, W. 1955. The 1954 control treatment of the Clear Lake gnat, *Chaoborus astictopus* D. S., in Clear Lake, California. Proc. and Papers, 23rd Ann. Conf. Calif. Mosq. Control Assoc., pp. 108–110.

Burchfield, H. P., and E. E. Sterrs. 1953. Partition of insecticides between N, N-Dimethylformamide and hexane. Contrib. Boyce Thompson Inst., Vol. 17, pp. 333–334.

Davidow, B. 1950. Isolation of DDT from fats. Jour. A.D.A.C., Vol. 33, No. 1, pp. 130–132.

DeWitt, J. J. 1955. Effects of chlorinated hydrocarbon insecticides upon quail and pheasants. Jour. Agr. Food Chem., Vol. 3, No. 8, pp. 672–676.

1957. H-bomb in the pea patch. Wildlife in North Carolina, Vol. 21, No. 9, pp. 4–6.

Genelly, R. E., and R. L. Rudd. 1956. Effects of DDT, toxaphene and dieldrin on pheasant reproduction. Auk., Vol. 73, No. 4, pp. 529–539.

Hammerstrom, R. J. 1958. Insect resistance to insecticides. Publ. Health Repts., Vol. 73, No. 12, pp. 1126–1131.

Henderson, C., Q. H. Pickering, C. M. Tarzwell. 1958. The relative toxicity of ten chlorinated hydrocarbon insecticides to four species of fish. Trans. Am. Fisheries Soc., Vol. 88, No. 1, pp. 23–32.

Herms, W. B. 1937. The Clear Lake gnat. U.S. Agr. Exp. Sta. Bull., No. 607, 22 pp.

Lagler, F. K. 1952. Freshwater fishery biology. Wm. C. Brown, Publ., Dubuque, Iowa, 360 pp.

Lawrence, E. G. 1950. The diving and feeding activity of the Western grebe on the breeding grounds. Condor, Vol. 52, No. 1, pp. 3–16.

Lindquist, A. W., and C. C. Deonier. 1943. Flight and oviposition habits of the Clear Lake gnat. Jour. Econ. Ento., Vol. 35, No. 3, pp. 441–451.

Lindquist, A. W., and A. R. Roth. 1950. Effect of dichlorodiphenyl dichloroethane on larva of the Clear Lake gnat in California. Jour. Econ. Ento., Vol. 43, No. 3, pp. 328–332.

Lindquist, A. W., A. R. Roth, and John R. Walker. 1951. Control of the Clear Lake gnat in California. Jour. Econ. Ento., Vol. 44, No. 4, pp. 572–577.

Marzolf, C. R. 1955. Use of pectoral spines and vertebrae for determining age and rate growth of the channel catfish. Jour. Wildl. Mgt., Vol. 19, No. 2, pp. 243–249.

Metcalf, R. L. 1957. Advances in pest control research. Vol. 1, Intersci. Publ. Inc., New York, 514 pp.

Murphy, G. I., and H. P. Chandler. 1948. The effects of TDE on fish and on the plankton and litoral fauna in lower Blue Lake, Lake County, California. Calif. Fish and Game, Inland Fisheries Admin. Rept., No. 48–14, June 1948.

Pontoriero, L. P., and J. N. Ginsburg. 1953. An abridged procedure in the Schechter Method for analyzing DDT residues. Jour. Econ. Ento., Vol. 46, No. 5, pp. 903–904.

Radeleff, R. O., and G. T. Woodward. 1955. The diagnosis and treatment of chemical poisoning of animals with particular reference to insecticides. Proc. Am. Vet. Med. Assn. 92nd meeting, pp. 109–113.

Rudd, R. L., and R. E. Genelly. 1956. Pesticides: their use and toxicity in relation to wildlife. Calif. Fish and Game, Game Bull. No. 7, 209 pp.

Rudd, R. L. 1958. The indirect effect of chemicals in nature. Talk presented at 54th Conv. Nat. Audubon So., N.Y., Nov. 10, 1958.

Shepard, H. H. 1958. Methods of testing chemicals on insects. Burgess Publ. Co., Minn. 356 pp.

Springer, Paul F. 1956. Insecticides boon or bane. Audubon, Vol. 58, No. 3, pp. 128–130; No. 4, pp. 176–178.

Tarzwell, C. M. 1950. Effects of DDT mosquito laviciding on wildlife. V. Effects on fishes of the routine manual and airplane application of DDT and other mosquito larvicides. Publ. Health Repts., Vol. 65, No. 8, pp. 231–255.

U.S. Dept. Health, Education and Welfare. 1955. Clinical memoranda on economic poisons. (Revised April 1, 1955), 56 pp.

Walker, John R. 1949. The Clear Lake gnat, *Chaoborus astictopus* D. S. Staff Communication, Calif. Dept. Publ. Health. mimeo 15 pp.

Wallace, George J. 1959. Insecticides and birds. Audubon, Vol. 61, No. 1, pp. 10–12–13–35.

Hunt and Bischoff's cautious evaluation of the data from the Clear Lake study has been amply supported by subsequent work. Residues of persistent pesticides have been found in all regions of the globe. Transfer and progressive concentration of fat soluble chlorinated hydrocarbons has been studied in a variety of biotic communities. The progressive concentration of the residues in the organisms of a food chain is another reflection of the trophic level structure of communities. Top level carnivors such as fish eating birds (or men) are receiving and storing in their fat the partial sum of the tiny residues accumulated by the millions of organisms forming the base of the food pyramid.

Reports of the development of pesticide-resistant strains of insects have been frequent. Under the conditions described at Clear Lake, the application of a new selective force, DDD, sufficient to kill 90 percent of the target population, provides an open niche which can be filled by the offspring of surviving individuals. If, among these survivors were individuals with a genetic resistance to DDD, that resistance becomes

*of great survival value. Additional applications of the pesticide will
continue the process of selecting a DDD resistant strain.*

*Hunt and Bischoff's concern that variation in resistance to pesticide
residues would lead to the production of "poisonous fishes" is given
substance in the following paper by Peter Rosato and Denzel Ferguson.
This brief research report demonstrates that the development of resistance
by a small fish does indeed allow the fish to accumulate amounts of
pesticide sufficient to pose a threat to much larger species. The toxicity
in this case is acute and dramatic. Slower, chronic effects such as those
observed in the Clear Lake population of Grebes, have also been studied
extensively. As the research on DDT and related compounds is pushed
to the cellular and biochemical level, evidence emerges of interference
with sex hormone and calcium metabolism, both of which suggest
explanations for the chronic effect on bird populations.*

THE TOXICITY OF ENDRIN-RESISTANT
MOSQUITOFISH TO ELEVEN SPECIES
OF VERTEBRATES

Peter Rosato and Denzel E. Ferguson

In 1963, a DDT-resistant population of mosquitofish, *Gambusia affinis*,
was discovered near heavily-sprayed cotton fields in Mississippi (Vinson
et al., 1963). Subsequent studies revealed resistance in five additional
species of fish and demonstrated that such fish are resistant to a variety
of pesticides, but particularly to the more persistent chlorinated hydrocarbon compounds (Ferguson, 1967; Ferguson and Bingham, 1966).

Wide-spread contamination of aquatic environments with pesticides
places a premium on the survival value of resistance. However, resistant
fish tolerate massive body burdens of pesticide residues and these have
become a matter of concern. A single endrin-treated resistant mosquitofish is able to release enough endrin into 10 liters of water to kill five
susceptible mosquitofish in 43 hours (Ferguson et al., 1966). Susceptible

Reprinted with permission from *BioScience*, Vol. 18, No. 8, 1968, pp. 783–784. Peter
Rosato is a graduate student at the University of Mississippi. Dr. Ferguson is with
the Biology Department of Portland State University, Portland, Ore.

green sunfish died in an average of 2 hours after consuming living resistant mosquitofish containing 1041.66 ppm endrin (Ferguson, 1967).

The present study demonstrates the potential hazard of endrin-exposed resistant mosquitofish to several natural piscivorous predators and certain other vertebrates.

MATERIALS AND METHODS

Groups of 100 mosquitofish from near Belzoni, Humphreys County, Mississippi were exposed to 2 ppm endrin solution for 7 days. The fish were placed in 20 liters of endrin solution which was replaced on the 2nd, 4th, and 6th days. Approximately 50% of the mosquitofish survived the 7-day treatment.

A single survivor was force-fed to individuals of 11 species of vertebrates, including redfin pickerel (*Esox americanus vermiculatus*), largemouth bass (*Micropterus salmoides*), bluegills (*Lepomis macrochirus*), bullfrogs (*Rana catesbeiana*), red-eared turtles (*Pseudemys scripta elegans*), yellow-bellied water snakes (*Natrix erythrogaster flavigaster*), diamond-backed water snakes (*Natrix rhombifera*), cottonmouths (*Ancistrodon piscivorus*), purple grackles (*Quiscalus quiscula*), starlings (*Sturnus vulgaris*), and coturnix quail (*Coturnix coturnix japonicum*). These animals were obtained from areas of minimal pesticide use; the coturnix quail were from a laboratory colony. Endrin-treated mosquitofish were selected without regard to size except where the "predator" to be force-fed was very small. All mosquitofish were rinsed thoroughly in tap water to remove adhering endrin solution. After consuming a mosquitofish, the animals were observed hourly and those that survived 24 hours were given a second endrin-treated mosquitofish; 48-hour survivors received a third fish. Specimens still alive after 2 weeks were discarded. Occasionally, the "predator" immediately regurgitated the endrin-treated fish and it was force-fed again. Regurgitation by animals exhibiting symptoms of endrin poisoning was ignored. Mosquitofish were weighed before use; "predators" were weighed at death.

Controls, two of each species tested, were fed endrin-susceptible mosquitofish from a population free of detectable pesticide contamination.

RESULTS AND DISCUSSION

All controls survived and exhibited no symptoms of discomfort.

Sample sizes for "predators" fed endrin-treated mosquitofish, mortality data, weight relationships of "predators" and prey (i.e., mosquitofish), and survival times are shown in Table 1. Approximately 95% of the predators died from consuming one endrin-treated fish. As previously

Table 1
Mortality, time, and weight data for experiments in which 11 species of vertebrates (predators) were force-fed living, resistant mosquitofish (prey) containing endrin

"Predator"	N	Per cent mortality	Survival time (hr) Mean±SD (Range)	Ratio of predator: prey Mean wt	Predator weight (g) Mean±SD (Range)	Prey weight (g) Mean±SD (Range)
Redfin pickerel	10	100	7.1±3.54 (3–12)	35:1	9.4±3.43 (3.42–15.2)	0.268±0.062 (0.21–.39)
Largemouth bass	10	100	12.6±3.01 (8–20)	168:1	101.6±139.76 (15–474)	0.600±0.393 (0.19–1.26)
Bluegills	10	100	9.4±4.01 (5–12)	113:1	57.7±16.75 (37–85)	0.513±0.108 (0.35–0.69)
Bullfrogs	10	100	15.6±5.03 (12–24)	418:1	155.0±84.78 (64–355)	0.377±0.104 (0.24–0.57)
Red-eared turtles	14	72	112.8±72.00 (24–264)	757:1	670.2±409.27 (66–1406)	0.885±0.197 (0.33–2.12)
Yellow-bellied water snakes	10	100	65.4±68.08 (18–192)	402:1	302.8±225.09 (47–744)	0.758±0.209 (0.25–2.72)
Diamond backed water-snakes	4	100	54.0±45.43 (24–120)	714:1	473.3±365.29 (81–793)	0.662±0.514 (0.34–1.43)
Cottonmouths	11	91	27.1±7.58 (24–48)	311:1	199.5±32.28 (100–469)	0.639±0.273 (0.43–1.39)
Purple grackles	5	100	8.2±12.01 (1–36)	77:1	79.0±2.50 (71.3–83.5)	1.020±0.791 (0.55–2.55)
Starlings	5	100	1.0±1.17 (.5–2)	93:1	63.0±6.32 (54.2–69.6)	0.676±0.238 (0.30–1.10)
Coturnix quail	10	100	1.3±0.41 (1–2)	134:1	86.1±11.46 (74–113)	0.639±0.481 (0.43–0.95)

noted by Ferguson (1967), some specimens regurgitated their fish, but died nevertheless.

Analyses by gas chromatography of a pooled sample of the mosquito-fish fed to the controls revealed no detectable pesticide residue. A pooled sample of four field-collected resistant mosquitofish, prior to endrin exposure, contained 9.65 ppm DDT and its metabolites. A steady diet of field-collected mosquitofish killed pesticide-susceptible green sunfish in an average of 62 days (Finley, unpublished). A sample of four endrin-treated mosquitofish contained 890.02 ppm (1958 μg) of endrin.

Our findings show that resistant mosquitofish tolerate endrin residues sufficient to kill potential predators several hundred times their own weight. Although the level of endrin exposure used in these experiments exceeds that normally encountered in the field, such levels might occur from direct spraying of water, unusual runoff, washing of equipment, discarded containers, or possibly mischievous contamination. We believe these mosquitofish represent a hazard to residents of the area, both human and nonhuman. Although mosquitofish are not considered to be food fish, they might be consumed by children or under other unusual circumstances. Furthermore, other species of fish in the area are resistant and many of these are popular food fish (e.g., bluegills, green sunfish, yellow and black bullheads). The hazard to native piscivorous predators is demonstrated in our findings.

ACKNOWLEDGMENT

This investigation was supported in part by Public Health Service Research Grant No. UI 00348-01 from the National Center for Urban and Industrial Health. We are indebted to Mr. J. Larry Ludke for the gas chromatographic analyses.

REFERENCES

Ferguson, D. E. 1967. The ecological consequences of pesticide resistance in fishes. *Trans. 32nd N. Am. Wildl. Conf.*, **1967**: 103–107.

Ferguson, D. E., and C. R. Bingham. 1966. The effects of combinations of insecticides on susceptible and resistant mosquito fish. *Bull. Environ. Contamination and Tox.*, **1**: 97–103.

Ferguson, D. E., J. L. Ludke, and G. G. Murphy. 1966. Dynamics of endrin uptake and release by resistant and susceptible strains of mosquitofish. *Trans. Am. Fisheries Soc.*, **95**: 335–344.

Vinson, S. B., C. E. Boyd, and D. E. Ferguson. 1963. Resistance to DDT in the mosquitofish, *Gambusia affinis. Science*, **139** (3551): 217–218.

A decade elapsed between the third application of DDD to Clear Lake and the preparation of William Niering's review, The Effects of Pesticides. *The literature on the environmental effects of pesticides had grown rapidly, as had the controversy over the use of these compounds. Almost any statement which could be made by the proponents of the use of persistent compounds could be countered by an equally impressive statement from the opponents.*

The herbivorus insects are surely man's most serious competitor for the energy stored by green plants. Insects and related invertebrates are also significant vectors of plant and animal diseases. Niering indicates that there are some 3000 species of insect pests in North America, an impressive figure—but only a fraction of the total number of species, the remainder often being both helpful to man and susceptible to pesticides.

DDT and related compounds are valuable pesticides because they are effective in low concentration and because their effectiveness persists, sometimes for years. If DDT applied to kill a pest species did, in fact, only that, its strength and persistence would be of unquestioned value. But if a compound applied to control one species kills many and its effect lasts beyond the period of activity of the pest species, then perhaps it is too good a pesticide.

The "sound use" of pesticides requires that there be enough information available to enable the conflicting claims to be evaluated. Conflicts over the use of pesticides are not often decided by one side proving the other wrong. In most cases both sides have been technically correct but have been assigning different values to the elements of the controversy. How do we compare, for example, the value of 350–400 robins with a life expectancy of 1–2 years with a possible 5–10-year extension of a grove of campus elms 50–75 years old? And what value should be assigned to the probable damage done by the pesticide residue as it is passed through the food chain of the community? We should be reminded of the question raised by Garrett Hardin in The Tragedy of the Commons: *How do we make incommensurables commensurable?*

THE EFFECTS OF PESTICIDES

William A. Niering

The dramatic appearance of Rachel Carson's *Silent Spring* (1962) awak-
ened a nation to the deleterious effects of pesticides. Our technology had
surged ahead of us. We had lost our perspective on just how ruthlessly
man can treat his environment and still survive. He was killing pesty
insects by the trillions, but he was also poisoning natural ecosystems all
around him. It was Miss Carson's mission to arrest this detrimental use
of our technological achievements. As one might have expected, she was
criticized by special vested industrial interests and, to some degree, by
certain agricultural specialists concerned with only one aspect of our
total environment. However, there was no criticism, only praise, from the
nation's ecosystematically oriented biologists. For those who found *Silent
Spring* too dramatic an approach to the problem, the gap was filled two
years later by *Pesticides and the Living Landscape* (1964) in which Rudd
further documented Miss Carson's thesis but in more academic style.

The aim of this chapter is to summarize some of the effects of two
pesticides—insecticides and herbicides—on our total environment, and to
point up research and other educational opportunities for students of
environmental science. The insecticide review will be based on representative studies from the literature, whereas the herbicide review will represent primarily the results of the author's research and experience in
the Connecticut Arboretum at Connecticut College. Although some consider this subject controversial, there is really no controversy in the mind
of the author—the issue merely involves the sound ecological use of
pesticides only where necessary and without drastically contaminating
or upsetting the dynamic equilibrium of our natural ecosystems. I shall
not consider the specific physiological effects of pesticides, but rather
their effects on the total environment—plants, animals, soil, climate, man
—the biotic and abiotic aspects.

Environmental science or ecosystematic thinking should attempt to
coordinate and integrate all aspects of the environment. Although ecosystems may be managed, they must also remain in a relative balance or
dynamic equilibrium, analogous to a spider's web, where each strand is
intimately interrelated and interdependent upon every other strand.

Reprinted with permission from *BioScience*, Vol. 18, No. 9, 1967, pp. 869–875. Dr.
Niering is Professor of Botany at Connecticut College, New London, Conn.

THE IMPACT OF INSECTICIDES

Ecologists have long been aware that simplifying the environment to only a few species can precipitate a catastrophe. Our highly mechanized agricultural operations, dominated by extensive acreages of one crop, encourage large numbers of insect pests. As insurance against insect damage, vast quantities of insecticides are applied with little regard for what happens to the chemical once it is on the land. Prior to World War II, most of our insecticides were nonpersistent organics found in the natural environment. For example, the pyrethrins were derived from dried chrysanthemum flowers, nicotine sulphate from tobacco, and rotenone from the tropical derris plants. However, research during World War II and thereafter resulted in a number of potent persistent chlorinated hydrocarbons (DDT, dieldrin, endrin, lindane, chlordane, heptachor and others) to fight the ever-increasing hordes of insects, now some 3000 species plaguing man in North America.

In 1964, industries in the United States produced 783 million lb. of pesticides, half insecticides and the other half herbicides, fungicides, and rodenticides. The application of these chemicals on the nation's landscape[1] has now reached the point where one out of every ten acres is being sprayed with an average of 4 lb. per acre (Anonymous, 1966).

POSITIVE EFFECTS ON TARGET ORGANISMS

That market yields and quality are increased by agricultural spraying appears to have been well documented. Data from the National Agricultural Chemical Association show net increased yields resulting in from $5.00 to $100.00 net gains per acre on such crops as barley, tomatoes, sugar beets, pea seed, and cotton seed. However, Rudd (1964) questions the validity of these figures, since there is no explanation just how they were derived. His personal observations on the rice crop affected by the rice leaf miner outbreak in California are especially pertinent. The insect damage was reported as ruining 10% to 20% of the crop. He found this to be correct for some fields, but most of the fields were not damaged at all. In this situation, the facts were incorrect concerning the pest damage. It appears that not infrequently repeated spraying applications are merely insurance sprays and in many cases actually unnecessary. Unfortunately, the farmer is being forced to this procedure in part by those demanding from agriculture completely insect-free produce. This has now reached ridiculous proportions. Influenced by advertising, the house-

[1] Dr. George Woodwell estimates that there are 1 billion lbs. of DDT now circulating in the biosphere.

wife now demands perfect specimens with no thought of or regard for how much environmental contamination has resulted to attain such perfection. If we could relax our standards to a moderate degree, pesticide contamination could be greatly reduced. Although it may be difficult to question that spraying increases yields and quality of the marketable products, there are few valid data available on how much spraying is actually necessary, how much it is adding to consumer costs, what further pests are aggravated by spraying, and what degree of resistance eventually develops.

NEGATIVE EFFECTS ON NONTARGET ORGANISMS

Although yields may be increased with greater margins of profit, according to available data, one must recognize that these chemicals may adversely affect a whole spectrum of nontarget organisms not only where applied but possibly thousands of miles from the site of application. To the ecologist concerned with the total environment, these persistent pesticides pose some serious threats to our many natural ecosystems. Certain of these are pertinent to review.

1. Killing of nontarget organisms.   In practically every spray operation, thousands of nontarget insects are killed, many of which may be predators on the very organisms one is attempting to control. But such losses extend far beyond the beneficial insects. In Florida, an estimated 1,117,000 fishes of at least 30 species (20 to 30 tons), were killed with dieldrin, when sand flies were really the target organism. Crustaceans were virtually exterminated—the fiddler crabs survived only in areas missed by the treatment (Harrington and Bidlingmayer, 1958).

In 1963, there was a "silent spring" in Hanover, New Hampshire. Seventy per cent of the robin population—350 to 400 robins—was eliminated in spraying for Dutch elm disease with 1.9 lb. per acre DDT (Wurster et al., 1965). Wallace (1960) and Hickey and Hunt (1960) have reported similar instances on the Michigan State University and University of Wisconsin campuses. Last summer, at Wesleyan University, my students observed dead and trembling birds following summer applications of DDT on the elms. At the University of Wisconsin campus (61 acres), the substitution of methoxychlor has resulted in a decreased bird mortality. The robin population has jumped from three to twenty-nine pairs following the change from DDT to methoxychlor. Chemical control of this disease is often overemphasized, with too little attention directed against the sources of elm bark beetle. Sanitation is really the most important measure in any sound Dutch elm disease control program (Matthysse, 1959).

One of the classic examples involving the widespread destruction of nontarget organisms was the fire ant eradication program in our southern states. In 1957, dieldrin and heptochlor were aerially spread over two and one-half million acres. Wide elimination of vertebrate populations resulted; and recovery of some populations is still uncertain (Rudd, 1964). In the interest of science, the Georgia Academy of Science appointed an ad hoc committee to evaluate this control-eradication program (Bellinger et al., 1965). It found that reported damage to crops, wildlife, fish, and humans had not been verified, and concluded, furthermore, that the ant is not really a significant economic pest but a mere nuisance. Here was an example where the facts did not justify the federal expenditure of $2.4 million in indiscriminate sprays. Fortunately, this approach has been abandoned, and local treatments are now employed with Mirex, a compound with fewer side effects. Had only a small percentage of this spray expenditure been directed toward basic research, we might be far ahead today in control of the fire ant.

2. *Accumulation in the food chain.*   The persistent nature of certain of these insecticides permits the chemical to be carried from one organism to another in the food chain. As this occurs, there is a gradual increase in the biocide at each higher trophic level. Many such examples have been reported in the literature. One of the most striking comes from Clear Lake, California, where a 460,000-acre warm lake, north of San Francisco, was sprayed for pesty gnats in 1949, 1954, and 1957, with DDD, a chemical presumably less toxic than DDT. Analyses of the plankton revealed 250 times more of the chemical than originally applied, the frogs 2000 times more, sunfish 12,000, and the grebes up to an 80,000-fold increase (Cottam, 1965; Rudd, 1964). In 1954 death among the grebes was widespread. Prior to the spraying, a thousand of these birds nested on the lake. Then for 10 years no grebes hatched. Finally, in 1962, one nestling was observed, and the following year three. Clear Lake is popular for sports fishing, and the flesh of edible fish now caught reaches 7 ppm, which is above the maximum tolerance level set by the Food and Drug Administration.

In an estuarine ecosystem, a similar trend has been reported on the Long Island tidal marshes, where mosquito control spraying with DDT has been practiced for some 20 years (Woodwell et al., 1967). Here the food chain accumulation shows plankton 0.04 ppm, shrimp 0.16 ppm, minnows 1 to 2 ppm, and ring-billed gull 75.5 ppm. In general, the DDT concentrations in carnivorous birds were 10 to 100 times those in the fish they fed upon. Birds near the top of the food chain have DDT residues about a million times greater than concentration in the water. Pesticide levels are now so high that certain populations are being subtly eliminated by food chain accumulations reaching toxic levels.

3. *Lowered reproductive potential.*   Considerable evidence is available to suggest a lowered reproductive potential, especially among birds,

where the pesticide occurs in the eggs in sufficient quantities either to prevent hatching or to decrease vigor among the young birds hatched. Birds of prey, such as the bald eagle, osprey, hawks, and others, are in serious danger. Along the northeast Atlantic coast, ospreys normally average about 2.5 young per year. However, in Maryland and Connecticut, reproduction is far below this level. In Maryland, ospreys produce 1.1 young per year and their eggs contain 3 ppm DDT, while in Connecticut, 0.5 young ospreys hatch and their eggs contain up to 5.1 ppm DDT. These data indicate a direct correlation between the amount of DDT and the hatchability of eggs—the more DDT present in the eggs, the fewer young hatched (Ames, 1966). In Wisconsin, Keith (1964) reports 38% hatching failure in herring gulls. Early in the incubation period, gull eggs collected contained over 200 ppm DDT and its cogeners. Pheasant eggs from DDT-treated rice fields compared to those from unsprayed lands result in fewer healthy month-old chicks from eggs taken near sprayed fields. Although more conclusive data may still be needed to prove that pesticides such as DDT are the key factor, use of such compounds should be curtailed until it is proved that they are not the causal agents responsible for lowering reproductive potential.

4. *Resistance to sprays.*   Insects have a remarkable ability to develop a resistance to insecticides. The third spray at Clear Lake was the least effective on the gnats, and here increased resistance was believed to be a factor involved. As early as 1951, resistance among agricultural insects appeared. Some of these include the codling moth on apples, and certain cotton, cabbage, and potato insects. Over 100 important insect pests now show a definite resistance to chemicals (Carson, 1962).

5. *Synergistic effects.*   The interaction of two compounds may result in a third much more toxic than either one alone. For example, Malathion is relatively "safe" because detoxifying enzymes in the liver greatly reduce its toxic properties. However, if some compound destroys or interrupts this enzyme system, as certain organic phosphates may do, the toxicity of the new combination may be increased greatly. Pesticides represent one of many pollutants we are presently adding to our environments. These subtle synergistic effects have opened a whole new field of investigation. Here students of environmental science will find many challnging problems for future research.

6. *Chemical migration.*   After two decades of intensive use, pesticides are now found throughout the world, even in places far from any actual spraying. Penguins and crab-eating seals in the Antarctic are contaminated, and fish far off the coasts of four continents now contain insecticides ranging from 1 to 300 ppm in their fatty tissues (Anonymous, 1966).

The major rivers of our nation are contaminated by DDT, endrin, and dieldrin, mostly in the parts per trillion range. Surveys since 1957 reveal that dieldrin has been the main pesticide present since 1958. Endrin reached its maximum, especially in the lower Mississippi River, in the fall of 1963 when an extensive fish kill occurred and has since that time decreased. DDT and its cogeners, consistently present since 1958, have been increasing slightly (Breidenbach et al., 1967).

7. *Accumulation in the ecosystem.*   Since chlorinated hydrocarbons like DDT are not readily broken down by biological agents such as bacteria, they may not only be present but aslo accumulate within a given ecosystem. On Long Island, up to 32 lb. of DDT have been reported in the marsh mud, with an average of 13 lb. presumed to be correlated with the 20 years of mosquito control spraying (Woodwell et al., 1967). Present in these quantities, burrowing marine organisms and the detritus feeders can keep the residues in continuous circulation in the ecosystem. Many marine forms are extremely sensitive to minute amounts of insecticides. Fifty per cent of a shrimp population was killed with endrin 0.6 parts per billion (ppb). Even 1 ppb will kill blue crabs within a week. Oysters, typical filter feeders, have been reported to accumulate up to 70,000 ppm (Loosanoff, 1965). In Green Bay along Lake Michigan, Hickey and Keith (1964) report up to 0.005 ppm wet weight of DDT, DDE, and DDD in the lake sediments. Here the accumulation has presumably been from leaching or run-off from surrounding agricultural lands in Door County, where it is reported that 70,000 pounds of DDT are used annually. Biological concentration in Green Bay is also occurring in food chain organisms, as reported at Clear Lake, California. Accumulation of biocides, especially in the food chain, and their availability for recycling pose a most serious ecological problem.

8. *Delayed response.*   Because of the persistent nature and tendency of certain insecticides to accumulate at toxic levels in the food chain, there is often a delayed response in certain ecosystems subjected either directly or indirectly to pesticide treatment. This was the case at Clear Lake, where the mortality of nontarget organisms occurred several years after the last application. This is a particularly disturbing aspect, since man is often the consumer of those food chain organisms accumulating pesticide residues. In the general population, human tissues contain about 12 ppm DDT-derived materials. Those with meatless diets, and the Eskimos, store less; however, agricultural applicators and formulators of pesticides may store up to 600 ppm DDT or 1000 ppm DDT-derived components. Recent studies indicate that dieldrin and lindane are also stored in humans without occupational exposure (Durham, 1965). The possibility of synergistic effects involving DDT, dieldrin, lindane, and other pollutants to which man is being exposed may result in unpredictable hazards. In fact, it is now believed that pesticides may pose a genetic hazard. At the recent conference of the New York Academy of Science. Dr. Onsy G.

Fahmy warned that certain chlorinated hydrocarbons, organophosphates and carbamates were capable of disrupting the DNA molecule. It was further noted that such mutations may not appear until as many as 40 generations later. Another scientist, Dr. M. Jacqueline Verrett, pointed out that certain fungicides (folpet and captan) thought to be nontoxic have chemical structures similar to thalidomide.

We are obviously dealing with many biological unknowns in our widespread use of presumably "safe" insecticides. We have no assurance that 12 ppm DDT in our human tissue, now above the permissible in marketable products for consumption, may not be resulting in deleterious effects in future generations. As Rudd warns (1964): ". . . it would be somewhat more than embarrassing for our 'experts' to learn that significant effects do occur in the long term. One hundred and eight million human guinea pigs would have paid a high price for their trust."

Of unpredicted delayed responses, we have an example in radiation contamination. In the Bravo tests on Bikini in 1954, the natives on Rongelap Atoll were exposed to radiation assumed to be safe. Now more than a decade later, tumors of the thyroid gland have been discovered in the children exposed to these presumably safe doses (Woodwell et al., 1966). Pesticides per se or synergisms resulting from their interaction could well plague man in now unforeseen or unpredictable ways in the future.

THE SOUND USE OF HERBICIDES

In contrast to insecticides, herbicides are chemical weed-killers used to control or kill unwanted plants. Following World War II, the chlorinated herbicide 2, 4-D began to be used widely on broadleaf weeds. Later, 2, 4, 5-T was added, which proved especially effective on woody species. Today, over 40 weed-killers are available. Although used extensively in agriculture, considerable quantities are used also in aquatic weed control and in forestry, wildlife, and right-of-way vegetation management. Currently, large quantities are being used as defoliators in Vietnam.

Although herbicides in general are much safer than insecticides in regard to killing nontarget organisms and in their residual effects, considerable caution must be exercised in their proper use. One of the greatest dangers in right-of-way vegetation management is their indiscriminate use, which results in habitat destruction. Drift of spray particles and volatility may also cause adverse effects on nontarget organisms, especially following indiscriminate applications. In the Connecticut Arboretum shade trees have been seriously affected as a result of indiscriminate roadside sprays (Niering, 1959). During the spring of 1957, the town sprayed the marginal trees and shrubs along a roadside running through the Arboretum with 2, 4-D and 2, 4, 5-T (1 part chemical: 100 parts water). White oaks overarching the road up to 2 feet in diameter were most seriously affected. Most of the leaves turned brown. Foliage of scarlet and black oaks of similar size exhibited pronounced leaf curling. Trees were affected up to 300 feet back from the point of application within the natural area of the Arboretum. White oak twigs near the sprayed belt also developed a striking weeping habit as twig elongation occurred—a growth abnormality still conspicuous after 10 years.

The effectiveness of the spray operation in controlling undesirable woody growth indicated a high survival of unwanted tree sprouts. Black birch and certain desirable shrubs were particularly sensitive. Shrubs affected were highly ornamental forms often planted in roadside beautification programs. The resulting ineffectiveness of the spray operation was indicated by the need for cutting undesirable growth along the roadside the following year.

In the agricultural use of herbicides, drift effects have been reported over much greater distances. In California, drift from aerial sprays has been reported up to 30 miles from the point of application (Freed, 1965).

Although toxicity of herbicides to nontarget organisms is not generally a problem, it has been reported in aquatic environments. For example, the dimethylamine salt of 2, 4-D is relatively safe for bluegill at 150 ppm, but the butyl, ethyl, and isopropyl esters are toxic to fish at around 1 ppm (R. E. Johnson, personal communication). Studies of 16 aquatic herbicides on *Daphnia magna*, a microcrustacean, revealed that 2, 4-D (specific derivative not given) seemed completely innocuous but that several others (Dichlone, a quinone; Molinate, a thiolcarbamate; Propanil, an anilide; sodium arsenite and Dichlopenil, a nitrile) could present a real hazard to this lower food chain organism (Crosby and Tucker, 1966).

Effects on rights-of-way. The rights-of-way across our nation comprise an estimated 70,000,000 acres of land, much of which is now subjected to herbicide treatment (Niering, 1967). During the past few decades, indiscriminate foliar applications have been widespread in the control of undesirable vegetation, erroneously referred to as brush (Goodwin and Niering, 1962). Indiscriminate applications often fail to root-kill undesirable species, therefore necessitating repeated retreatment, which results in the destruction of many desirable forms. Indiscriminate sprays are also used for the control of certain broadleaf weeds along roadsides. In In New Jersey, 19 treatments were applied during a period of 6 years in an attempt to control ragweed (Dill, 1963). This, of course, was ecologically unsound, when one considers that ragweed is an annual plant typical of bare soil and that repeated sprayings also eliminate the competing broadleaved perennial species that, under natural successional conditions, could tend to occupy the site and ntaurally eliminate the ragweed. Broadcast or indiscriminate spraying can also result in destruction of valuable wildlife habitat in addition to the needless destruction of our native flora—wildflowers and shrubs of high landscape value.

Nonselective spraying, especially along roadsides, also tends to produce a monotonous grassy cover free of colorful wildflowers and interesting shrubs. It is economically and aesthetically unsound to remove these valuable species naturally occurring on such sites. Where they do not occur, highway beautification programs plant many of these same shrubs and low-growing trees.

Recognizing this nation-wide problem in the improper use of herbicides, the Connecticut Arboretum established, over a decade ago, several right-of-way demonstration areas to serve as models in the sound use of herbicides (Niering, 1955; 1957; 1961). Along two utility rights-of-way and a roadside crossing the Arboretum, the vegetation has been managed following sound ecological principles (Egler, 1964; Goodwin and Niering, 1959; Niering, 1958). Basic techniques include basal and stump treatments. The former involves soaking the base of the stem (root collar) and continuing up the stem for 12 inches; the stump technique involves soaking the stump immediately after cutting. Effective formulations include 2, 4, 5-T in a fuel oil carrier (1 part chemical: 20 parts oil). Locally, stem-foliage sprays may be necessary, but the previous two techniques form the basic approach in the selective use of weed-killers. They result in good root-kill and simultaneously preserve valuable wildlife habitat and aethetically attractive native species, all at a minimum of cost to the agency involved when figured on a long-range basis. In addition to these gains, the presence of good shrub cover tends to impede tree invasion and to reduce future maintenance costs (Pound and Egler, 1953; Niering and Elger, 1955).

Another intriguing use of herbicides is in naturalistic landscaping. Dr. Frank Egler conceived this concept of creating picturesque natural settings in shrubby fields by selectively eliminating the less attractive species and accentuating the ornamental forms (Kenfield, 1966). At the Connecticut Arboretum we have landscaped several such areas (Niering and Goodwin, 1963). This approach has unlimited application in arresting vegetation development and preserving landscapes that might disappear under normal successional or vegetational development processes.

FUTURE OUTLOOK

Innumerable critical moves have recently occurred that may alter the continued deterioration of our environment. Secretary Udall has banned the use of DDT, chlordane, dieldrin, and endrin on Department of the Interior lands. The use of DDT has been banned on state lands in New Hampshire and lake trout watersheds in New York State; in Connecticut, commercial applications are limited to dormant sprays. On Long Island, a temporary court injunction has been granted against the Suffolk County Mosquito Control Board's use of DDT in spraying tidal marshes. The Forest Service has terminated the use of DDT, and in the spring of 1966 the United States Department of Agriculture banned the use of endrin and dieldrin. Currently, the Forest Service has engaged a top-level research team in the Pacific Southwest to find chemicals highly selective to individual forest insect pests and that will break down quickly into harmless components. The Ribicoff hearing, which has placed Congressional focus on the problem of environmental pollution and Gaylord Nelson's bill to ban the sale of DDT in the United States are all enlightened endeavors at the national level.

The United States Forest Service has a selective program for herbicides in the National Forests. The Wisconsin Natural Resources Committee has instituted a selective roadside right-of-way maintenance program for the State. In Connecticut, a selective approach is in practice in most roadside and utility spraying.

Although we have considerable knowledge of the effects of biocides on the total environment, we must continue the emphasis on the holistic approach in studying the problem and interpreting the data. Continued observations of those occupationally exposed and of residents living near pesticide areas should reveal invaluable toxicological data. The study of mirgrant workers, of whom hundreds have been reported killed by pesticides, needs exacting investigation.

The development of more biological controls as well as chemical formulations that are specific to the target organism with a minimum of side effects needs continuous financial support by state and federal agencies and industry. Graduate opportunities are unlimited in this field.

As we look to the future, one of our major problems is the communication of sound ecological knowledge already available rather than pseudoscientific knowledge to increase the assets of special interest groups (Egler, 1964; 1965; 1966). The fire ant fiasco may be cited as a case in point. And as Egler (1966) has pointed out in his fourth most recent review of the pesticide problem: "... 95% of the problem is not in scientific knowledge of pesticides but in scientific knowledge of human behavior. ... There are power plays ... the eminent experts who deal with parts not ecological wholes."

One might ask, is it really good business to reduce the use of pesticides? Will biological control make as much money? Here the problem integrates political science, economics, sociology, and psychology. Anyone seriously interested in promoting the sound use of biocides must be fully cognizant of these counter forces in our society. They need serious study, analysis, and forthright reporting in the public interest. With all we know about the deleterious effects of biocides on our environment, the problem really challenging man is to get this scientific knowledge translated into action through the sociopolitical pathways available to us in a free society. If we fail to communicate a rational approach, we may find that technology has become an invisible monster as Egler has succinctly stated (1966).

Pesticides are the greatest single tool for simplifying the habitat ever conceived by the simple mind of man, who may yet prove too simple to grasp the fact that he is but a blind strand of an ecosystem web, dependent not upon himself, but upon the total web, which nevertheless he has the power to destroy.

Here environmental science can involve the social scientist in communicating sound science to society and involve the political scientist in seeing that sound scientific knowledge is translated into reality. Our survival on this planet may well depend on how well we can make this translation.

REFERENCES

Ames, P. L. 1966. DDT residues in the eggs of the osprey in the northeastern United States and their relation to nesting success. *J. Applied Ecol.*, **3** (suppl.): 87–97.

Anonymous. 1966. Fish, wildlife and pesticides. U.S. Dept. of Interior, Supt. of Doc., 12 p.

Bellinger, F., R. E. Dyer, R. King, and R. B. Platt. 1965. A review of the problem of the imported fire ant. *Bull. Georgia Acad. Sci.*, Vol. 23, No. 1.

Breidenbach, A. W., C. G. Gunnerson, F. K. Kawahara, J. J. Lichtenberg, and R. S. Green. 1967. Chlorinated hydrocarbon pesticides in major basins, 1957–1965. *Public Health Rept.* **82**: 139–156.

Carson, Rachel. 1962. *Silent Spring.* Houghton Mifflin, Boston, 368 p.

Cottam, C. 1965. The ecologists' role in problems of pesticide pollution. *BioScience*, **15**: 457–463.

Crosby, D. G., and R. K. Tucker. 1966. Toxicity of aquatic herbicides to *Daphnia magna*. *Science*, **154**: 289–290.

Dill, N. H. 1962–63. Vegetation management. *New Jersey Nature News*, **17**: 123–130; **18**: 151–157.

Durham, W. F. 1965. Effects of pesticides on man. *In* C. O. Chichester, ed., *Research in Pesticides.* Academic Press, Inc., New York.

Egler, F. E. 1954. Vegetation management for rights-of-way and roadsides. *Smithsonian Inst. Rept. for 1953*: 299–322.

———. 1964a. Pesticides in our ecosystem. *Am. Scientist*, **52**: 110–136.

———. 1964b. Pesticides in our ecosystem: communication II: *BioScience*, **14**: 29–36.

———. 1965. Pesticides in our ecosystem: communication III. *Assoc. Southeastern Biologist Bull.*, **12**: 9–91.

———. 1966. Pointed perspectives. Pesticides in our ecosystem. *Ecology*, 47: 1077–1084.

Freed, V. H. 1965. Chemicals and the control of plants. *In* C. O. Chichester, ed., *Research in Pesticides.* Academic Press, Inc., New York.

Goodwin, R. H., and W. A. Niering. 1959. The management of roadside vegetation by selective herbicide techniques. *Conn. Arboretum Bull.*, 11: 4–10.

———. 1962. What is happening along Connecticut's roadsides. *Conn. Arboretum Bull.*, 13: 13–24.

Harrington, R. W., Jr., and W. L. Bidlingmayer. 1958. Effects of dieldrin on fishes and invertebrates of a salt marsh. *J. Wildlife Management*, 22: 76–82.

Hickey, J. J., and L. Barrie Hunt. 1960. Initial songbird mortality following a Dutch elm disease control program. *J. Wildlife Management*, 24: 259–265.

Hickey, J. J., and J. A. Keith. 1964. Pesticides in the Lake Michigan ecosystem. *In* The Effects of Pesticides on Fish and Wildlife. U.S. Dept. Interior Fish and Wildlife Service.

Keith, J. A. 1964. Reproductive success in a DDT-contaminated population of herring gulls, pp. 11–12. *In* The Effects of Pesticides on Fish and Wildlife. U.S. Dept. Interior Fish and Wildlife Service.

Kenfield, W. G. 1966. *The Wild Gardner in the Wild Landscape*. Hafner, New York, 232 p.

Loosanoff, V. L. 1965. Pesticides in sea water. *In* C. O. Chichester, ed., *Research in Pesticides*. Academic Press, Inc., New York.

Matthysse, J. G. 1959. An evaluation of mist blowing and sanitation in Dutch elm disease control programs. N.Y. State Coll. of Agric. Cornell Misc. Bull. 30, 16. p.

Niering, W. A. 1955. Herbicide research at the Connecticut Arboretum. *Proc. Northeastern Weed Control Conf.*, 9: 459–462.

———. 1957. Connecticut Arboretum right-of-way demonstration area progress report. *Proc. Northeastern Weed Control Conf.*, 11: 203–208.

———. 1958. Principles of sound right-of-way vegetation management. *Econ. Bot.*, 12: 140–144.

———. 1959. A potential danger of broadcast sprays. *Conn. Arboretum Bull.*, 11: 11–13.

———. 1961. The Connecticut Arboretum right-of-way demonstration area—its role in commercial application. *Proc. Northeastern Weed Control*, 15: 424–433.

———. 1967. Connecticut rights-of-way—their conservation values. *Conn. Woodlands*, 32: 6–9.

Niering, W. A., and F. E. Egler. 1955. A shrub community of *Viburnum lentago*, stable for twenty-five years. *Ecology*, 36: 356–360.

Niering, W. A., and R. H. Goodwin. 1963. Creating new landscapes with herbicides. *Conn. Arboretum Bull.*, 14: 30.

Pound, C. E., and F. E. Egler. 1963. Brush control in southeastern New York: fifteen years of stable treeless communities. *Ecology*, 34: 63–73.

Rudd, R. L. 1964. *Pesticides and the Living Landscape*. University of Wisconsin Press, 320 p.

Wallace, G. J. 1960. Another year of robin losses on a university campus. *Audubon Mag.*, 62: 66–69.

Woodwell, G. M., W. M. Malcolm, and R. H. Whittaker, 1966. A-bombs, bug bombs & us. Brookhaven National Lab. 9842.

Woodwell, G. M., C. F. Wurster, Jr., & P. A. Isaacson. 1967. DDT residues in an east coast estuary: a case of biological concentration of a persistent insecticide. *Science*, 156: 821–824.

Wurster, Doris H., C. F. Wurster, Jr., & W. N. Strickland. 1965. Bird mortality
    following DDT spray for Dutch elm disease. *Ecology,* **46:** 488–499.

*If the arguments about the benefits and dangers of pesticides is a
question of competing values as well as a question of fact, then to change
pesticide policies we must change values. Niering emphasized the
growing consumer demand for 100 percent insect-free, undamaged food
products. It is highly probable that the bulk of pesticides applied to some
crops is for "cosmetic" purposes rather than for increasing yield.*

*It is possible to encourage people to have a higher tolerance for insects
in and on agricultural products? I had an uncle who was especially fond
of eating a small fish found along the Maine coast. The fish were
commonly infected with roundworms which encysted in the meat. Once
when he expressed a desire for a meal of these little fish a friend
protested, "But what about the worms?" "When I eat Tommy-cod,"
my uncle replied, "the worms have to look out for themselves!"*

*It may not be possible to return the American consumer to this degree
of tolerance for the nonhuman members of his biotic community. We
should all be willing, however, to accept an occasional accidental insect
in packaged food as a natural event and not the occasion for a law suit.
We could all be willing to wash and pick over food from the market
as we would if it came from a home garden.*

*There are, of course, questions of fact as well as of value.
Ray Manley's brief report of an interview with five University of
California entomologists makes it clear that many of the opportunities
for research described by Niering still exist. The interview further
emphasizes that it is salesmanship as well as research which determines
the actual level of pesticide application. Even if the value of a pesticide
is clearly demonstrated, the agent is highly specific, and the application
well controlled, a "when in doubt, spray" attitude can not be defended.*

*Just as each natural biotic community is unique, each of the many
agricultural communities of plants, invertebrate and vertebrate animals,
and soil organisms is unique. Each agricultural community deserves its
own integrated program of control. It is only prudent that the persistent
pesticide component of such a program be minimized in favor of other
available methods.*

INTEGRATED BIOLOGICAL-CHEMICAL PEST CONTROL SOUGHT

Ray Manley

Five University of California entomologists believe that pest controls should be invoked only when their use is economically—and ecologically—justified. They have tested their theory and found it works in California's cotton control program.

"It was very apparent to those of us involved in cotton entomology that the development of valid economic thresholds, at least for the two major pests, was an imperative first step in the development of an integrated control program," they said.

Plumping for integrated pests control programs involving the use of more than one means for controlling pests, including cultural, biological and chemical methods, are Drs. Thomas F. Leigh, Robert van den Bosch, Vernon M. Stern, Louis A. Falcon, and Daniel Gonzalez.

In an interview with *Biomedical News*, Leigh, speaking in particular of Californians, said:

"Too often growers will ignore long-range economics if one dollar for pest controls will give a five dollar yield. In the past, California cotton growers had a good profit margin and therefore had no need to closely investigate the economics of pest control programs. But now the price of cotton is way down and the yields are also down. Now growers must see if they're getting a return on the money they spend for pest controls."

In California, reliable economic thresholds have never existed for the two major pests, the mirid *Lygus hesperus* and the bollworm *Heliothis zea*. This has been at the root of problems with California's $200-million cotton program, according to Leigh. Actually, the group says, specific levels of abundance of the two pests have previously determined insecticide treatment levels. Their research has shown this to be a costly indicator of when controls should be applied.

As for other pests, such as the cabbage looper (*Trichoplusia ni*), beet armyworm (*Spodoptera exigua*), and spider mites (*Tetranychidae*), there are no guides for applying pesticides. Rather they are applied upon grower whim or apprehension, salesmen's persuasion, and other reasons.

In assessing the overall pest situation (in the San Joaquin Valley, where 90 per cent of the state's cotton is grown), researchers learned that extensive early and midseason treatments for *Lygus* control were causing damaging outbreaks of lepidopterous pests and spider mites. So first

Reprinted with permission from *Biomedical News*, May, 1970, p. 9. Copyright 1970 by Biomedical News Publishing Company, Inc., Falls Church, Va. The author is on the staff of *Biomedical News*.

priority was placed on a study of *Lygus* injury. Control of the pest was necessary to develop a realistic economic threshold for it.

The existing treatment level of 10 bugs per 50 net sweeps was quickly judged invalid. A new threshold was developed which, in essence, says that an infestation level of 10 bugs per 50 net sweeps is valid only during the period from June 1 to July 20, and then only if the level is sustained over two sampling dates of four to five days interval. Subsequent to the heavy squaring (flower budding) stage, a much higher *Lygus* infestation can be tolerated if the plants are fruiting normally. Growers applying this philosophy in 1969 reported good to excellent yields at greatly reduced pest control costs. As a side benefit, their fields were essentially free of lepidopterous pests.

In related studies, researchers were unable to correlate density of the pest with crop loss.

In fact, in a number of experiments, the untreated controls produce yields equal to those obtained from plots in which bollworms were significantly eradicated by insecticides, and on occasion the controls outyielded the chemically-treated plots.

Several factors, the researchers said, are involved:

• The bollworm larvae in untreated cotton are ordinarily under extreme pressure from biotic mortality agents. Most chemical insecticides are extremely destructive to these natural enemies. So deaths caused by insecticides simply replace those caused by the predators.

• The bulk of the larvae surviving the insecticides are free to develop to maturity because of their release from predators and parasites.

• Certain organophosphates—and a carbamate (carbaryl) and the toxaphene-DDT mixture—cause the plants to develop vegetatively and results in delayed maturity of the bolls.

• Bollworms often feed on surplus buds, flowers, and small bolls not destined to contribute to ultimate crop yield. These parts simply act as a buffer against injurious feeding by the pest.

In other findings, it was determined that:

• In cotton fields not previously treated with insecticides, *H. zea* will rarely develop to economically significant status because its populations are repressed by predators and parasites.

• Moth activity can be reliably predicted on the basis of moon phase.

• More research is needed on using a nuclear polyhedrosis virus of *H. zea*, despite encouraging results last year.

• In tests against bollworm, the bacterium *Bacillus thuringiensis* has shown some promise.

• *Lygus* is also an alfalfa pest. Researchers found that maintaining alternate alfalfa growth cycles in the fields will prevent emigration of some bugs from the fields at harvest time to the cotton crops. This, however, involves special care and is expensive.

• There is a critical need for supervisors in the integrated control program.

PART FOUR

OTHER CULTURAL PRESSURES ON THE ENVIRONMENT

It's Only a Metal World

Cast, poured, molded. Stamped out. Extruded, annealed.
Peeled off the mold. Spread, splayed.
Red hot rivet laid in place, headed,
turned. Driven home. Bam-bam-bammed in tinny
drum. Pneumatic, hydrolic, steam-driven—Wham!

Formed, forged. Rolled, drawn, shaped, milled.
Pressed. Abraded, sanded, sandblasted. Buffed,
polished, waxed. Cleaned, greased, oiled. Primed, sprayed.
Rustoleum red. Battleship gray. Flamingo
blue. Old fashioned apple. Harmony green.

Bent. Curled. Sprung. Hammered, dented, cut.
Bolted, cracked. Welded, soldered, glued.
Busted, wired, screwed. Canned, carted,
dumped, discarded. Buried, burned, drowned. Rusted.
Soil, air, water, roots, leaves, grass somewhere.

Robert M. Chute

Reprinted from *Epos*, Vol. 18, No. 1, 1969, p. 24.

The four papers in this section all deal with pollution. If we define pollution as a concentration effect, too much of something per unit of volume, we can see some of the common features of these problems, as well as their direct relationship to the problems of population, technology, modern agriculture, and urbanization. More and more people require more and more food, shelter, transportation, consumer goods, and energy. The pressure is worsened by the nature of much of our production and consumption. Much of that which we say we "consume" is really only used, then discarded. Studies indicate that the per capita production of trash and garbage is increasing at a rate greater than that of the production of goods. Added to this is the stimulating effect of the advertising industry, which seems intent on maximizing the level of created needs.

The first paper in this series deals with cultural eutrophication or the excessive fertilization of waters with wastes containing nutrients. These nutrients are "natural" products. The process of eutrophication is a "natural" process. The problem is a rate of production and a concentration of wastes too great to be adsorbed by existing biogeochemical cycles.

The second and third papers discuss pollution by oil and by radioactive materials. Although the direct effects of oil and radioisotope pollution are quite different, both are of increasing concern because of man's rising demand for energy to drive our machines. In any discussion of these two sources of energy you are apt to be told of the necessity of ever increasing rates of energy production—of the demand for energy which makes the expanded use of oil and atomic power essential. They must be developed or . . . or what?

It is instructive to ask yourself, what would have been the consequence for our world if no workable way of generating electric power from atomic energy had ever been discovered? What if petroleum as a fuel had not existed? The world would be quite different, but I find no evidence that this different world would have been either a better or a worse place to live. To ask a more modest question based on the same approach, what if the additional oil reserves under the Alaskan north slope had not been discovered now but 100 years from now? Would our civilization have survived to use that oil in 2070? What do these questions suggest about the argument that such "finds" must be developed as rapidly as possible—or else? Invention and discovery creates its own necessity.

The fourth paper in this series, Effects of Pollution on the Structure and Physiology of Ecosystems, by George Woodwell, attempts to bring together the studies of various types of pollution and to provide a *unified explanation. His model may not hold for all cases, but it shows, I think, an example of science "doing what it should." It provides us with another way of thinking about the complexities of our world.*

CULTURAL EUTROPHICATION IS REVERSIBLE

Arthur D. Hasler

Many lakes the world over are becoming less desirable places on which to live because of nutrient wastes pouring into them from a man-changed environment. Human activities, through population and industrial growth, intensified agriculture, river-basin development, recreational use of waters, and domestic and industrial exploitation of shore properties, are contributing to excessive nutrient enrichment of lakes, streams, and estuaries. This accelerated process of enrichment (cultural eutrophication) causes undesirable changes in plant and animal life, reduces the aesthetic qualities and economic value of the body of water, and threatens the destruction of precious water resources. Overwhelming excessive scums of blue-green algae and aquatic plants choke the open water, rendering the water turbid and nonpotable. The algae and aquatic plants die and rot, yielding a repugnant odor, and the organic matter from this crop sinks and consumes the deep-water oxygen vital for fish and other animal life.

Under natural conditions lakes proceed toward geological extinction at varying rates through eutrophication or bog formation. Many lakes, in unpopulated temperate zones and lying in sandy granite drainage basins, are still pristine and clear (oligotrophic) even though 10,000 years have elapsed since their formation. Other lakes in the same area, such as shallow bog lakes which were also formed during the same glacial epoch, are already extinct. They are grown over with mats of sphagnum moss interspersed with orchids and pitcher plants. Brown-colored water lies below the mat which deteriorates and slowly fills in the basin. In some, the terminal stages of bog formation are evident because these former lakes

Reprinted with permission from *BioScience*, Vol. 19, No. 5, 1969, pp. 425–431. The author is with the Laboratory of Limnology, University of Wisconsin, Madison.

are now covered with shrubs, tamarack, and black spruce forests, but this type of extinction is not eutrophication. How this succession or continuum proceeds from open lake to forest is too complex to be developed in this brief essay.

Archeological studies by G. E. Hutchinson and R. Patrick of cores of lake sediments of the Italian lake, *Lago di Monterosi*, reveal that the Romans, by constructing roads, inadvertently increased the nutrient drainage of a landscape by cutting the trees and exposing limestone strata. The erosion from these nutrient-richer strata was followed by a eutrophic period in the lake's history as recognized by the kinds of diatoms found in the cores. E. S. Deevey, Yale University, also recognized prehistoric changes of climate and rate of eutrophication in Linsley Pond, Conn., which are correlated with the abundance and variety of fossil organisms in the different strata.

The rate of eutrophication of lakes in geological time can often be predicted by examining the soil and vegetation of their drainage basins. If the drainage area is large, the vegetation pristine, and the soil rich and erodible, the lake water will be rich in algae and fish; if poor, the water will produce little and will retain its clarity.

THE ALGAL COMMUNITY (PHYTOPLANKTON)

Algae are microscopic one-celled plants which require for their growth the same nutrients as do garden flowers and lawns. If fertilized richly in spring and summer, they flourish; if impoverished, they grow sparsely. A community of free-floating algae is richer and more diverse than is any garden.

Pure cultures of algae grown in the laboratory multiply and grow rapidly if nitrogen and phosphorus-bearing chemicals are added. Algae in identical cultures will grow even more luxuriantly when small amounts of sewage effluent are added demonstrating that in addition to P and N, there are ingredients (probably vitamins and growth hormones) in sewage which promotes growth.

A nutrient-poor, temperate zone lake will be clear; hence, one might collect thousands of miniscule algae cells at depths of 150 ft and more. In a nutrient-rich lake, on the other hand, the high numbers of algae will lend a greenish cast to the surface water, restrict the penetration of sunlight, and therefore limit photosynthesizing algae and rooted aquatic plants to the shallower depths.

The onset of eutrophicated (nutrient-enriched) conditions has adverse ramifications. When the enriched conditions are due to man-made effluents, the algae grow so profusely that the water fleas (the basic food of all larval fishes) cannot consume the algae fast enough to reduce their numbers significantly; hence, abnormal amounts die uneaten.

The biological communities of a lake become upset when bacteria are unable to convert dead organic matter into plant and animal food.

Not only is oxygen in the deep, cool water exhausted by organic products, but hydrogen sulfide (rotten egg gas) accumulates to poisonous levels.

The finale in these despoiled depths is the demise of all noble fishes, e.g., whitefish, trout, and cisco, which require oxygen-rich water depths for life. Moreover, some noble fishes such as cisco spawn in the fall—their eggs must incubate throughout winter—but an enriched lake, having lost its oxygen in the deep layers (under the ice), cannot nourish the eggs for hatching in the spring.

SOURCES OF NUTRIENTS

Phosphate additions appear to be one of the major factors in pollution of European and North American lakes although the rate at which nutrients pass through chemical and biological cycles is also important. Sources of plant nutrients are principally from human sewage and industrial wastes, including the phosphate-rich detergents (Table 1). Drainage from farmland is second in importance as a nutrient source in temperate zones, where farm manure, spread on frozen ground in winter, is flushed into streams during spring thaws and rains. A shocking statistic

Table 1
Summary of estimated nitrogen and phosphorus reaching Wisconsin surface waters

Source	N	P	N	P
	Lbs. per year		(% of total)	
Municipal treatment facilities	20,000,000	7,000,000	24.5	55.7
Private sewage systems	4,800,000	280,000	5.9	2.2
Industrial wastes[a]	1,500,000	100,000	1.8	0.8
Rural sources				
Manured lands	8,110,000	2,700,000	9.9	21.5
Other cropland	576,000	384,000	0.7	3.1
Forest land	435,000	43,500	0.5	0.3
Pasture, woodlot & other lands	540,000	360,000	0.7	2.9
Ground water	34,300,000	285,000	42.0	2.3
Urban runoff	4,450,000	1,250,000	5.5	10.0
Precipitation on water areas	6,950,000	155,000	8.5	1.2
Total	81,661,000	12,557,500	100.0	100.0

[a] Excludes industrial wastes that discharge to municipal systems. Table does not include contributions from aquatic nitrogen fixation, waterfowl, chemical deicers and wetland drainage.

which points up the gravity of our contemporary situation is that farm animals in the Midwest alone provide unsewered and untreated excrement which is equivalent to that from a population of 350 million people. Also, it is surprising that substantial quantities of nitrates of combustion engine and smokestack origin augment these sources (see rain and groundwater, Table 1). City streets also provide sources of phosphates and nitrates that must be dealt with.

In toto, the results of man-induced eutrophication are catastrophic as noted in the case history of Lake Zürich, Switzerland, where all noble, deep-water fishes, which had provided gourmet specimens for generations, disappeared within 20 years after sewage disposal in surrounding villages was changed from the "Chick Sale" type to flush toilets.

A CASE HISTORY

The Zürichsee, a lake in the foothills of the Alps, offers a sad example of the effects of sewage effluent. It is composed of two distinct basins, the Obersee (50 m) and the Untersee (141 m), separated only by a narrow passage. In the past five decades the deeper of the two, at one time a decidedly clear and oligotrophic lake, has become strongly eutrophic, owing to urban effluents originating from a group of small communities totaling about 110,000 people. The shallower of the two received no major urban drainage and retained its oligotrophic characteristics for a longer period. Thus we have an experimental and reference lake side by side.

HISTORY OF FISHING

Dr. L. Minder (Zürich, Switzerland) observed that, hand in hand with domestic fertilization, the Zürichsee changed from a whitefish (coregonid) lake to a coarse fish lake. In fact, the trout, *Salmo salvelinus,* and a whitefish, *Coregonus exignus,* disappeared from the Untersee and are no longer common in the Obersee; restocking has not been successful. An upsurge of cyprinid fishes (minnow-carp family), chiefly *Abramis brama* and *Leuciscus rutilus,* have also become abundant with the progressive eutrophication.

HISTORY OF PLANKTON SUCCESSION

Minder is convinced that the decided increase of plankton is not an expression of a natural ripening process, but is due to plant nutrients, principally P and N, from domestic sources. The diatom *Tabellaria fenestra* appeared explosively in 1896. Two years later an eruption of the blue-green alga *Oscillatoria rubescens* occurred. The latter had been known from the eutrophic Murtenersee for 70 years, but otherwise had been recorded only from the Baldeggersee in spring and winter 1894. It had not been seen in the Zürichsee plankton until the 1896 eruption when it replaced the usually dominant *Fragilaria capucina*. When Minder studied the lake during 1920–24, *Oscillatoria rubescens* appeared in quantities in the surface plankton, with a maximum in fall and winter, while flourishing in the deeper water of the lake in summer. In 1936 Minder observed a red scum over most of the lake. An odor of fish oil is frequently noticeable in summer. There were 1.75 g wet weight of algae per liter, chiefly *Oscillatoria*, on 5 May 1899.

Further evidence for a recent sudden increase in biological productivity can be found in bottom sediment studies. These demonstrate that *Tabellaria* occurs in only the most recent layers. Moreover, the modern layers are laminated, at least in the deeper parts of the lake, and everywhere are darker than the underlying sediment. The dark, laminated character of the sediments is especially pronounced from 1896 onward, the date being determined by counting the seasonal laminae.

Minder cites some comparative plankton analyses on the Untersee and Obersee: first, in no series were the biocoenoses of the two sections identical; second, *Oscillatoria rubescens* was never found in the Obersee and *Tabellaria*, very infrequently; third, quantitatively the entire plankton of the Untersee was vastly richer; and fourth, plankton quantities are greater in the Untersee downstream from the town of Rapperswil where most of the sewage enters. Minder also observed the rotifer *Keratella Quadrata* as appearing first in 1900. *Bosmina longirostris* largely replaced *B. coregoni* after 1911. Since 1920 one of the Ulotricales has become common in summer.

HISTORY OF OTHER LIMNOLOGICAL FACTORS

Chemical analyses by Minder have shown that certain elements of domestic sewage origin, notably chloride ion, have increased gradually over a relatively few decades. Analyses in 1888 showed the water contained 1.3 mg Cl/liter, by 1916 it had risen to 4.9 mg/liter. The organic matter as measured by loss on ignition also rose from 9 mg/liter in 1880 to 20 in 1914. Vollenweider gives as a rule of thumb 0.2–0.5 $g/m^2/yr$ of P and 5–10 $g/m^2/yr$ of N as the levels of these nutrients which are associated with nuisance blooms of algae in European lakes.

Minder gives comparisons of the changes in transparency (average of 100 readings)

	Maximum disc reading	Minimum disc reading
Before 1910	16.8	3.1
1905–10	10.0	2.1
1914–28	10.0	1.4

It is significant also that O_2 values in the deep water have decreased in the last four decades. Midsummer values at 100 m were nearly 100% saturation from 1910–30; from 1930–42, however, they averaged about 50% saturation but did occur as low as 9%.

MAN-MADE LAKES

Lakes are more adversely affected by sewage effluent than are flowing streams, chiefly because rapidly flowing water is not conducive to the growth and attachment of algae and rooted aquatic plants. Hence, the diversion of sewage around lakes and into streams is the lesser evil. Nevertheless, while alleviating the lake problem, it places an increasing burden upon the stream's biological system and upon the communities downstream which must purify it. In modern times most large streams have man-made dams for impounding the water and the outflow provides energy for hydroelectric power. If such a reservoir receives sewage, the quality of the water deteriorates as does a lake, and the cost of water purification and odor control rises for downstream communities. There is therefore a finite limit. Permissible levels of impurities will have to decrease, hence the technological improvement to obtain more complete nutrient removal must become more efficient.

LIMNOLOGICAL FEATURES OF EUTROPHICATED LAKES

Figure 1 shows the data obtained by Edmondson and his associates during their continuing long-term investigation of Lake Washington at Seattle. Changes in chlorophyll concentration in the epillimnion correspond with the trend of phosphate accumulation, reduced transparency, and increase in the O_2 deficit, and are all therefore expressions of racing eutrophication.

Findenegg (Fig. 2) has used the ^{14}C method (radioactive carbon) to evaluate the degree of eutrophication. A eutrophic lake fixes carbon principally in the near-surface water because its turbidity prevents light from supplying essential photosynthetic energy to the deeper layers. Higher nutrient levels in a eutrophic lake also serve to stimulate higher rates of ^{14}C fixation in the surface waters (see example No. 4, Fig. 2).

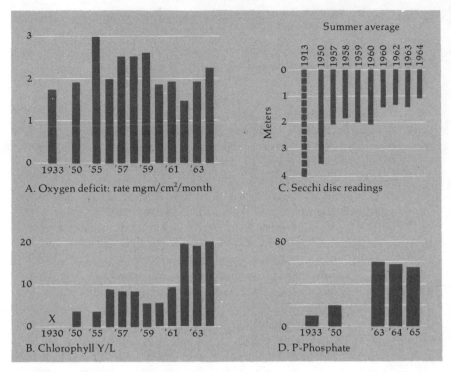

Fig. 1
Changes that have occurred in Lake Washington. (A) Rate of development of relative areal oxygen deficit below 20 m depth between 20 June and 20 September. (B) Mean concentration of chlorophyll in top 10 m of lake during same period of time. (C) Mean Secchi disc transparency, June–September. (D) Maximum concentration of phosphate phosphorous in surface water during winter. (After Edmondson, 1968)

Dr. Findenegg's example demonstrates a general principle in biology that in senility the older animal often consumes as much food as when he was young, but utilizes it less efficiently. In jargon we say, "He spins his wheels." With increasing levels of eutrophication there is a steady increase in carbon fixed, but as turbidity rises, photosynthesis is restricted to the surface waters, hence less depth can be used for production and the utilization drops off—frankly the lake is overfed and obese, perhaps also physiologically senile, and it is spinning its wheels.

Reduction in transparency (Secchi Disc) of Lakes Washington and Zürich appears to be characteristic for rapidly eutrophicated oligotrophic lakes. Hypereutrophication of a natural eutrophic lake, Lake Mendota, has not changed the average transparency nor the average hypolimnetic deficit although other characteristics such as loss of cisco, increase in macrophytes, and increase in algal blooms are conspicuous features.

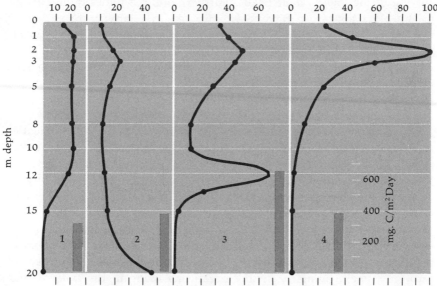

Fig. 2
The production of carbon by photosynthesizing algae in four alpine lakes (1.
Millstätter; 2. Klöpeiner; 3. Worther; and 4. Lower part of the Lake of Con-
stance) expressed as mg C per m^3 per day. The columns give the total production below 1 m^2 in mg C per m^2 per day. Note the restriction of production to
the surface waters in the most eutrophic lake, No. 4.

PHYTOPLANKTON

Comparisons of algal diversity of oligotrophic Trout Lake and eutrophic
Lake Mendota show the latter to have fewer species, but the size of the
organisms is considerably larger indicating higher levels of production
than in the oligotrophic lake.

Often the low species diversity of the phytopyankton in eutrophic
lakes is a result of high populations of blue-green algae such as *Aphani-
zomenon flosaquae* and *Anabaena spiroides*. In some seasons *Fragilaria
crotonensis and Stephanodiscus astrae* become dominant.

In many eutrophicated northeastern U.S. lakes, rooted aquatic plants
Myriophyllum and *Ceratophyllum* become festooned with the filamen-
tous alga *Cladophora* and form dense mats in shallow areas.

GREAT LAKES

Until recently it was thought that eutrophication would not be a major
problem in large lakes because of the vast diluting effect of their size.

However, evidence is accumulating that indicates eutrophication is occurring in the lower Great Lakes. Furthermore, the undesirable changes in the biota appear to have been initiated in relatively recent years. Charles C. Davis, utilizing long-term records from Lake Erie, has observed both qualitative and quantitative changes in the phytoplankton owing to cultural eutrophication. Total numbers of phytoplankton have increased more than threefold since 1920, while the dominant genera have changed from *Asterionella* and *Synedra* to *Melosira, Fragilaria,* and *Stephanodiscus.*

Other biological changes usually associated with the eutrophication process in small lakes have also been observed in the Great Lakes. Alfred M. Beeton recently summarized the literature pertaining to the trophic status of the Great Lakes in terms of their biological and physiochemical characteristics and indicated that of the five lakes Lake Erie has undergone the most noticeable changes due to eutrophication. In terms of the annual harvests, commercially valuable species of fish such as the lake herring or cisco, sauger, walleye, and blue pike have been replaced by less desirable species such as the freshwater drum or sheepshead, carp, and smelt. Similarly, in the organisms living in the bottom sediments, drastic changes in species composition have been observed. Where formerly the mayfly nymph *Hexagenia* was abundant to the extent of 500 organisms per square meter, it presently occurs at levels of five and less per square meter. Chironomid midges and tubificid worms now are dominant members in this community.

WHAT CAN BE DONE TO REDUCE THE GALLOPING RATE OF EUTROPHICATION?

The deterioration of our lakes proceeds at such a galloping pace that there is insufficient time to raise an enlightened younger generation which could cope with the causes of eutrophication. Every effort must be undertaken to convince government officials and voters that action, even though expensive, must be taken immediately to avoid catastrophe. In attempting to obtain positive returns, time operates negatively against delay. To insure a brighter future, universities, colleges, churches, service clubs, the press, radio, and television must acquire a knowledge of the causes, prevention, and cure and begin without delay to help disseminate factual information.

Provided they are given the facts, preachers and rabbis could preach sin against the environment as convincingly as they preach sin against the soul.

Decision makers such as legislators, state, county, and village officials, decision planners such as architects, decision formulators such as lawyers and judges, decision executors such as realtors, engineers, and contractors must all receive enlightenment about the implication of possible perturbations of the landscape whose environmental health influences the well-being of the lake into which the land's effluents flow.

I urge that every educational body, in every community, organize week-long intensive clinics, seminars, or working groups to which experienced limnologists and ecologists are invited as teachers, lecturers, demonstrators, and guides. I urge journalists and editors, television and radio directors to send their personnel to clinics, or to meet with experienced ecologists in order to obtain facts and illustrations, to provide bases on which readable and effective articles and programs can be prepared. They should be taken on field trips to areas where the reality of a eutrophied lake can be demonstrated, in order to capture their enthusiasm and stimulate their originality toward preparation of dynamic and imaginative programs. I would urge legislative lawyers to draft critical legislation for water usage in regions where the legal procedures are inadequate and encourage them to draft laws which will provide adequate protection of a lake or reservoir from perturbations.

The processes of eutrophication are too rapid to risk delay in taking legal action. In applying new concepts of water law to the alleviation of eutrophication, there is a need for proper zoning ordinances and forthright public initiative in modernizing the law when the scientific data, even if not complete, suggest action. Public planners recommend the formation of a County or Drainage Basin Authority, which can act for the towns, counties, and municipalities to deal with all problems of water quality. It would have authority to make water and sewage assessments, control erosion, create zoning ordinances, conduct studies toward evaluation of problems and evolve improvements.

In Wisconsin the late Jacob Beuscher, through his association with ecologists and landscape architects, drafted unique zoning legislation for Wisconsin which now has been passed (Wisconsin Water Resources Law, 1965).

If a dwelling or resort is planned, it must meet exact specifications for sewage disposal so that no offluent can seep into the water. Some soils are less able to absorb effluents than others, hence the setback of a planned hotel or dwelling might need to be at the extreme end of the 1000-ft maximum setback on lakes, 300 on rivers. His legislation also specified beauty for this zoned corridor as a 'quality to be preserved.' Vilas County, rich in lakes, prohibits cutting the natural vegetation from more than 10% of the shoreline fronting a property.

SOCIAL, LEGAL, AND ECONOMIC ASPECTS

In the preceding discussion emphasis was placed upon the effectiveness of various management procedures. Of equal importance are comprehensive economic analyses of new approaches to management. Included should be studies to develop methods to quantify costs and benefits and to analyze public opinion so that the management programs developed are acceptable to society.

Beuscher writes:

Since resource management requires not only scientific knowledge and techniques but also governmental and legal structures by which desired management can be achieved, the entire field of legal and governmental structure is a necessary research area. Wisconsin's assertion that it is trustee of all navigable waters of the state is one of the strongest examples of a state's assertion of its rights and duty to protect public interests in natural resources, and this could form a basis for a variety of strong regulatory policies. Potential conflicts between the asserted trusteeship and the rights of private littoral and riparian owners exist, however, and should be investigated as a guide both to the potentials for regulation and to the limitations on regulation without compensation.

Zoning is one type of regulatory action which is likely to be of significant value in attacking the problems associated with inland lakes. As for other water resources, the Wisconsin Legislature has acted, and the counties are presently required by law to enact river and lakeshore zoning ordinances. Research is needed to review the powers of the counties under present statutes, especially noting where powers which seem necessary to accomplish desired regulation are lacking or unclear. Creative proposals and careful analyses are needed concerning the present procedures for administration of zoning by the counties. Projects in various areas of scientific research could be undertaken with a view toward producing facts and testing procedures which the counties might employ to guide and defend their regulation of stream and lakeshore lands.

Owing to the traditional lack of compensation for regulations imposed, zoning is a limited device for the control of lakeshore lands. Imaginative legal research is needed on a broad range of new control devices, such as compensable regulation and partial condemnation, some of which are being tried in some parts of the country. Finally, the powers of all levels of government and the potential powers of private groups and resource control and management corporations should be analyzed as means toward proposing more systematic and creative methods of management than exist presently.

EXAMPLES OF SUCCESS

Our knowledge of what causes eutrophication is sufficiently good that firm and effective precautions can be recommended. They may be expensive to achieve, but the predictive facts are at hand. With improvement, methods can be made more economical, but it is not a lack of knowledge which prevents us from action. Three case histories are at hand.

LAKE MONONA

Complaints about the unpleasant odors arising from Madison's Lake Monona were published in the newspapers as early as 1850. Sewage effluents were impuned as the villain in 1885 when a consultant J. Nader advised ". . . that the lakes were not properly used as receptacles for sewage in the crude state." In 1895 a 1½-mill sewer tax was imposed on assessed valuation, but the sewage treatment plant built from these funds failed in 1898. Septic tanks and cinder filter beds were then constructed but reached capacity in 1906, and it was not until 1914 that a modern sewage treatment plant was constructed. Its effluent entered Lake Monona and continued to feed the algae and weeds. The process of eutrophication accelerated in Lake Monona and in 1920 the city council minutes read: "Winds . . . drive detached masses of putrefying algae onto shores . . . if stirred with a stick, look like human excrement and smell exactly like odors from a foul and neglected pig sty."

In 1921 consideration was given to piping the effluent to the Wisconsin River, but another plant was built below Lake Monona in 1928. One-half of Madison's effluent then first passed into Lake Waubesa; later (1936), all of it. In spite of heavy applications of the algal poison $CuSO_4$ to the lake, the build-up of offensive and obnoxious odors in Waubesa and Kegonsa worsened. Anti-pollution legislation was introduced in 1941, but was vetoed because of conflicting opinions on whether sewage or rural runoff was the culprit.

In 1942 the Burke Plant, which had been discontinued in the '30s, was reopened to accommodate the military needs of Truax Field in World War II. The need for more copper sulfate during this period is obvious from the graph (Fig. 3). In 1943 the Lewis Anti-Pollution law was passed, to take effect one year after the war.

In actuality, the effluent did not bypass the lakes until 1950. During this century of time, buck passing, economy measures, false information from communications, inconclusive action, and lack of cooperation between government and citizens hampered progress.

The fact that copper sulfate treatment of the lake dropped from car-load quantities to minimal local treatments (Fig. 3) is proof that even though agricultural drainage unfortunately continues, the diversion of city sewage produced a change for the better.

LAKE WASHINGTON

Lake Washington was used first for the disposal of raw sewage and later treated sewage from the City of Seattle. About 1930, the last major source of raw sewage was removed from the lake, but up until 1959 untreated sewage still entered the lake in relatively small quantities

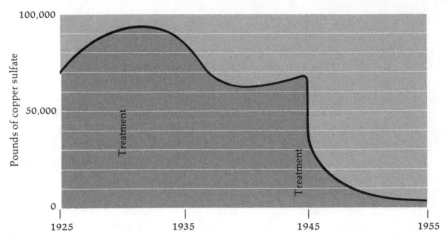

Fig. 3
The amount of copper sulfate required to control alga nuisances in Lake Monona near Madison, Wisconsin, in the period 1925–56. The amount used is a function both of the abundance of algae and the degree of public disturbance; thus small differences are probably unimportant, but large changes are significant. The main trend is shown by the solid line.

through storm sewer overflows and seepage from septic tanks. In 1959 there were 10 sewage treatment plants, serving 64,000 people, putting treated effluent into Lake Washington.

While biologists and engineers warned the community of the impending doom of the lake, it took dense blooms of *Oscillatoria rubescens*, the same lavender-colored alga that produced nuisances in Lake Zürich, to awaken the citizens to the reality of these warnings. While some argued as they did in Madison that the run-off from fertile land was causing the nuisances, others contended that the major source (city sewage) could be diverted. A powerful combination of radio and television debates, citizens' group meetings, and door-to-door campaigning culminated in arousing sufficient public support for a bond issue. This amounted to an expenditure of $121 million for diversion of 50 million gallons of sewage from Lake Washington to Puget Sound. While the diversion is not yet entirely complete, a major part of the sewage has now (1968) been diverted, with subsequent improvement of the quality and clarity of water in Lake Washington.

LAKE TAHOE

To protect the pristine beauty and crystal clarity of Lake Tahoe, several sanitary engineers (P. McGauhey, G. Rohlich, and others) made a study

of the sewage disposal problems of Lake Tahoe and published a comprehensive study in 1963. They described the problem and projected the
rate of growth of the communities and tourist facilities whose sewage
from treatment plants and septic tanks enters the lake. The lake's great
size and immense depth meant that it could absorb some sewage without
showing general signs of deterioration. However, objectionable accumulations of green algae at sewage outlets indicated that it was only a
matter of time before the increased sewage load from a skyrocketing
population would change this clearest of all North American lakes to one
of lesser esthetic value.

In spite of the 70-odd governmental units in Nevada and California
which surround the lake, this initial limnological and engineering evaluation inspired the creation of citizen-governmental action committees and
associations which went into action. South Tahoe (1968) has built a $19
million sewage treatment plant in which the treated effluent is pumped
over a 7000 ft pass to a reservoir, where the fertile .water will be used
for irrigation. Some $10 million of the total budget was in federal grants
acquired by the South Tahoe Public Utility District to help offset this
cost—a demonstration of cooperative action by federal and local government in solving a local and national problem. Acknowledging the
imminent danger of despoiling this esthetic and financial resource, other
communities are facing reality in an action program. The small community of Round Hill in Nevada with only 42 voting citizens, albeit
many are owners of gaming houses, has bonded itself for $5.8 million
to treat its sewage and pump it out of the basin. We can only hope that
the hotel and residential sewage can be similarly diverted from other
parts of this once gin-clear lake in time to avoid the certain despoliation
of Sierra Nevada's most magnificent landscape gem.

Two European lakes, Schliersee and Tegernsee in Germany's Bavarian
Alps, were eutrophicated by hotel sewage, but are now slowly reverting
to more tolerable conditions following diversion of sewage to the outlets.
Lake d'Annecy, France (near Lake Geneva) is following suit. All lakes
from which sewage has been diverted have shown improvement (see case
for Lake Monona, Fig. 3), thereby demonstrating that ingredients in
sewage contribute greatly to eutrophication. These facts negate the argument "Why divert sewage at great cost if rainwater and rural drainage
is so rich in nitrogen?" The "healing" is, of course, more rapid in lakes
in oligotrophic and high rainfall landscapes. The Madison, Wis., lakes
are naturally eutrophic; nevertheless the hypereutrophic, repulsive conditions have been alleviated following diversion, as demonstrated by a
shift from single-species to multi-species blooms in lakes Waubesa and
Kegonsa.

HARVESTING AND UTILIZATION OF EXCESS CROPS OF PLANTS AND FISH

More machinery is needed for harvesting large aquatic plants. Removal of this crop, which contains significant quantities of phosphorus and nitrogen, will aid in impoverishing the water. It also improves esthetic quality, opens the water area to boating and swimming, and creates better shoreline sanitation. Development of new and more effective harvesting machines is needed, and research is also needed to find a commercial outlet for the harvested vegetation. Eutrophicated lakes produce large crops of fish which should also be harvested more intensively, by commercial fishermen if necessary, because the unharvested fish die and decompose, adding nutrients to the already over-rich environment.

In Lake Mendota in late 1966, 40 lb./acre (44 kg/ha) of carp alone were harvested in a single seine haul. Yields of 250/lb./acre/yr (280 kg/ha/yr) of fish of all species could be harvested easily from this lake without damaging the fishery. In terms of nitrogen and phosphorus, 1000 lb. of rotting fish would yield to the lake 25 lb. (11.3 kg) of N and 2 lb. (0.9 kg) of P.

CHEMICAL CONTROL OF NUISANCE GROWTHS

Chemicals which poison unwanted aquatic plants and algae have deleterious effects in and around treated areas. Moreover, the killed weeds rot and add to the nutrient supply. This is a bad conservation practice because no good is accomplished. Chemicals distort the structure of multi-species aquatic communities and hence are less useful in lakes than they are in agriculture where weeds are to be eradicated from a single-species crop such as wheat. Herbicide usage cannot be justified in a lake ecosystem. In addition, chemicals are more difficult to manage than on land, for they are soon drifted to other areas. The toxic actions of these chemicals on other species in the lake have not been tested, nor have the possible insidious side effects of sublethal actions over longer periods. At present, the use of chemicals to combat algal blooms or rooted aquatic vegetation can be no more than a palliative and should be used only as a last resort. What is eradicated is sure to be replaced by something else that may be more difficult to poison.

UTILIZATION OF SEWAGE AND FARM MANURE

Each human produces 1.5 to 4 lb./yr (0.7–1.8 kg/yr) of phosphorus; Chicago's effluent amounted to 30 tons (27,000 kg) of phosphorus per day in 1960. After sewage has undergone secondary treatment it still contains phosphorus. The average P content of sewage after secondary treatment is 8 mg/l. Hormones, vitamins, and growth substances are also fertilizing ingredients. Moreover, phosphate-rich detergents now added are not entirely removed. In fact, in most treatment plants secondary treatment removes only about 80% of the P and high costs deter removing more. An increasing human population adds to the total residual left in sewage effluent after treatment. "We seem to be on a treadmill," comments G. A. Rohlich, an eminent engineer, who states further that in spite of new advances we are not much further ahead of the problem than at the turn of the century.

The price of clean water may rise to a point where we may have to insist upon and want to afford evaporation of the effluents in order to obtain a dry solid for use as a farm fertilizer. Secondary treatment of sewage does not remove organic growth factors but probably produces them; hence, evaporation looms as a likely though expensive treatment.

In temperate climates of North America it is customary to scatter farm manure on the frozen land. Large amounts of valuable fertilizer are flushed into streams and lakes during early spring thaws and spring rains. Because a cow produces 6 lb. (3 kg) nitrogen and 1.5 lb. (0.7 kg) phosphorus per year, it is clear that this source is important. Modernization of the European method of fluidizing dairy cow manure, storing it in huge tanks, and distributing it with a "honey wagon" as soon as the soil can absorb it is now being recommended. However, economic limitations inhibit progress in converting to a more efficient method of manuring. Fortunately, forest and agricultural soils have a remarkable tenacity for phosphorus. Agricultural and forest crops could profit from the fertilizers from our domestic wastes, but the technology for processing and distributing them are still very expensive when compared with artificial fertilizers.

The volume and weight of dried sewage to be disposed of will have staggering proportions. Settlings from primary treatment of sewage abound near every city, but a farmer can buy and distribute sacked fertilizer cheaper than he can haul dried sewage sludge which is available free of charge. We are too affluent to be able to afford the use of our "night soil."

The City of Milwaukee markets a dried sludge called Milorganite from its primary settlings which is rich in organic matter. Every city could do this, but instead it piles up and presents a disposal problem because Milwaukee's product satisfies the available market for this product.

BENEFITS OF GUIDED EUTROPHICATION

All eutrophication is not necessarily bad. Well-planned enrichment could increase the production of food organisms for fish and hence raise the protein productivity of a natural or man-made lake. Many lakes in Canada, Alaska, and USSR are candidates for this potential. Because of the complexity of interactions at various depths and seasons, more knowledge than we now have is needed before we can guide eutrophication and harvest the increase in fish produced without exceeding the fertility levels that destroy the esthetics of a lake.

PREDICTIONS

Predicting the consequences of eutrophication would be highly desirable for decision-makers. Systems analysis offers new techniques in multi-factorial analysis which may be employed in constructing models of drainage basins in order to evaluate the impact of various eutrophicating factors.

IN SUMMARY

It is now of the greatest urgency to prevent further damage to water resources and to take corrective steps to reverse present damages. Suggested preventive and corrective measures include removing nutrients from municipal, industrial, and agricultural wastes; diversion of treated effluents from lakes; harvesting algae, aquatic plants, and fish from lakes in order to help impoverish the water and to improve esthetic qualities; and establishing regulations for shoreland corridors in order to protect lakes from further damage.

GENERAL REFERENCES (Not referenced in text)

Edmondson, W. T. 1968. Water-quality management and lake eutrophication: The Lake Washington case. Reprinted from *Water Resources Management and Public Policy*, Thomas H. Campbell and Robert O. Sylvester (eds.), University of Washington Press, Seattle, p. 139–178.

Findenegg, I., 1964. Bestimmung des Trophiegrades von Seen nach der Radiocarbonmethod. *Naturwissenschaften*, **51**: 368–369.

Hasler, Arthur D. 1947. Eutrophication of lakes by domestic drainage. *Ecology*, **28** (4):383–395.

International Symposium on Eutrophication. 1968. National Academy of Sciences-National Research Council, Washington, D.C.

McGaughey, P. H., R. Eliassen, G. A. Rohlich., H. F. Ludwig, and E. A. Pearson. 1963. Comprehensive study of protection of water resources of Lake Tahoe. To Lake Tahoe Area Council Engineering-Sciences, Inc., Arcadia, Calif.

Minder, Leo. 1938. Der Zürichsee als Eutrophierungsphänomen. Summarische

Ergebnisse aus fünfzig Jahren Zürichseeforschung. *Geol. Meere Binnenge-wässer,* **2** (2): 284–299.

Rohlich, G. A., and K. Stewart. 1967. Eutrophication—a review. California State Water Quality Control Board. Publ. No. 34. 188 p.

SOME BIOLOGICAL EFFECTS OF OIL POLLUTION

Eric B. Cowell

The problems of investigating the biological effects of oil pollution and the subsequent shore-cleaning operations are complex because the eco-system is a complicated system of inter-related reactions between the abiotic environment and the organisms that are dependent upon it.

Oil pollution due to natural seepage of crude oil from oil bearing rocks has been known since Biblical times, but the first documented pollution from a shipping accident was in the 1700s. The problem came into prominence in the 1930s when increasing numbers of ships converted their boilers from coal to oil firing. It was the damage to birds that brought oil pollution to the pubilc eye. Oil pollution incidents in Britain, Europe and the United States involved bird lovers in attempts to wash and clean sea birds. Their well-intentioned efforts usually resulted in failure and frustration and submitted countless birds to processes of cleaning involving pain and suffering. These frustrations produced a barrage of uninformed protest that often bordered on hysteria and made excellent material for the news media. Ecologists concerned with the whole environment began to take an interest but official support for long-term research work was lacking while Government interest was centered upon the problems of oiled beaches and angry holiday makers.

In January 1967 the damaged tanker Chrissi P. Goulandris spilled 250–500 tons of light Arabian crude oil into the confined waters of Milford Haven, Pembrokeshire, South Wales. Once again birds stole the headlines and almost the entire swan population of the area either died or had to be humanely destroyed. While the cleaning-up operations

Reprinted by permission from *Your Environment,* Vol. 1, No. 3, 1970, pp. 84 and 93–94. Copyright 1970 by *Your Environment.* The author is Director of the Oil Pollution Research Unit, Orielton Field Studies Centre (England).

were being carried out, ecologists were being asked to assess the extent of the damage and the time that would be needed for recovery. The only honest answer to such questions was that no one knew. Talks with the oil industry through the good offices of the Institute of Petroleum resulted in the establishment of the Orielton Oil Pollution Research Unit which is partly supported financially by a substantial grant from the Institute of Petroleum Jubilee Fund and partly by the World Wildlife Fund.

In March 1967 the Torrey Canyon Disaster resulted in the world's largest oil-pollution incident up to that time and oil was deposited on beaches along huge stretches of the Cornish Coast. Thousands of sea birds died, holiday beaches were blackened. Sadly, almost all attempts to clean and rehabilitate oiled sea birds failed due to a complicated set of factors that are not yet fully understood. Birds unfortunately attempt to clean themselves by preening; in doing so they ingest quantities of oil, producing internal lesions often resulting in the sloughing of gut linings and the bird's digestion system working on the bird itself. The resulting death is slow and painful.

Even if preening is prevented, cleaning removes natural oils from the feathers and the fine feather structure of interlocking barbs is destroyed. The water repellant properties of the plumage are lost and the birds cannot be returned to the water without risk of them sinking. To overcome this the birds must be kept on land for prolonged post-cleaning care. During this time secondary infections are likely to occur, especially lung diseases such as Aspergillosis. These infections cause even further mortality. Bone deformations are common when sea birds are kept on land for long periods; these result from undue stresses on the birds' leg structures which are adapted for swimming, with the weight of the body supported by water. Even if birds survive these and other difficulties they can become so dependent upon people for food that they may lose their drive to support themselves when released. In Britain private organisations that have attempted to rescue, clean and rehabilitate oiled birds have had variable success. It is ironic that the success rate is lowest for those species showing the greatest decline in numbers. Swans, gulls and some ducks are easy to clean and keep in captivity and almost 75 per cent of those rescued from the sea are successfully returned to it after treatment. Other species, and particularly those most vulnerable to oiling, are extremely difficult to rehabilitate and the success rate is 5 per cent or less. The RSPCA and other conservation organisations have recently recommended the humane killing of all poor-risk species instead of attempted rehabilitation. In such species cleaning only prolongs suffering and causes a particularly slow and painful death.

It is comforting to realise that the populations of most sea bird species are robust and have the potential to rapidly regain optimal population levels in equilibrium with food supply and other related factors. Following disasters they will recover if the environment itself recovers. If there is widespread damage to the ecosystem then food supplies will be diminished. Saving birds for release into a devastated ecosystem would only result in further mortality. For these reasons the Orielton approach to oil pollution-research is not primarily concerned with birds but with the effects on the whole ecosystem particularly in the intertidal zone.

Quite early in the research programme it was established that the volatile aromatic compounds in crude oil were the most toxic components to wild life. For this reason oil reaching shores within a few minutes from spillage was demonstrated to be more biologically damaging than oil that had been at sea for some time and from which the low boiling-point fractions had evaporated. The Torrey Canyon oil was almost biologically inert when it was stranded on the Cornish beaches. The real damage to the shores was done by panic cleaning measures motivated by a desire to placate public feeling, prepare Cornwall for the coming holiday season and to salve stricken consciences. The detergent/emulsifier beach-cleaning materials used were highly toxic formulations of wetting agents and aromatic solvents. These materials have been shown to be toxic to some forms of marine life in concentrations as low as five parts per million and lethal in concentrations as low as 25 parts per million. The main problems however arose from the misuse of the cleaning materials and from their application by misinformed teams without expert supervision. If oil reaches shores biologists prefer that they remain untreated since eventually it will disappear by weathering, ultra-violet breakdown, abrasion and bacterial action. Weathered oil does little real harm to shore life. However, oiled beaches are understandably unacceptable to bathers, boat users and fishermen. Most biologists are not fanatics, many swim, sail and fish and recognise that action is necessary under many circumstances. The second approach is to remove the oil by mechanical methods, pumping, shovelling or absorption by straw, ash, chalk or brushwood, etc. The third choice and the one most widely used is the one least favoured by biologists and this is the spraying of toxic emulsifiers to form emulsions which are hastily washed into the sea and out of sight. The damage that can be done by shore cleaning chemicals was known before the Torrey Canyon disaster but the warnings of experienced ecologists and harbour authorities went unheeded.

The paradox is that until recently the only materials that would effectively clean a beach were extremely toxic to marine life. Hopefully new materials are being developed by the petrolum industry that are effective beach cleaners and up to 1,000 times less toxic than the materials available at the time of the Torrey Canyon accident. At present most marine ecologists agree that it is better to treat oil spills while still afloat, when dilution of detergent to non-toxic levels will take place rapidly. The system of harbour cleaning adopted at Milford Haven, now Britain's largest oil port, seems to work well and measurable damage on the port's beaches is negligible. In Milford Haven most oil spills are fortunately small and are emulsified before they can reach shore. Should oil reach the shore then cleaning is done in consultation with the harbour authority, the local oil industry and conservation organisations. Only amenity beaches are automatically cleaned and inaccessible shores are not cleaned at all.

Recent work at Orielton has established that oil and emulsifier damage may be more severe at some seasons than at others and will also vary according to the type of animal or plant community that is contaminated. On rocky shores in winter, animals may suffer more mortality than in summer while salt-marsh communities within sheltered areas may be resistant to winter pollutions but susceptible in spring and early summer. These phenomena are being investigated and recommendations for future cleaning operations will vary according to season and the type of ecosystem involved. It is strange that some animals may resist damage from neat detergent but be killed by diluted material. In plants on salt marshes neat detergent penetrates the plant in seconds, damages the cell membranes and causes death. In general, however, it is the concentration of the detergent which is critical rather than the actual total amount present and the greatest damage occurs at concentrations above 10–15 per cent.

The degree of detergent damage varies due to a wide range of variable factors. Animals on wave-exposed shores may be killed more readily than on sheltered ones due to the numbers of anaesthetised specimens that release their hold onto the rocks and become washed away from their food supply. Such animals may recover later in deeper water and crawl upwards again, reappearing on the damaged site weeks later, while others perish in the process. The shores may therefore appear to be more severely damaged immediately after detergent treatment than they do some weeks later. The assessment of the severity of damage may therefore entail long term observations on shores. Due to the complicated factors involved, laboratory toxicity tests can give misleading information and must be backed up by long term ecological work of the type currently being conducted by the Field Studies Council at Orielton.

One of the complications that has been elucidated at Orielton is that of the role played by the limpet *Patella vulgata* in controlling the general shore ecology. The limpet is the principal grazing animal responsible for controlling the population of seaweed since it crawls over the rocks eating algal sporelings. If in the process of beach cleaning, limpets are killed in large numbers then the rock surface will become covered by seaweeds, firstly the quick growing green weeds and then the slower growing brown ones like the bladder wrack. Once the rock is covered then new

limpet settlement is impossible since the limpet will not crawl about on
the seaweed itself. Barnacles also fail to settle and then dog whelks which
feed on barnacles also fail to thrive. Only when some of the new large
weed growths die can limpets become established in the space created.
It follows therefore that even if only limpets are killed in substantial
numbers during shore cleaning, then the ecological chain reaction that
follows will ensure widespread damage to the system and recovery will
be slow. Work done at the Marine Biological Station at Port Erin in the
Isle of Man enables us to predict that it could be 8–10 years from complete shore devastation until a normal situation is reached. The Cornish
beaches following Torrey Canyon are undergoing cycles of changes very
similar to those produced experimentally by workers in the Isle of Man.
Recent work by our unit has shown that we may well be able to assess
shore damage and recovery by using the limpet as an indicator organism.
If the limpet population is normal in its community structure both in its
numbers and its size/age relationships, then it is likely that the whole
shore ecology will be returned to normal.

While accidents such as the Torrey Canyon disaster make headline
news, I now feel that such accidents are not a major threat to our shores
(with the exception of bird populations). It is unlikely that another major
accident will happen on such shores before recovery. I am much more
concerned with the effects of chronic pollutions in which repeated or continual damage occurs at a low level but one at which the rate of damage
may exceed the rate of ecosystem recovery. Such chronic effects are possible within the vicinity of fixed installations such as oil terminals and
ports where small spillages may be commonplace or where processing-
plant effluents contain small but continual levels of oil, amounting ultimately to considerable volumes. Damage of this sort can result in slow
but progressive ecosystem decline. A few instances of this type of pollution are known and are being studied both where they occur and in
controlled experiments. We have been able to simulate these effects experimentally in salt-marsh communities, using small but repeated doses
of oil. Where the dilution rate may be as low as 10 parts per million but
the effluent volume is 11,000 gallons per minute, the amount of oil per
day may be 1,500 galls. In one refinery installation near Southampton
Water this level of oil in the effluent water has resulted in the total
death of areas of salt marsh and subsequent erosion of the hitherto stable
mud banks colonised by the vegetation.

Finally I would like to put oil pollution into perspective in relation to
other pollution threats. Oil is considered to be a serious environmental
threat mainly because it is visible and unaesthetic. It is probably not as
serious in its effects and dangers as many other materials that are invisible. Industrial effluents such as polychlorinated biphenyls and chlorinated hydrocarbons (DDT, Aldrin and Dieldrin) are being found in wildlife

on a world-wide scale; heavy-metal poisoning such as that caused by methyl mercury has rendered fish catches in the Baltic unfit for human consumption and has killed people in Japan. Already our oceans are suffering chronic pollution of various kinds and our normal situation is a polluted one. It is vital that we establish the norm, the rate of ecosystem decline, assess the potential threats and take action to prevent a worsening situation. Oil pollution is probably the least of our dangers since being a visible one we demand immediate action to prevent it, understand it and reduce its consequences.

HAZARDS OF RADIOACTIVE WASTE

Walter C. Patterson

When you don't want something, you throw it away. You pour it down the sink or toss it in the dustbin, and somehow or other it disappears. That's the last you see of it, and the last you think of it. Unfortunately, this casual, carefree approach to waste disposal is becoming increasingly indefensible. The situation is serious enough when the waste in question can be successfully recycled by the biosphere—the overworked bacteria in the sewage plants are already hard pressed to keep up with us. But the problem acquires a new and even more challenging dimension when the waste is radioactive.

NATURAL BACKGROUND

The radioactivity of our surroundings is by no means entirely our own doing. Human beings have always eaten, drunk and breathed radioactive substances which are part of the natural environment. Your body contains about one ten-thousand-millionth of a gram of radium. That may not sound like much; but in each second about four of these atoms of radium undergo radioactive disintegration, firing destructive alpha-particles through your body-tissues. The familiar element potassium, essential to your physiology, includes with its stable atoms a significant propor-

Reprinted by permission from *Your Environment*, Vol. 1, No. 3, 1970, pp. 99–104. Copyright 1970 by *Your Environment*. The author is a co-editor of *Your Environment*, 10 Roderick Rd., London NW 3, England.

tion of radioactive ones, emitting beta particles at a rate of perhaps four thousand per second inside you. Like it or not, you yourself are radioactive. You are also exposed to a steady crossfire from outside, cosmic rays from above and beta- and gamma- radiation from uranium and thorium products in the earth and air.

These various internal and external radiations make up what is called the natural background. On average your body-tissues receive a dose of about 0.3 millirads (see accompanying table of units) per day from this natural background—that is, they absorb about 0.03 ergs of energy per gram of body weight. Is this harmful? In a sense the question is academic: the natural background is an inescapable part of the biophysical system we share. Nonetheless there is abundant evidence that energy absorbed from so-called 'ionizing' radiations like these is invariably disruptive to the delicate structures of living tissue. Evidence from Hiroshima and Nagasaki and from accidents involving radioactive materials indicates that a whole body exposure to 600 rads will kill 95 out of 100 human beings, death coming within two weeks of the irradiation.

THE GENETIC QUESTION-MARK

In the seventy-five years since Roentgen discovered X-rays man has been generating ionizing radiation in addition to the natural background. The International Commission on Radiological Protection (ICRP) maintains a continuing review of all available information on the biological effects of radiation. As we shall see, British standards for the control of man-made radioactivity are based on ICRP recommendations. But agreement on such standards is far from unanimous. If it were possible to demonstrate convincingly that here is a threshold radiation-dose level below which no damage to tissue occurs, it would be relatively easy to establish guidelines for man-made radiation. But no such demonstration has been achieved. On the contrary it seems probable that the amount of tissue damage is proportional to the dosage, and that even very low doses may cause damage which we are simply unable to measure, whose consequences may not materialize for many years.

Radiation requires peculiarly stringent control not only because of the possible harm to individuals but also because of the long-term genetic effects. A fleeting exposure to radiation may have no noticeable significance for the person exposed; but the radiation may nonetheless produce minute alterations in the genetic information stored in his reproductive cells. If one of these altered cells participates in the formation of his offspring the genetic alterations will be perpetuated in the next generation, with unforeseeable results. Experiments dating back to the Nobel Prize-winning work of Muller in the 1920s indicate that irradiation of chromosomes increases the rate of mutations in succeeding generations. The odds against such occurrences are extremely high in single instances; but the collective effect of even a small increase in the radiation-exposure of a whole population may not be negligible. We don't know, nor can we in honesty make any valid predictions. In such a context, the question of radioactive waste becomes a matter for urgent concern.

MAN-MADE RADIOACTIVITY

By far the largest man-made addition to the radioactive burden of the earth has been the fallout from detonation of nuclear explosives. The additional radioactivity released into the environment during the years of active nuclear weapons-testing in the atmosphere amounted to thousands of millions of curies. A considerable proportion of this nuclear debris consists of isotopes with a long 'half-life', whose radioactivity will persist for decades. Nuclear explosions are still being triggered; France and China test nuclear weapons, and the American Atomic Energy Commission proceeds with its programme, persuasively named Plowshare, for industrial use of nuclear explosives, with the eager backing of French, Belgian and West German descendants of the vast Nobel armaments complex.

Such massive injections of added radioactivity into our surroundings demonstrate an appalling lack of concern for the possible consequences, and must be deplored. But as the build-up of environmental radioactivity from nuclear explosions slows somewhat, a new factor is beginning to enter the picture: the 'planned release'. Many industrial, medical and research applications of radioactivity involve the production of waste material which has become radioactive. This waste can be anything from a paper handkerchief used in a radiotherapy ward to intensely radioactive fission products from the spent fuel elements of a nuclear reactor. The difficulty is that radioactivity, once turned on, cannot be turned off. You can pour radioactive wishwater down the sink, but wherever it goes it will still be radioactive, and potentially dangerous. The radioactivity of many materials will die away rapidly; if you store the waste for a few weeks its activity will then be nothing to worry about. But the radioactivity of some substances remains almost undiminished for centuries, and the requirements for storage are of a wholly different order. If you pour such substances down the sink, literally or figuratively, you are executing a 'planned release', adding new radioactvity to the environment.

RADIOACTIVE WASTE IN BRITAIN

In Britain radioactive waste is produced by hospitals, universities, some industries, the Central Electricity Generating Board, the South of Scotland Electricity Board, the Royal Navy, and—about all—the United Kingdom Atomic Energy Authority. Such waste is subdivided into three grades: low activity (such as the paper handkerchief aforementioned), medium activity (such as liquid body waste from the same ward), and high activity (such as fission products from reactor fuel). The waste is also subdivided into solid, liquid and gaseous.

An abundant literature details handling and disposal procedures for the various classes of wastes. The most important are the Nuclear Installations (Licensing and Insurance) Act 1959, and the Radioactive Substances Act 1960. The former Act lays down the regulations as they apply to the electricity generating boards and the Atomic Energy Authority, the latter as they apply otherwise. These Acts are administered by the Ministry of Housing and Local Government; in the case of nuclear installations the responsibility is shared with the Ministry of Agriculture, Fisheries and Food.

Elaborate directives specify procedures for disposal and limits on amounts. An explanatory memorandum entitled Radioactive Substances Act 1960, available from HMSO for 1s 6d, gives details. Low activity radioactive waste is disposed of, with certain restrictions, just like other waste; gaseous waste is discharged through chimneys and liquid waste into sewers; solid waste is buried on local-authority dumping-sites. But more active wastes receive more careful handling, as will be described shortly.

Prosecution and penalties are provided for failure to comply with regulations, although evasions seem relatively infrequent; a Ministry spokesman could recall only a single case in 1969, an illegal disposal of used luminous material that resulted in a fine of £100. Agencies of the Ministeries carry out spot checks on liquid and gaseous discharges; but the main responsibility for monitoring major discharge lies with the producers themselves, especially the nuclear reactor plants and related installations.

THE LANGUAGE OF RADIOACTIVITY

The **curie:** describes how radioactive a source is (how much radiation it gives off); one curie (originally the activity of one gram of radium) represents thirty-seven thousand million atoms undergoing 'decay' (emitting radiation) per second.

The **roentgen:** describes how effectively a beam 'ionizes' (knocks electrons off) molecules; strictly applicable only to air.

The **rad:** describes how much energy is delivered to living tissue by ionizing radiation; one rad delivers 100 ergs per gram of tissue, about equivalent to one dental X-ray. A beam of one roentgen produces an exposure of one rad for most radiation.

THE LOWESTOFT REPORTS

Independent monitoring of radioactive discharges from these sources is carried out by the Fisheries Radiobiological Laboratory in Lowestoft, under the direction of the Ministry of Agriculture, Fisheries and Food. Since 1967, the Lowestoft laboratory have published a yearly report, Radioactivity in Surface and Coastal Waters of the British Isles. The three reports issued thus far suggest that the control of radioactive discharges is subject to much more scrupulous and stringent policing than any other type of waste discharge. Each separate discharge is followed through its subsequent dispersal in the environment; all special circumstances of possible reconcentration by biological processes are taken into account before the permitted level of discharge is set according to the guidelines of the ICRP.

The most famous example is the small group of people in Wales who eat a type of bread called laverbread, made partly from seaweed. The seaweed used in laverbread concentrates certain radioactive isotopes from the coastal waters where the seaweed grows. These isotopes originate primarily from the Windscale establishment of the UKAEA in Cumberland. A spokesman of the UKAEA observes accordingly that the laverbread-eaters of south Wales determine the permitted level of effluent radioactivity from Windscale: this level is set to assure that the so-called 'critical group' eating laverbread do not under any imaginable dietary circumstances ingest an amount of radioactivity approaching the ICRP recommended maximum for safety. Similar individual assessments are applied to each separate discharge.

In view of the possible hazards this intensive scrutiny is entirely appropriate; but if other industries were compelled to maintain similar standards of effluent-control there's no doubt that the air and water of Britain would be much cleaner and healthier than they are. The nuclear industry and its government monitors could teach their colleagues some valuable lessons. Nonetheless, there must be no resting on laurels. The number of major sources recorded in the Lowestoft report has increased every year. The ICRP recommendations are cautious in the extreme; but environmental radioactivity can never be regarded as completely innocuous.

ATLANTIC DUMPING

A major problem with low activity waste is its sheer bulk. Broken glassware from radiochemical laboratories, contaminated paper and fabric, et cetera, accumulate at a rate which can make adequate burial difficult. In 1965 the European Nuclear Energy Agency, a sub-section of the Organisation for Economic Co-operation and Development, undertook a massive project ultimately reported under the title of 'Radioactive Waste Disposal into the Atlantic 1967'.

Preliminary consideration of the dumping project involved oceanographers, marine biologists, fishery experts and radiation protection specialists drafted from the top levels of the professions in several countries. The feasibility of the project was established by the initial Hazard Assessment (the capitals are in the report). A team of waste-treatment specialists convened to determine the best procedure, and laid down detailed specifications for preparation of the material to be dumped. Land and sea transport men from the fire participating countries, Britain, France, West Germany, Belgium and the Netherlands, set out elaborate logistical time-tables for movement of the cargo to the ports; in the event these time-tables were adhered to with few and minor deviations. Scrupulous monitoring throughout the various road and rail journeys and five sea voyages indicated that exposure of personnel and public remained well below ICRP-recommended levels.

The dumping itself took place from 30 May 1967 to 14 August 1967. A total of 35,790 specially sealed oil-drums with a gross weight of 10,895 tonnes and a measured radioactivity (at the time) of 7,889 curies were dumped overboard in a location in 'the North East Atlantic Ocean' where the depth exceeded 5,000 metres. The precise location of the dumping area is one of the few details not given in the report.

At the time, and since, understandable doubts have been expressed about operations of this kind. The long-term effects of such dumping cannot be foreseen with any guarantee of completeness. But a fair appraisal of this report suggests that virtually no possible detail was overlooked or undervalued. The report makes absorbing reading. It is commendably direct and forthright, free of jargon and unexpectedly reassuring.

Nevertheless, there is no room for complacency. Dumping of radioactive wastes at sea has not by any means always been subject to such scrupulous care. Furthermore, by any criterion eight thousand curies is a substantial addition to the radioactive burden of the environment. Another dump under ENEA auspices took place in 1969, and was mentioned casually as being 'about the same' as the 1967 dump. It's true that the tonnage dumped in 1969 was lower than that dumped in 1967; but this is trivial. On the other hand, the measured radioactivity dumped in 1969 was some 22,600 curies, nearly three times the activity dumped in 1967. The 1969 dump was referred to only in a brief subsection of an ENEA report; and the question arises whether deep-ocean dumping is coming to be taken for granted. If so, if familiarity makes such undertakings routine, we are incurring an environmental debt that may have to be paid, with incalculable interest, by our children's children.

HIGH ACTIVITY WASTE

Waste from the various processes involved in operating reactors comes into a separate category, and is a much more serious problem than the low activity waste thus far mentioned. The nuclear reactions occurring in the core of a reactor create a build-up of fission products in the fuel elements. These fission products reduce the efficiency of the reactor until it becomes necessary to reprocess the fuel chemically, to retrieve the unused uranium or plutonium and remove the accumulated fission products. This involves dissolving the spent fuel in acid and treating the solution thus obtained. The unused fuel is recovered for re-use; but the remaining solution is now intensely radioactive, including some isotopes of long 'half-life' whose high activity will persist for tens of thousands of years.

What to do with waste of this kind has been an acutely troublesome question ever since the first plutonium-production reactors went into operation at Hanford, Washington, in the north-western U.S., more than twenty-five years ago. High activity waste from the Hanford plant was stored in underground tanks; the urgency of the wartime Manhattan Project for development of the atomic bomb led to over-hasty planning, the awesome implications of which have been publicised only in recent months. The vast storage 'farm' (officials avoid the term 'burial ground') at Hanford is in fact situated over a major geological fault. If an earthquake were to rupture the tanks the radioactivity released would have an effect fully as devastating as a global nuclear war.

The Hanford tanks underline dramatically the central problem of high activity fission-product waste: it doesn't go away. The Hanford tanks are no longer in active service, but they will continue to boil under their own internally-generated heat for many generations. They will require maintenance, cooling and replacement of corroded tank-walls when the obliteration of Hiroshima is as remote as the fall of Constantinople. Human history offers no prior examples of stewardship whose reliability can be foreseen on a time-scale like this; the prognosis is—to put it mildly—not good.

WINDSCALE

The United Kingdom Atomic Enery Authority operates a fuel-reprocessing plant at Windscale. Waste-handling at this plant represents much the most serious challenge to the safety-consciousness of the British nuclear industry. The UKAEA takes a great deal of pride in its safety record, which—with the classical exception of the Windscale reactor accident in October 1957—compares favourably with those of other British industries. The Authority is far from reluctant to discuss its operations, and seems to feel that it has a responsibility to provide the public with relevant information. Such an attitude is certainly to be commended, offering as it does an opportunity for rational evaluation of problems and prospects. One of the most pressing of these problems is certainly that of the handling of high activity waste.

Fuel reprocessing at Windscale produces two kinds of high-activity waste, solid and liquid. The outer casings of used fuel elements must be stripped off; these casings, severely contaminated with fission products, are stored underwater in concrete silos on the grounds of the Windscale establishment. After the spent fuel has been dissolved and the reusable uranium and plutonium extracted, the remaining solution is fed into storage tanks elsewhere in the grounds. There are at present nine of these tanks, eight with capacities of 70 m³ each and one with a capacity of 158 m³. Each tank has an inner wall of ½ in. stainless steel, enclosed in a separate outer wall of stainless steel and surrounded by reinforced concrete 5 ft. thick. The intense radioactivity of the liquid makes it boil with its own internally-generated heat; each tank is equipped with duplicated water cooling circuits. One of the tanks is a stand-by tank; the radioactive liquid can be pumped from tank to tank if the need arises.

In the last three years the contents of the tanks have increased by 120 m³; the rate of increase is now about 45 m³ per year. The total radioactivity of the liquid now in the tanks is *several hundred million curies*. For comparison it's worth mentioning that the estimated total radioactivity of all the oceans of the earth is several hundred thousand million curies: the tanks at Windscale already contain about one tenth of one per cent of this activity in a volume less than that of one detached house.

As more and more reactors come into service in Britain the high-activity waste is accumulating ever more rapidly in the silos and tanks at Windscale. The UKAEA also reprocesses fuel from British-built reactors in Italy and Japan; the waste goes into the Windscale tanks. The UKAEA comments, with disarming casualness, that the Windscale tanks will have to be tended 'for 500–1,000 years'. It is difficult to believe that they themselves look upon the situation with such aplomb. Precious few of the works of man have even survived for such a length of time, much less been tended with the assiduousness required to pamper the furious contents of the high-activity tanks.

Needless to say alternative methods of handling high-activity waste are under urgent investigation. Glassification—concentration and sealing of the waste into solid ceramic bricks—appears the most promising. Once glassified, the waste will no longer be capable of escaping into the environment as a result of accident or natural catastrophe. But glassification is still early in the development stage. Furthermore, even if glassified, the high activity waste will continue to accumulate as long as reactors are operating and creating it.

THE ENERGY DILEMMA

Our technological culture demands ever more power: were you one of the many uttering imprecations at the Central Electricity Generating Board when your electric fires dimmed last winter? Power must come from somewhere. Fossil-fuel power plants create their own hazards: these include atmospheric pollution with sulphur dioxide, and disturbance of the carbon dioxide balance in the biosphere. Furthermore, the earth's remaining reserves of irreplaceable fossil fuel are limited, and could be better employed as raw materials for many manufacturing processes. Against these considerations must be weighed the increasing burden of man-made radioactivity created by nuclear power-generation. Controlled thermonuclear fusion, the technologists' dream, seems likely to remain a dream for the foreseeable future. Solar power is unlikely ever to make much contribution during a British winter.

If we must have more power, there is certainly a strong case in favour of nuclear power. But its drawbacks must also be recognised. As must now be stressed in every industrial picture take into account not only the current balance-sheet but also the long-term environmental debt, which may well be extremely difficult to quantify. At the time of writing, the UKAEA has an application pending, to increase the level of effluent discharge from Windscale into the Solway Firth: from 450 curies per quarter to 2000 curies per quarter. The Ennerdale Rural District Council has registered vigorous opposition to the increase. Asked what would be the consequence of refusal of the application, a UKAEA spokesman said simply, 'We'd have to cut back the nuclear power programme'.

If we want the undoubted benefits of nuclear power, radiotherapy and the many other applications of man-made radioactivity that are becoming part of our everyday life, we must recognise what we are buying, and what we are paying for it. Unfortunately, some of the bills may not arrive until it's no longer possible to return undesired goods.

EFFECTS OF POLLUTION ON THE STRUCTURE AND PHYSIOLOGY OF ECOSYSTEMS

G. M. Woodwell

The accumulation of various toxic substances in the biosphere is leading to complex changes in the structures and function of natural ecosystems. Although the changes are complex, they follow in aggregate patterns that are similar in many different ecosystems and are therefore broadly predictable. The patterns involve many changes but include especially simplification of the structure of both plant and animal communities, shifts in the ratio of gross production to total respiration, and loss of part or all of the inventory of nutrients. Despite the frequency with which various pollutants are causing such changes and the significance of the changes for all living systems (1), only a few studies show details of the pattern of change clearly. These are studies of the effects of ionizing radiation of persistent pesticides, and of eutrophication. The effects of radiation will be used here to show the pattern of changes in terrestrial plant communities and to show similarities with the effects of fire, oxides of sulfur, and herbicides. Effects of such pollutants as pesticides on the animal community are less conspicuous but quite parallel, which shows that the ecological effects of pollution correspond very closely to the general "strategy of ecosystem development" outlined by Odum (1) and that they can be anticipated in considerable detail.

The problems caused by pollution are of interest from two viewpoints. Practical people—toxicologists, engineers, health physicists, public health officials, intensive users of the environment—consider pollution primarily as a direct hazard to man. Others, no less concerned for human welfare but with less pressing public responsibilities, recognize that toxicity to humans is but one aspect of the pollution problem, the other being a threat to the maintenance of a biosphere suitable for life as we know it. The first viewpoint leads to emphasis on human food chains; the second leads to emphasis on human welfare insofar as it depends on the integrity of the diverse ecosystems of the earth, the living systems that appear to have built and now maintain the biosphere.

The food-chain problem is by far the simpler; it is amenable at least in part to the pragmatic, narrowly compartmentalized solutions that industrialized societies are good at. The best example of the toxicological approach is in control of mutagens, particularly the radionuclides. These

Reprinted by permission from *Science*, Vol. 168, 1970, pp. 429–433. Copyright 1970 by the American Association for the Advancement of Science. The author is Senior Zoologist at the Brookhaven National Laboratory, Upton, N.Y.

present a specific, direct hazard to man. They are much more important to man than to other organisms. A slightly enhanced rate of mutation is a serious danger to man, who has developed through medical science elaborate ways of preserving a high fraction of the genetic defects in the population; it is trivial to the rest of the biota, in which genetic defects may be eliminated through selection. This is an important fact about pollution hazards—toxic substances that are principally mutagenic are usually of far greater direct hazard to man than to the rest of the earth's biota and must be considered first from the standpoint of their movement to man through food webs or other mechanisms and to a much lesser extent from that of their effects on the ecosystem through which they move. We have erred, as shown below, in assuming that all toxic substances should be treated this way.

Pollutants that affect other components of the earth's biota as well as man present a far greater problem. Their effects are chronic and may be cumulative in contrast to the effects of short-lived disturbances that are repaired by succession. We ask what effects such pollutants have on the structure of natural ecosystems and on biological diversity and what these changes mean to physiology, especially to mineral cycling and the long-term potential for sustaining life.

Although experience with pollution of various types is extensive and growing rapidly, only a limited number of detailed case history studies provide convincing control data that deal with the structure of ecosystems. One of the clearest and most detailed series of experiments in recent years has been focused on the ecological effects of radiation. These studies are especially useful because they allow cause and effect to be related quantitatively at the ecosystem level, which is difficult to do in nature. The question arises, however, whether the results from studies of ionizing radiation, a factor that is not usually considered to have played an important role in recent evolution, have any general application. The answer, somewhat surprisingly to many biologists, seems to be that they do. The ecological effects of radiation follow patterns that are known from other types of disturbances. The studies of radiation, because of their specificity, provide useful clues for examination of effects of other types of pollution for which evidence is much more fragmentary.

The effects of chronic irradiation of a late successional oak-pine forest have been studied at Brookhaven National Laboratory in New York. After 6 months' exposure to chronic irradiation from a ^{137}Cs source, five well-defined zones of modification of vegetation had been established. They have become more pronounced through 7 years of chronic irradiation. The zones were:

1) A central devastated zone, where exposure were > 200 R/day and no higher plants survived, although certain mosses and lichens survived up to exposures > 1000 R/day.

2) A sedge zone, where *Carex pensylvanica* (2) survived and ultimately formed a continuous cover (> 150 R/day).

3) A shrub zone in which two species of *Vaccinium* and one of *Gaylussacia* survived, with *Quercus ilicifolia* toward the outer limit of the circle where exposures were lowest (> 40 R/day).

4) An oak zone, the pine having been eliminated (> 16 R/day).

5) Oak-pine forest, where exposures were < 2 R/day, and there was no obvious change in the number of species, although small changes in rates of growth were measurable at exposures as low as 1 R/day.

The effect was a systematic dissection of the forest, strata being removed layer by layer. Trees were eliminated at low exposures, then the taller shrubs (*Gaylussacia baccata*), then the lower shrubs (*Vaccinium* species), then the herbs, and finally the lichens and mosses. Within these groups, it was evident that under irradiation an upright form of growth was a disadvantage. The trees did vary—the pines (*Pinus rigida*) for instance were far more sensitive than the oaks without having a conspicuous tendency toward more upright growth, but all the trees were substantially more sensitive than the shrubs (3). Within the shrub zone, tall forms were more sensitive; even within the lichen populations, foliose and fruticose lichens proved more sensitive than crustose lichens (4).

The changes caused by chronic irradiation of herb communities in old fields show the same pattern—upright species are at a disadvantage. In one old field at Brookhaven, the frequency of low-growing plants increased along the gradient of increasing radiation intensity to 100 percent at > 1000 R/day (5). Comparison of the sensitivity of the herb field with that of the forest, by whatever criterion, clearly shows the field to be more resistant than the forest. The exposure reducing diversity to 50 percent in the first year was $\sim$1000 R/day for the field and 160 R/day for the forest, a greater than fivefold difference in sensitivity (3).

The changes in these ecosystems under chronic irradiation are best summarized as changes in structure, although diversity, primary production, total respiration, and nutrient inventory are also involved. The changes are similar to the familiar ones along natural gradients of increasingly severe conditions, such as exposure on mountains, salt spray, and water availability. Along all these gradients the conspicuous change is a reduction of structure from forest toward communities dominated by certain shrubs, then, under more severe conditions, by certain herbs, and finally by low-growing plants, frequently mosses and lichens. Succession, insofar as it has played any role at all in the irradiated ecosystems, has simply reinforced this pattern, adding a very few hardy species and allowing expansion of the populations of more resistant indigenous species. The reasons for radiation's causing this pattern are still not clear (3, 6), but the pattern is a common one, not peculiar to ionizing radiation, despite the novelty of radiation exposures as high as these.

Its commonness is illustrated by the response to fire, one of the oldest and most important disruptions of nature. The oak-pine forests such as those on Long Island have, throughout their extensive range in eastern North America been subject in recent times to repeated burning. The changes in physiognomy of the vegetation follow the above pattern very closely—the forest is replaced by communities of shrubs, especially bear oak (*Quercus ilicifolia*), *Gaylussacia*, and *Vaccinium* species. This change is equivalent to that caused by chronic exposure to 40 R/day or more. Buell and Cantlon (7), working on similar vegetation in New Jersey, showed that a further increase in the frequency of fires resulted in a differential reduction in taller shrubs first, and a substantial increase in the abundance of *Carex pensylvanica*, the same sedge now dominating the sedge zone of the irradiated forest. The parallel is detailed; radiation and repeated fires both reduce the structure of the forest in similar ways, favoring low-growing hardy species.

The similarity of response appears to extend to other vegetations as well. G. L. Miller, working with F. McCormick at the Savannah River Laboratory, has shown recently that the most radiation-resistant and fire-resistant species of 20-year-old fields are annuals and perennials characteristic of disturbed places (8). An interesting sidelight of his study was the observation that the grass stage of long leaf pine (*Pinus palustris*), long considered a specific adaptation to the fires that maintain the southeastern savannahs, appears more resistant to radiation damage than the mature trees. At a total acute exposure of 2.1 kR (3 R/day), 85 percent of the grass-stage populations survived but only 55 percent of larger trees survived. Seasonal variation in sensitivity to radiation damage has been abundantly demonstrated (9), and it would not be surprising to find that this variation is related to the ecology of the species. Again it appears that the response to radiation is not unique.

The species surviving high radiation-exposure rates in the Brookhaven experiments are the ones commonly found in disturbed places, such as roadsides, gravel banks, and areas with nutrient-deficient or unstable soil. In the forest they include *Comptonia peregrina* (the sweet fern), a decumbent spiny *Rubus*, and the lichens, especially *Cladonia cristatella*. In the old field one of the most conspicuously resistant species was *Digitaria sanguinalis* (crabgrass) among several other weedy species. Clearly these species are generalists in the sense that they survive a wide range of conditions, including exposure to high intensities of ionizing radiation —hardly a common experience in nature but apparently one that elicits a common response.

With this background one might predict that a similar pattern of devastation would result from such pollutants as oxides of sulfur released from smelting. The evidence is fragmentary, but Gorham and Gordon (10) found around the smelters in Sudbury, Ontario, a striking reduction in the number of species of higher plants along a gradient of

62 kilometers (39 miles). In different samples the number of species ranged from 19 to 31 at the more distant sites and dropped abruptly at 6.4 kilometers. At 1.6 kilometers, one of two randomly placed plots (20 by 2 meters) included only one species. They classified the damage in five categories, from "Not obvious" through "Moderate" to "Very severe." The tree canopy had been reduced or eliminated within 4.8 to 6.4 kilometers of the smelter, with only occasional sprouts of trees, seedlings, and successional herbs and shrubs remaining; this damage is equivalent to that produced by exposure to 40 R/day. The most resistant trees were, almost predictably to a botanist, red maple (*Acer rubrum*) and red oak (*Quercus rubra*). Other species surviving in the zones of "Severe" and "Very severe" damage included *Sambucus pubens, Polygonum cilinode, Comptonia peregrina*, and *Epilobium angustifolium* (fire weed). The most sensitive plants appeared to be *Pinus strobus* and *Vaccinium myrtilloides*. The pine was reported no closer than 25.6 kilometers (16 miles), where it was chlorotic.

This example confirms the pattern of the change—first a reduction of diversity of the forest by elimination of sensitive species; then elimination of the tree canopy and survival of resistant shrubs and herbs widely recognized as "seral" or successional species or "generalists."

The effects of herbicides, despite their hoped for specificity, fall into the same pattern, and it is no surprise that the extremely diverse forest canopies of Viet Nam when sprayed repeatedly with herbicides are replaced over large areas by dense stands of species of bamboo (*11*).

The mechanisms involved in producing this series of patterns in terrestrial ecosystems are not entirely clear. One mechanism that is almost certainly important is simply the ratio of gross production to respiration in different strata of the community. The size of trees has been shown to approach a limit set by the amount of surface area of stems and branches in proportion to the amount of leaf area (*12*). The apparent reason is that, as a tree expands in size, the fraction of its total surface devoted to bark, which makes a major contribution to the respiration, expands more rapidly than does the photosynthetic area. Any chronic disturbance has a high probability of damaging the capacity for photosynthesis without reducing appreciably the total amount of respiration; therefore, large plants are more vulnerable than species requiring less total respiration. Thus chronic disturbances of widely different types favor plants that are small in stature, and any disturbance that tends to increase the amount of respiration in proportion to photosynthesis will aggravate this shift.

The shift in the structure of terrestrial plant communities toward shrubs, herbs, or mosses and lichens, involves changes in addition to those of structure and diversity. Simplification of the plant community involves also a reduction of the total standing crop of organic matter and a corresponding reduction in the total inventory of nutrient elements held within the system, a change that may have important longterm implications for the potential of the site to support life. The extent of such losses has been demonstrated recently by Bormann and his colleagues in the Hubbard Brook Forest in New Hampshire (*13*), where all of the trees in a watershed were cut, the cut material was left to decay, and the losses of nutrients were monitored in the runoff. Total nitrogen losses in the first year were equivalent to twice the amount cycled in the system during a normal year. With the rise of nitrate ion in the runoff, concentrations of calcium, magnesium, sodium, and potassium ions rose severalfold, which caused eutrophication and even pollution of the streams fed by this watershed. The soil had little capacity to retain the nutrients that were locked in the biota once the higher plants had been killed. The total losses are not yet known, but early evidence indicates that they will be a high fraction of the nutrient inventory, which will cause a large reduction in the potential of the site for supporting living systems as complex as that destroyed—until nutrients accumulate again. Sources are limited; the principal source is erosion of primary minerals.

When the extent of the loss of nutrients that accompanies a reduction in the structure of a plant community is recognized, it is not surprising to find depauperate vegetation in places subject to chronic disturbances. Extensive sections of central Long Island, for example, support a depauperate oak-pine forest in which the bear oak, *Quercus ilicifolia*, is the principal woody species. The cation content of an extremely dense stand of this common community, which has a biomass equivalent to that of the more diverse late successional forest that was burned much less recently and less intensively, would be about 60 percent that of the richer stand, despite the equivalence of standing crop. This means that the species, especially the bear oak, contain, and presumably require, lower concentrations of cations. This is an especially good example because the bear oak community is a long-lasting one in the fire succession and marks the transition from a high shrub community to forest. It has analogies elsewhere, such as the heath balds of the Great Smoky Mountains and certain bamboo thickets in Southeast Asia.

The potential of a site for supporting life depends heavily on the pool of nutrients available through breakdown of primary minerals and through recycling in the living portion of the ecosystem. Reduction of the structure of the system drains these pools in whole or in part; it puts leaks in the system. Any chronic pollution that affects the structure of ecosystems, especially the plant community, starts leaks and reduces the potential of the site for recovery. Reduction of the structure of forests in Southeast Asia by herbicides has dumped the nutrient pools of these large statured and extremely diverse forests. The nutrients are carried to the streams, which turn green with the algae that the nutrients support. Tschirley (*11*), reporting his study of the effects of herbicides in Viet Nam, recorded "surprise" and "pleasure" that fishing had improved in treated areas. If the herbicides are not toxic to fish, there should be little surprise at improved catches of certain kinds of fish in heavily enriched waters adjacent to herbicide-treated forests. The bamboo thickets that replace the forests also reflect the drastically lowered potential of these sites to support living systems. The time it takes to reestablish a forest with the original diversity depends on the availability of nutrients, and is probably very long in most lateritic soils.

In generalizing about pollution, I have concentrated on some of the grossest changes in the plant communities of terrestrial ecosystems. The emphasis on plants is appropriate because plants dominate terrestrial ecosystems. But not all pollutants affect plants directly; some have their principal effects on heterotrophs. What changes in the structure of animal communities are caused by such broadly toxic materials as most pesticides?

The general pattern of loss of structure is quite similar, although the structure of the animal communities is more difficult to chart. The transfer of energy appears to be one good criterion of structure. Various studies suggest that 10 to 20 percent of the energy entering the plant community is transferred directly to the animal community through herbivores (*14*). Much of that energy, perhaps 50 percent or more, is used in respiration to support the herbivore population; some is transferred to the detritus food chain directly, and some, probably not more than 20 percent, is transferred to predators of the herbivores. In an evolutionarily and successionally mature community, this transfer of 10 to 20 percent per trophic level may occur two or three times to support carnivores, some highly specialized, such as certain eagles, hawks, and herons, others less specialized, such as gulls, ravens, rats, and people.

Changes in the plant community, such as its size, rate of energy fixation, and species, will affect the structure of the animal community as well. Introduction of a toxin specific for animals, such as a pesticide that is a generalized nerve toxin, will also topple the pyramid. Although the persistent pesticides are fat soluble and tend to accumulate in carnivores and reduce populations at the tops of food chains, they affect every trophic level, reducing reproductive capacity, almost certainly altering behavioral patterns, and disrupting the competitive relationships between species. Under these circumstances the highly specialized species, the obligate carnivores high in the trophic structure, are at a disadvantage because the food chain concentrates the toxin and, what is even more important, because the entire structure beneath them becomes unstable. Again the generalists or broad-niched species are favored, the gulls, rats, ravens, pigeons and, in a very narrow short-term sense, man. Thus, the pesticides favor the herbivores, the very organisms they were invented to control.

Biological evolution has divided the resources of any site among a large variety of users—species—which, taken together, confer on that site the properties of a closely integrated system capable of conserving a diversity of life. The system has structure; its populations exist with certain definable, quantitative relationships to one another; it fixes energy and releases it at a measurable rate; and it contains an inventory of nutrients that is accumulated and recirculated, not lost. The system is far from static; it is subject, on a time scale very long compared with a human lifespan, to a continuing augmentive change through evolution; on a shorter time scale, it is subject to successsion toward a more stable state after any disturbance. The successional patterns are themselves a product of the evolution of life, providing for systematic recovery from any acute disturbance. Without a detailed discussion of the theory of ecology, one can say that biological evolution, following a pattern approximating that outlined above, has built the earth's ecosystems, and that these systems have been the dominant influence on the earth throughout the span of human existence. The structure of these systems is now being changed all over the world. We know enough about the structure and function of these systems to predict the broad outline of the effects of pollution on both land and water. We know that as far as our interests in the next decades are concerned, pollution operates on the time scale of succession, not of evolution, and we cannot look to evolution to cure this set of problems. The loss of structure involves a shift away from complex arrangements of specialized species toward the generalists; away from forest, toward hardy shrubs and herbs; away from the phytoplankton of the open ocean that Wurster (15) proved so very sensitive to DDT, toward those algae of the sewage plants that are unaffected by almost everything including DDT and most fish; away from diversity in birds, plants, and fish toward monotony; away from tight nutrient cycles toward very loose ones with terrestrial systems becoming depleted, and with aquatic systems becoming overloaded; away from stability toward instability especially with regard to sizes of populations of small, rapidly reproducing organisms such as insects and rodents that compete with man; away from a world that runs itself through a self-augmentive, slowly moving evolution, to one that requires constant tinkering to patch it up, a tinkering that is malignant in that each act of repair generates a need for further repairs to avert problems generated at compound interest.

This is the pattern, predictable in broad outline, aggravated by almost any pollutant. Once we recognize the pattern, we can begin to see the meaning of some of the changes occurring now in the earth's biota. We can see the demise of carnivorous birds and predict the demise of important fisheries. We can tell why, around industrial cities, hills that were once forested now are not; why each single species is important; and how the increase in the temperature of natural water bodies used to cool new reactors will, by augmenting respiration over photosynthesis, ultimately degrade the system and contribute to degradation of other interconnected ecosystems nearby. We can begin to speculate on where continued, exponential progress in this direction will lead: probably not to extinction—man will be around for a long time yet—but to a general degradation of the quality of life.

The solution? Fewer people, unpopular but increasing restrictions on technology (making it more and more expensive), and a concerted effort to tighten up human ecosystems to reduce their interactions with the rest of the earth on whose stability we all depend. This does not require foregoing nuclear energy; it requires that if we must dump heat, it should be dumped into civilization to enhance a respiration rate in a sewage plant or an argicultural ecosystem, not dumped outside of civilization to affect that fraction of the earth's biota that sustains the earth as we know it. The question of what fraction that might be remains as one of the great issues, still scarcely considered by the scientific community.

REFERENCES AND NOTES

1. E. P. Odum, *Science* **164**, 262 (1969).
2. Plant nomenclature follows that of M. L. Fernald in *Gray's Manual of Botany* (American Book, New York, ed. 8, 1950).
3. G. M. Woodwell, *Science* **156**, 461 (1967); ——— and A. L. Rebuck, *Ecol. Monogr.* **37**, 53 (1967).
4. G. M. Woodwell and T. P. Gannutz, *Amer. J. Bot.* **54**, 1210 (1967).
5. ——— and J. K. Oosting, *Radiat. Bot.* **5**, 205 (1965).
6. ——— and R. H. Whittaker, *Quart. Rev. Biol.* **43**, 42 (1968).
7. M. F. Buell and J. E. Cantlon, *Ecology* **34**, 520 (1953).
8. G. L. Miller, thesis, Univ. of North Carolina (1968).
9. A. H. Sparrow, L. A. Schairer, R. C. Sparrow, W. F. Campbell, *Radiat. Bot.* **3**, 169 (1963); F. G. Taylor, Jr., *ibid.* **6**, 307 (1965).
10. E. Gorham and A. G. Gordon, *Can. J. Bot.* **38**, 307 (1960); *ibid.*, p. 477; *ibid.* **41**, 371 (1963).
11. F. H. Tschirley, *Science* **163**, 779 (1969).
12. R. H. Whittaker and G. M. Woodwell, *Amer. J. Bot.* **54**, 931 (1967).
13. F. H. Bormann, G. E. Likens, D. W. Fisher, R. S. Pierce, *Science* **159**, 882 (1968).
14. These relationships have been summarized in detail by J. Phillipson [*Ecological Energetics* (St. Martin's Press, New York, 1966)]. See also L. B. Slobodkin, *Growth and Regulation of Animal Populations* (Holt, Rinehart and Winston, New York, 1961) and J. H. Ryther, *Science* **166**, 72 (1969).
15. C. F. Wurster, *Science* **159**, 1474 (1968).
16. G. M. Woodwell, *ibid.* **138**, 572 (1962).
17. Research carried out at Brookhaven National Laboratory under the auspices of the U.S. Atomic Energy Commission. Paper delivered at 11th International Botanical Congress, Seattle, Wash., on 26 August 1969 in the symposium "Ecological and Evolutionary Implications of Environmental Pollution."

PART FIVE

THE FATEFUL EXPONENT^{population}

Genesis
(and that God be directed
to cast one vote . . .)

God made Heaven and Earth
  with all its murderous
  mountainous features.
  With all its crawling
  and squirming creatures—
  equipped them with wings
  and musical screeches.
  And then he made man
  in His image
  and man said, "I move
  the nominations be closed . . ."

Robert M. Chute

The growth of the human population is a fact that has been amply documented. The rate and magnitude of growth in the historical past is known with decreasing accuracy as we recede from the present. Disagreeemnt about the exact rate of increase in a particular country or in the world as a whole is still possible but, with increasingly better data, the area for disagreement grows slim. Major disagreements arise about the future growth of the human population. Arguments on this latter point have obscured discussion of an even more fundamental issue, determination of optimum population level.

All predictions about the future of our population are based on extrapolation from past and present data. This does not mean that any prediction is mere speculation—at least no more so than any other rational prediction. All our judgments relating to future events are consciously or unconsciously probabilistic and are rooted in our estimation of the degree to which past events will repeat themselves and our knowledge of any rules, laws, or principles which allow us to predict the manner in which any changes will occur.

Given the present level of population and the present rate of increase, what will be the population 100 years from today? This is not a difficult problem if one remembers how to calculate compound interest. A convenient set of figures to remember is that if a population increases at an annual rate of 2.0 percent, the time required for the population to double is 35 years. Any rate of increase, continued over a long enough period of time, can produce any population level specified. Any rate of increase will, in time, overpopulate the world.

In general terms there are two opinions regarding the seriousness of the population problem and the type of response that should be made. Garrett Hardin (see page 6) speaks for one group, feeling that the past rate of increase has brought us to a critical point and that society can not afford to depend upon voluntary or "natural" population control. Harald Frederiksen, author of the following article, Feedbacks in Economic and Demographic Transition, presents a different point of view. He argues for a more optimistic view, based on the responses of various national populations to increasing levels of economic development. Frederiksen's paper may be difficult for those not familiar with the terminology or statistical methods used. The main structure of his argument should be clear even if you find it necessary to skim some of the more technical aspects of the way in which the data are presented.

FEEDBACKS IN ECONOMIC
AND DEMOGRAPHIC TRANSITION

Harald Frederiksen

Demographic transition and economic development are not independent phenomena. If there is such a thing as a "population problem," it cannot be understood and solved in isolation from the complex process of national development, of which economic development is but one aspect.

Needs and resources for health and family-planning programs evolve in the context of the successive stages of demographic transition and economic development. We have to agree on the nature and magnitude of the interactions between population and economic phenomen at the various stages of national development (called simply "development" hereafter) before we can agree on how much of what is most appropriate and effective in the circumstances in question.

NEO-MALTHUSIAN MODEL

A neo-Malthusian school believes that the process of development is impeded when the rate of population growth is high, and that this high rate of growth is the result of a rapid reduction in mortality, which in turn is the result of alien technology's increasing the effectiveness and efficiency of health services quite independently of levels of production and consumption. Let me quote from some writers who belong to this school.

The death rate in less-developed areas is dropping very rapidly . . . and without regard to economic change. . . .

The less-developed areas have been able to import low-cost measures of controlling disease, measures developed for the most part in the highly industrialized societies. The use of residual insecticides to provide effective protection against malaria at a cost of no more than 25 cents per capita per annum is an outstanding example. . . .

The death rate in Ceylon was cut in half in less than a decade and declines approaching this rapidity are almost commonplace. The result of a precipitous decline in mortality while birth rate remains essentially unchanged is, of course, a very rapid acceleration in population growth. . . .

Reprinted with permission from *Science*, Vol. 166, 1969, pp. 837–847. Copyright 1969 by the American Association for the Advancement of Science. The author is Chief of Analysis and Evaluation Division, Office of Population, Technical Assistance Bureau, Agency for International Development, Washington, D.C.

In the longer run, economic progress will eventually be stopped and reversed unless the birth rate declines *or the death rate increases* [1].

The higher the population growth, the harder becomes the task of breaking through the Malthusian trap. A vicious spiral is set into operation. Because of a high rate of population growth, industrialization is difficult to attain. Because there is no industrilization, the birth rtae and the rate of population growth remain high [2].

It may seem indecent to some to suggest that medical research first be concentrated on those diseases whose control will do most to improve the happiness and baliyit to work of people without reducing infant mortality. . . . [3]. . . . Public health measures which can save millions of lives should not be practiced in China on a nationwide scale until the stage is set for a concurrent reduction in the birth rate [4].

Another 10 to 15 points of the initial death rate of 40 per thousand may be attributable to inadequate diet, clothing and shelter, with malnutrition the primary cause. This is of direct concern to economic policy makers because it suggests that extra investments that do *not* increase the food supply, whether directly or indirectly through international trade, may temporarily be preferred to those that do [5].

Thus, a neo-Malthusian model of economic and demographic transition may seem quite plausible, at least when used to explain failure or to predict the probability of failure (Fig. 1). But in order to explain successful development, we have to explain how countries proceed from low to high levels of production and consumption, and from high to low levels of mortality and fertility.

A more humanitarian version of a neo-Malthusian model of successful development would allow some reduction in mortality, but not too rapid a reduction, so that a concurrent and commensurate reduction in fertility would keep population growth to a minimum and raise the formation of capital to a maximum (Fig. 2). Such a model of economic and demographic transition implies that high levels of production could be achieved when consumption, mortality, and fertility are, at best, still at intermediate levels.

Even if it were feasible to achieve high levels of production by some such shortcut, bypassing commensurate improvements in the levels of living and health and commensurate reductions in mortality and fertility, high levels of production alone would hardly meet the criteria for successful development. It remains to be seen, in the real world, whether the neo-Malthusian model is a shortcut to successful development. Yet, as a possible result of uncritical acceptance of the neo-Malthusian model, with its explanation of failure in development, "health programs," says Taylor (6), "which once represented a major effort in American technical assistance, are now being quietly downgraded or phased out in most [underdeveloped] countries except those that are obviously under-populated, such as Ethiopia."

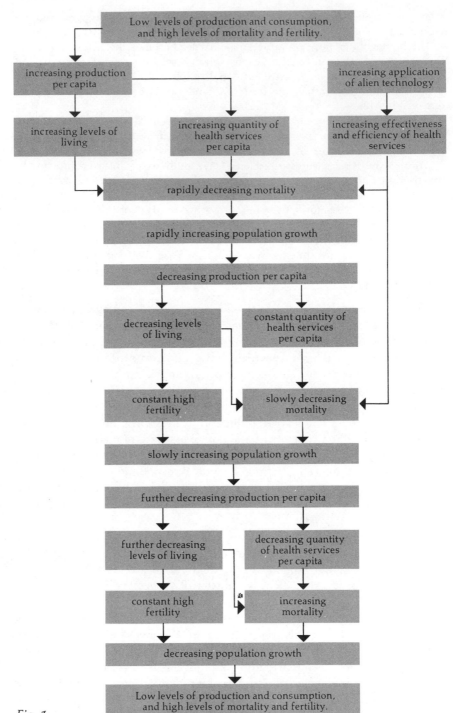

Fig. 1
Neo-Malthusian model of failure of economic and demographic transition.

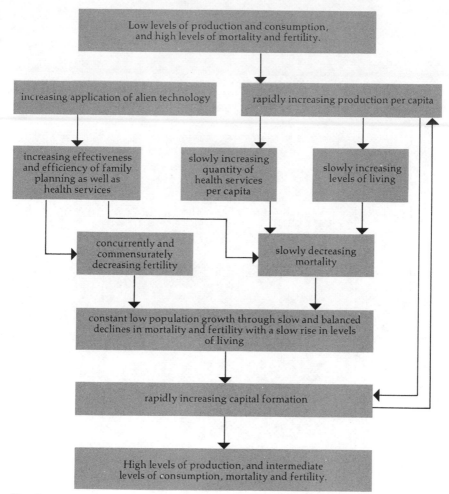

Fig. 2
Neo-Malthusian model of successful takeoff in economic and demographic transition.

ALTERNATIVE MODEL

An alternative model of successful economic and demographic transition would seem to explain more readily the transition from low to high levels of production and consumption, and from high to low levels of mortality and fertility (Fig. 3).

This alternative model assumes that improvements in the standard of living and decreases in the mortality and fertility rates are linked in a process of "concurrent, circular, and cumulative causation" (to use the language of Gunnar Myrdal). This model stresses the human factor in

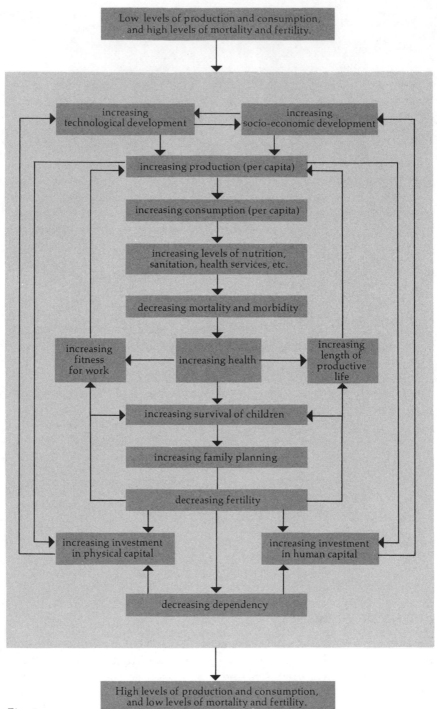

Fig. 3
Alternative model of successful economic and demographic transition from low to high levels of production and consumption, and from high to low levels of mortality and fertility.

development and views a drop in the mortality rate as part of the solution of the population problem, not as a cause.

A reduction in mortality is considered a necessary, although insufficient, condition for a reduction in fertility. Mortality trends may influence fertility trends by way of two mechanisms: (i) with reduction in mortality, compensatory reduction in fertility are required if the desired family size is to be achieved; (ii) when there is less uncertainty about survival, as well as a higher probability of survival, the desired family size may be reduced.

In regions where there had been considerable variation in the number of child deaths from family to family, a reduction in overall mortality might result in a reduction in fertility larger than that required to offset the reduced probability of child loss. Thus, a reduction, at the family level, in uncertainty concerning the survival of children might tend to make people want smaller families.

Let me quote from some of the writers who have arrived at similar conclusions.

. . . The removal of any of the particular causes of mortality can have no further effect upon population than the means of subsistence will allow. . . . Of its operation in tending to prevent marriage, by diminishing the demand for fresh supplies of children, I have no doubt [7].

To some extent the birth rate is influenced by the death rates in the lower age groups. . . . A reduction in child mortality would probably reduce birth rates after a lag of several decades [5].

Low death rates, or conditions underlying low death rates, merit consideration as contributory factors, if not as prerequisites, for low birth rates [8].

No efforts of social-economic development can be successful in a disease-ridden population, or will a desire for small families be likely to emerge [9].

Mortality varies inversely with economic indicators of the levels of living. In a balancing movement, fertility tends toward approximate equilibrium with mortality. . . . a deliberate reduction in fertility is a sequel to a reduction in mortality which develops individual and collective motivation as well as the need for a commensurate restraint of fertility [10].

High fertility has been an adjustment to high and unpredictable mortality. . . . Availability of birth control is largely irrelevant until the desired number of living children is secured [11].

The frequency of births in a population can be understood in terms of three groups of factors that influence parents' desires for births. First there is a family size goal or a number of surviving children that parents want. This goal is determined by a host of environmental factors that modify the relative attractiveness of many versus few children. Second is the incidence of death, mainly among offspring, which necessitates a compensating adjustment in birth rates to achieve any specific family size goal. Third is the effect of uncertainty in the family formation process where births, deaths, and remarriage are unpredictable [12].

In nations with traditionally high child mortality, this desire of fathers to have sons who will outlive them acts as a deterrent to restriction of family size [13].

It was generally agreed that in high mortality countries, the thing *not* to do is blanket the country with a massive family planning program. . . . programs will usually not emerge in countries where the population perceives that the high rate of infant mortality is either high by their standards or is not declining [14].

Although the world-wide population explosion has been created by a decline in death rates paradoxically a further decline in mortality in the less developed nations may be an invaluable aid for curbing the current rate of population growth [15].

The authors quoted above seem to support one or other of the basic assumptions (concerning the interactions between mortality, fertility, and levels of living) which underlie the alternative model of successful development. But those authors may or may not support the alternative model, which puts these basic interactions together in a concurrent, circular, and cumulative process of transition from low to high levels of production and consumption, and from high to low levels of mortality and fertility (Fig. 3).

COMPARISON OF THE MODELS

Comparison (Fig. 4) of the neo-Malthusian model (Fig. 2) and the alternative model (Fig. 3) indicates three essential differences.

The neo-Malthusian model views a reduction in mortality as an increase in population growth, whereas the alternative model notes the transitory nature of the "population explosion" and emphasizes the improvement in health, productivity, and longevity.

The neo-Malthusian model explicitly or implicitly assumes that levels of mortality are now *quite independent* of levels of living, whereas the alternative model assumes that levels of mortality are still *quite dependent* on levels of living, although the relative effectness of health services increases with increasing levels of living.

The neo-Malthusian model ignores any dependence of fertility trends on mortality trends, whereas the alternative model assumes that reductions in mortality develop the need and desire for family planning.

EMPIRICAL TEST OF THE MODELS

At any given point of development, the economic growth rate per capita, approximates the economic growth rate minus the population growth rate. This may have led some to equate the population problem with excessive population growth. But it does not follow that a decrease in the

Neo-Malthusian Model

Dependent variables	Independent variables		
	Levels of living	Mortality	Fertility
Levels of living		⊕	—
Mortality	◯		+
Fertility	—	◯	

Alternative Model

Dependent variables	Independent variables		
	Levels of living	Mortality	Fertility
Levels of living		⊖	—
Mortality	⊖		+
Fertility	—	⊕	

Fig. 4
Neo-Malthusian and alternative models of demographic and economic inter-action. The circles focus attention on those interactions which are essentially different in the two models. Plus or minus signs indicate a positive or negative association.

population growth rate would be associated with a commensurate increase in the economic growth rate per capita.

Cross-sectional comparison of nonlinear regression lines for population growth rates, economic growth rates, and economic growth rates per capita, for 67 countries, plotted by gross national product per capita, indictaes no obvious correlations between population growth rates and economic growth rates per capita (Fig. 5).

The *linear* correlation of the rate of population growth with the rate of economic growth *per capita* for the 67 countries was only weakly negative ($r = -0.32$), even though the population growth rate serves as denominator for the dependent variable. In contrast, the linear correlation of the rate of economic growth with the rate of economic growth per capita was strongly positive ($r = 0.88$). The linear correlation of the rate of population growth with the rate of economic growth was only slighty positive ($r = 0.15$).

A statistical significance test was performed only for the latter correlation—that between the rates of population growth and of economic growth—since only these two variables are not algebraically related to

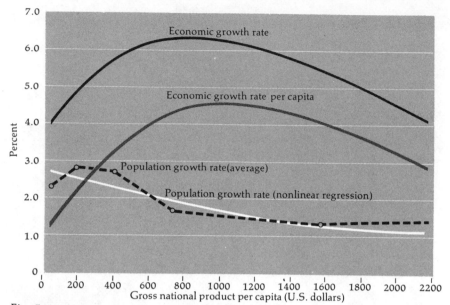

Fig. 5

Nonlinear regression lines (third degree) for population growth rates (1958–1966), economic growth rates (1960–1965), and economic growth rates per capita (1960–1965), by gross national product per capita (1965), for 67 countries. (Sources of basic data, United Nations and World Bank)

each other. The correlation ($r = 0.15$) was not significant even at the 5 percent level of probability.

Actually, the rate of *per capita* economic growth is a poor indicator of development. A low rate of economic growth per capita can be the result of a balance between high or low rates of economic and population growth and thus may be found in countries with *any* rate of economic growth, and with any rate, and at any level, of development.

Moreover, the rate of population growth is a poor indicator of the "population problem," or of its solution, since this rate tends first to rise and then to fall in the course of the modernization process.

Rather than rely exclusively or primarily on the population growth rate as a basis for understanding, measuring, and influencing the demographic transition, it would be better to rely on the birth rates and death rates from which the population growth rates are derived.

Thus, in the real world, successful development is associated with increasing levels of consumption and of capital formation with decreasing levels of mortality and fertility—first mortality, then fertility (Fig. 6).

Incidentally, the rise in the crude death rates toward the higher values for gross national product per capita is a result of the aging of the populations, which in turn is a result of the declining birth rates. If the death rates could have been adjusted for the differences in age distributions, there would not have been such an apparent rise in the death rates at the higher values for gross national product per capita. Unfortunately, not enough comparable detailed data were available to permit adjustment of the death rates for differences in the age distributions.

The objection might be raised that these comparisons are cross-sectional, and that these relationships that existed at a point in time would not hold true in longitudinal comparisons over a period of time.

The historical tendency for mortality trends to vary inversely with the standard of living and for fertility trends to maintain or restore approximate balance between mortality and fertility is indicated by the economic and demographic transition that has occurred in France over the past two centuries (Fig. 7).

A similar tendency toward approximate balance between mortality and fertility has been observed in Japan (Fig. 8), where the demographic transition began much later than it did in France. Whereas France was the first country to enter into the process of demographic transition, Japan was one of the latest countries to complete it.

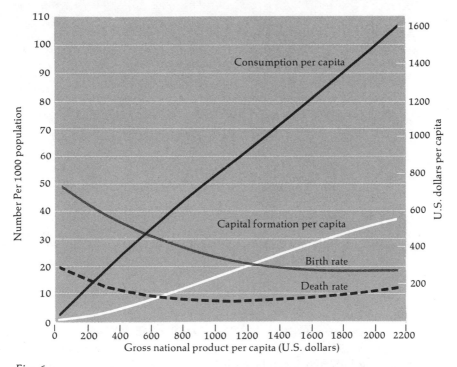

Fig. 6
Nonlinear regression lines (third degree) for economic and demographic variables by gross national product per capita (1965), for 67 countries. (Sources of basic data, United Nations and World Bank)

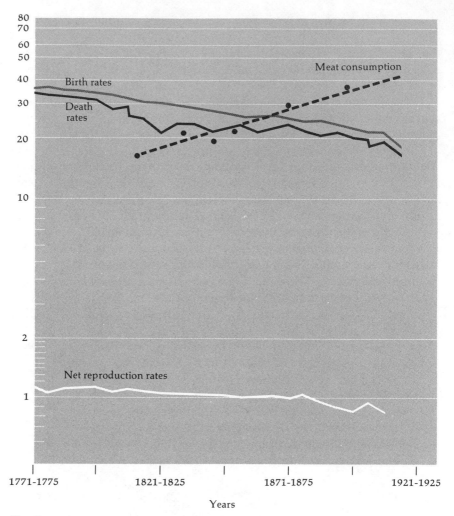

Fig. 7
Average annual number of births per 1000, number of deaths per 1000, and net reproduction rates in the 5-year periods 1771 to 1775 and 1906 to 1910, and annual consumption of meat and animal fat (in kilograms per capita) between 1812 and 1910, in France. [Four sources of basic data, see (22)]

When one compares the experience of France and of Japan, it seems that the process of transition has been accelerated. Whereas improvements in the standard of living and reductions in mortality have accelerated, the lag between mortality and fertility may have remained more or less constant. Thus, we are observing more violent, but transitory, "population explosions." Once the fertility trend turns downward, the reduction in fertility are also accelerated.

Japan, it might be argued, was a rapidly developing country at the time of its demographic transition, and it was for this reason that the transition could take place in Japan as late as it did, but modern medicine has since changed the course of demographic transition and the prospects for development in the less developed world.

Kirk has noted (*16*) that the later phases of the demographic transition (that is, definitive declines in birth rates to low or moderate fertility) have now reached almost all people of European ethnic background, but that Costa Rica and, until recently, Chile have been exceptions. Kirk made his statement in 1967; information subsequently made available indicates that Costa Rica and Chile are beginning to complete the historic process of demographic transition first observed in Europe. Thus, in the 5 years between 1962 and 1967, Costa Rica experienced about a 10 percent reduction, and Chile about a 20 percent reduction, in fertility.

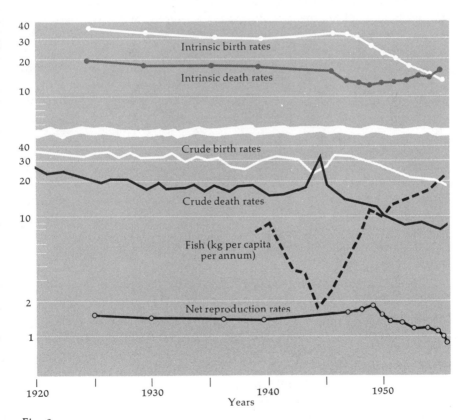

Fig. 8
Processed fishery products (in kilograms per capita per annum), crude and intrinsic birth rates and death rates (in number of births or deaths per 1000), and net reproduction rates, for Japan, for the period 1920 to 1957. [For sources, see (23)]

It might be objected that Costa Rica and Chile, while they may be developing countries, are of European ethnic background, and that their experience may differ from that of countries of non-European background. It is for this reason that the case histories of Ceylon and of Mauritius are cited here, since these countries were first selected by the neo-Malthusian school to bolster their views.

Many writers—too many to be cited here—have attributed the dramatic postwar decline in mortality in Ceylon solely or largely to the eradication of malaria. Newman (*17*), who has studied the case history of Ceylon more than most, has concluded that eradication of malaria has accounted for 42 percent of the postwar decline in the death rate of Ceylon. Titmuss and Abel-Smith (*18*) have attributed most of the dramatic decline in mortality between 1946 and 1947 in Maritius to eradication of malaria.

If the sequence of events in Ceylon and Mauritius had demonstrated that economic development is no longer a prerequisite for a decline in the death rate, it might have seemed plausible to postulate that modern public health measures would tend to reduce per capita income as well as mortality, should economic development lag; it might have seemed plausible to infer that per capita income would rise with a rise in mortality. But the postulation of such determinants and consequences of mortality trends is not confirmed by the experiences of Ceylon and Mauritius (*10*).

Although the postwar decline in the death rate in Ceylon, from 20 to 14 per 1000 in the single year from 1946 to 1947, approximately coincided with a campaign of spraying with insecticides, the spectacular decline in mortality was about the same for the area without malaria, not protected by insecticides, as for the area with malaria, protected by insecticides (*19*). It has also been shown (*8*) that the decline in mortality was associated with a commensurate development of the economy and rise in the standard of living.

Moreover, the birth rate declined from a postwar peak of 39.8 per 1000 in 1951 to 31.6 in 1967. In the 5 years between 1962 and 1967, Ceylon has experienced a greater than 10 percent decline in birth rate.

The postwar drop in the death rate in Mauritius, from 30 to 20 per 1000 in the single year from 1946 to 1947, was also attributed mainly to the use of insecticides. But the spraying campaign was started in 1949, 2 years after the dramatic 1947 decline in the death rate. Moreover, the per capita production of sugar, virtually the sole export of the island, rose sharply as mortality declined.

Mauritius may follow the pattern of demographic transition displayed in the course of history in the West.

First, the inverse relationship between (i) the mortality rate and (ii) the standard of living indicated by the per capita proceeds (in 1939 rupees) from sale of the principal cash crop suggests that reduction in mortality are still dependent on commensurate improvements in the standard of living. Improvements in health services may be involved, but only as a part of general improvements in living standards (Fig. 9).

Second, the fertility trend has now turned downward, decisively so, about 20 years after the dramatic downturn in the death rate. From a postward peak of 49.7 per thousand in 1950, the birth rate declined to 30.4 in 1967. In the 5 years between 1962 and 1967, Mauritius experienced about a 20 percent decline in the birth rate. This seems to confirm the experience of other countries: a reduction in mortality is a precursor of, and perhaps a prerequisite for, a reduction in fertility in the course of demographic transition (Fig. 10).

Thus, Mauritius experienced a population explosion. As the word implies, an explosion is a transitory phenomenon. The sharp increase in the rate of population growth calls for individual and collective decision making. With lower mortality, the traditional and practical family size can be achieved with lower fertility. Moreover, the lessening of uncer-

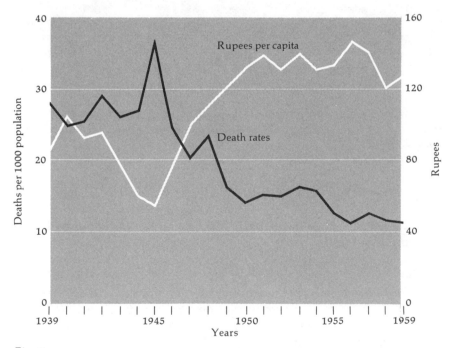

Fig. 9
Levels of mortality and levels of living, as indicated by the sales proceeds from sugar production (in constant rupees per capita) for Mauritius, for the period 1939 to 1959. (Constant rupees at 1939 prices were computed from the consumer price index for manual workers.) [Source of basic data, Yearbook of Statistics *(Central Statistical Office, Colony of Mauritius, 1946–1959)]*

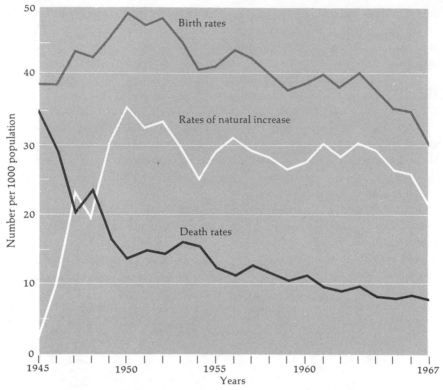

Fig. 10
Rates of birth, death, and natural increase for Mauritius, for the period 1945 to 1967. [Source of basic data, Demographic Yearbook *(United Nations, New York, 1954–1967)]*

tainty about whether one's children will survive, and the greater overall probability that they will, may induce parents to want fewer children than they have wanted in the past. Thus, reduction in mortality, by influencing the decision concerning family size as well as facilitating its realization, may operate by way of two mechanisms to develop motivation toward a reduction in fertility.

In the course of economic and demographic transition, a reduction in mortality induces a population explosion which may, in turn, induce a commensurate reduction in fertility, thereby restoring approximate balance between mortality and fertility.

The qualitative nature and directions of the feedbacks in the alternative model (Figs. 3 and 4) seem to be consistent with the relationships observed in the real world, as indicated by longitudinal as well as cross-sectional observations, and by historical as well as contemporary case histories (Figs. 5 and 10). Let me say again that case histories of Ceylon and Mauritius were first cited by those who wanted to bolster their neo-Malthusian views. But the actual events in these countries seem to refute the neo-Malthusian model and to support the alternative model of economic and demographic transition.

Additional empirical evidence for the alternative model has been presented elsewhere (*10, 20*).

DYNAMICS OF TRANSITION

The dynamic equilibrium of economic and demographic transition in the postwar era may be indicated by empirical equations describing the quantitative and qualitative relationships between changes in mortality, fertility, and living standards in 21 countries, for which comparable data were available.

The equations imply that the prospective rate of natural increase can be estimated on the basis of the rates of fertility and mortality in the base year and the relative change in per capita product at constant prices.

The relative change in natality n in year t can be expressed in terms of natality n and mortality m in the base year o:

$$\frac{n_t}{n_o} = \left[\frac{a}{(n_o - m_o)^b} \right]^{t-o}$$

(a and b are constants).

The relative change in mortality m in the year t can be expressed in terms of the relative change in per capita product (at constant prices) p in year t:

$$\frac{m_t}{m_o} = \left[\frac{c}{\left(\frac{p_t}{p_o} \right)^d} \right]^{t-o}$$

(c and d are constants).

When the equations for relative changes in natality and mortality are combined, the rate of natural increase, $n - m$, in year t can be expressed in terms of natality n and mortality m in the base year o and the relative change in per capita product (at constant prices) p in year t:

$$n_t - m_t = n_o \left[\frac{a}{(n_o - m_o)^b} \right]^{t-o} - m_o \left[\frac{c}{\left(\frac{p_t}{p_o} \right)^d} \right]^{t-o}$$

The empirical derivation of the equations and of the constants $a(= 1.028)$, $b(= 0.016)$, $c(= 1.085)$, and $d(= 0.018)$ are described eleswhere (*20*). The parameters can hardly be expected to predict the trends in vital events in all countries at all times, at least with any great degree of accuracy. For one thing, the values of the constants were derived from data uncorrected for differences in the age distributions. Second, the process of economic and demographic transition is constantly accelerating, as indicated by comparisons of the tempo of transition in developing countries with the tempo of the historical process in Europe.

But the equations were remarkably accurate in predicting or explaining the recent changes in the levels of fertility, mortality, and natural increase in Chile and Costa Rica. The recent dramatic turn in the trends of vital events in Chile and Costa Rica would have been missed had it simply been assumed "that current trends continue."

The population projections for Costa Rica, published by the United Nations in 1966 but based on data available in 1963, implied a rate of population growth of 3.9 percent in 1965 (an average annual rate of 4.0 percent between 1960 and 1965 and 3.8 percent between 1965 and 1970). The United Nations has since reported that the actual rate of population growth in 1965 was 3.1 percent. By substituting, in the foregoing equations, the birth rate and the death rate in 1960 and the relative change in per capita gross national product at constant prices between 1960 and 1965, we would estimate the 1965 population growth rate to be 3.3 percent in 1965.

Of course, the estimate of the death rate, and the rate of population growth derived therefrom, require economic data first available sometime after 1965, and for this reason this part of the equation is explanatory rather than predictive. But the estimate of the birth rate (number of births per 1000 population) obtained by means of this equation can be based solely on demographic data available in the base year. Such an estimate, for Costa Rica, based on the 1960 birth rate of 48.4 per 1000 and the 1960 death rate of 8.6, yields an estimated birth rate of 41.3 in 1965, which quite closely approximates the actual birth rate of 40.5 for that year.

Of course, no one factor in the equation can be successfully manipulated independently of the other factors, in the expectation that the other factors will automatically respond, as if this were simply a matter of arithmetic.

DEMOGRAPHIC POLICY FOR DEMOGRAPHIC TRANSITION

The solution of the "population problem" is not simply the achievement of a low rate of population growth, which could be the result of a balance between either high or low birth rates and death rates. All humanitarian considerations aside, only low death rates matched by low birth rates will provide maximum returns from investment in human resources and keep to a minimum the burden of child dependency.

Of course, the desired demographic changes are no more automatic than the desired economic changes. The systematic extension of information and facilities favoring the use of efficient, effective, and acceptable methods of regulating family size is the appropriate response to spontaneous motivation to limit family size—motivation which increases as rates of survival increase.

Thus, improvements in the standard of living, as well as desired changes in mortality and fertility rates, will result for an interplay of effort in both the demographic and the economic aspects of economic and demographic transition.

Health measures and family planning, by their effects on morbidity, mortality, and fertility, can accelerate the economic transition from low to high levels of production and consumption. They can also accelerate the demographic transition from high to low levels of mortality and fertility by restoring the balance between mortality and fertility at the lowest level of mortality attainable with the available resources. With such understanding, the allocations for health services would be limited by the availability of resources rather than by a fear that health services might be too effective.

The availability of resources for competing sectors of development would be decided by empirical review of the combinations of allocations to determine which combination had achieved a given level of development in the past and seemed to be necessary and feasible for achieving the next level.

RELATIVE COSTS AND BENEFITS

The question remains, How should we or can we plan optimum efforts in view of the unlimited needs competing for the limited resources available? If we are to set realistic health targets, we must consider political, social, economic, and demographic, as well as administrative, factors. We must consider noneconomic as well as economic costs and benefits, and we must start with the given set of circumstances, not with rarefied abstractions.

Health planners can dream of comprehensive and integrated health services, both curative and preventive, for achieving the ideal state of health as defined by the World Health Organization. But in the real world, available resources are limited. Moreover, it is in the less developed parts of the world that the needs are greatest, and the resources least.

In planning health services as integral parts of national development, it would be necessary or desirable to compare the costs and benefits of alternative programs, having different objectives, in different sectors of the economy, as well as the costs and benefits of alternative programs, having the same objectives, within the health sector. We must determine the optimum allocations for all sectors in the context of multiple needs competing for inadequate resources.

But, in practice, cost-benefit analysis may be neither a practical nor a valid method of deciding whether a more efficient and more effective program is an appropriate alternative for a less efficient and less effective program when the two do not have the same objective.

For one thing, we may lack a common unit of measurement for comparing the costs and benefits of programs in the health sector with those of programs having different objectives, in other sectors. In theory it may seem possible to quantify the various benefits in dollars, but what seems possible in theory may not prove feasible in practice.

Moreover, we lack understanding of, or agreement on, the innumerable interactions of the multiple factors in the complex process of development. For example, death control and birth control programs may be placed in competition for limited funds. In such a predicament, the dilemma can be resolved neither by moral arguments nor by cost-benefit analysis. Simple comparisons of the ratios of the costs and benefits of these arbitrary alternatives would be meaningless and misleading.

On the basis of simple arithmetic, we find that either more deaths or fewer births would lower the rate of population growth. But a low rate of population growth may be the result of a balance between either high or low birth rates and death rates. Only a balance between low birth and death rates will give the highest possible ratio between producers and dependents. And, as discussed above, only a prior reduction of mortality will develop the motivation needed for limiting family size.

Thus it is clear that cost-benefit analyses must be based on valid alternatives and not on simple assumptions and speculations which tend to ignore the dynamic nature and sequence of the interactions between economic and demographic factors. We might feel assured that a good analyst would take second- and third-order benefits into account. Yet, again, what seems possible in theory may not prove feasible in practice.

Again (to cite a comparison of the costs and benefits of another popular pair of specious choices), it has been variously calculated that the expenditure on a program of birth control of either $1 or $5 from each $100 spent on development can double the rate of per capita economic growth achieved by the whole expenditure. But could we really double economic growth merely by increasing our investment in contraception? If that were possible, we might concentrate on contraception and eliminate investments in all other sectors of development. Although the popular notion that an ounce of contraception is worth a pound of development has some validity, this does not mean that birth-control programs could or should invariably be substituted for programs that have a less favorable cost-benefit ratio. The setting of priorities is not simply a mathematical problem.

Of course, within a given sector, a more effective and efficient program may be substituted for one that has the same objective but a less favorable cost-benefit ratio, provided the proposed alternative is otherwise appropriate and acceptable.

Actually, there is little need for complex and controversial economic and demographic arguments to justify appropriate action in response to spontaneous motivation to restore the balance between mortality and fertility. We all know the absurd consequences projected by extrapolations of imbalances between current mortality and fertility trends.

Although intersectoral cost-benefit analyses may not be particularly feasible, such analyses may be undertaken intrasectorally in conjunction with an empirical method, described next, for intersectoral linking of budgeting in a multisectoral system of development.

PROFILES OF RELATIVE DEVELOPMENT

So far, no comprehensive model of development for obtaining the best possible allocations among the innumerable needs competing for limited resources has been generally accepted and successfully applied. In the absence of such a model, analysis of national and sectoral "profiles of the relative development" of human and natural resources provides an objective and practical method for setting realistic, although tentative, targets and budgets (21). Such profiles facilitate comparison between countries or regions with respect to a number of variables, each of which can serve as an indicator of the level of development (Fig. 11).

Profiles of individual countries are entered on global grids of development, which are constructed by ranking any number of variables from all countries for which comparable data are available; the deciles thus obtained are used to construct the grids.

For example, the first indicator in the global grid is the product per capita. Data for this variable from 120 countries are ranked in the first two horizontal rows of Fig. 11, from left to right. The top entry in the first vertical column (the 0-percentile column) indicates that none of the 120 countries had a per capita product of less than $35 in 1965. The top entry in the second vertical column (the 10-percentile column) indicates that 12 countries (10 percent of 120) had a per capita product of no more than $70. And the top entry in the last vertical column (the 100-percentile column) indicates that all 120 countries had a per capita product lower than $3300. The profile of the relative development of a particular country (Nepal, the U.S.S.R., and the United States) is indicated by the histogram in the grid. For example, Nepal had a product per capita of less than $70.

Variables have been included in the grid without regard to any hierarchy or classification. The variables or indicators are simply a diverse collection of characteristics of a society or economy, some of which

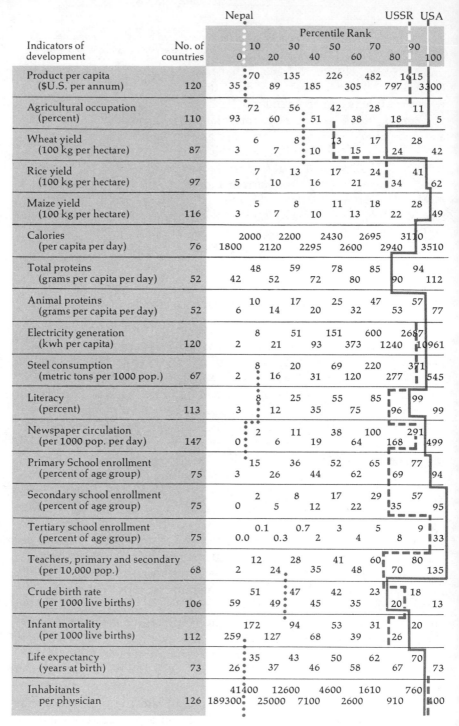

Indicators of development	No. of countries	Percentile Rank										
		0	10	20	30	40	50	60	70	80	90	100
Product per capita ($U.S. per annum)	120	35	70	89	135	185	226	305	482	797	1615	3300
Agricultural occupation (percent)	110	93	72	60	56	51	42	38	28	18	11	5
Wheat yield (100 kg per hectare)	87	3	6	7	8	10	13	15	17	24	28	42
Rice yield (100 kg per hectare)	97	5	7	10	13	16	17	21	24	34	41	62
Maize yield (100 kg per hectare)	116	3	5	7	8	10	11	13	18	22	28	49
Calories (per capita per day)	76	1800	2000	2120	2200	2295	2430	2600	2695	2940	3110	3510
Total proteins (grams per capita per day)	52	42	48	52	59	72	78	80	85	90	94	112
Animal proteins (grams per capita per day)	52	6	10	14	17	20	25	32	47	53	57	77
Electricity generation (kwh per capita)	120	2	8	21	51	93	151	373	600	1240	2687	10961
Steel consumption (metric tons per 1000 pop.)	67	2	8	16	20	31	69	120	220	277	371	545
Literacy (percent)	113	3	8	12	25	35	55	75	85	96	99	99
Newspaper circulation (per 1000 pop. per day)	147	0	2	6	11	19	38	64	100	168	291	499
Primary School enrollment (percent of age group)	75	3	15	26	36	44	52	62	65	69	77	94
Secondary school enrollment (percent of age group)	75	0	2	5	8	12	17	22	29	35	57	95
Tertiary school enrollment (percent of age group)	75	0.0	0.1	0.3	0.7	2	3	4	5	8	9	33
Teachers, primary and secondary (per 10,000 pop.)	68	2	12	24	28	35	41	48	60	70	80	135
Crude birth rate (per 1000 live births)	106	59	51	49	47	45	42	35	23	20	18	13
Infant mortality (per 1000 live births)	112	259	172	127	94	68	53	39	31	26	20	13
Life expectancy (years at birth)	73	26	35	37	43	46	50	58	62	67	70	73
Inhabitants per physician	126	189300	41400	25000	12600	7100	4600	2600	1610	910	760	400

Fig. 11

Profiles of the relative development of Nepal, the U.S.S.R., and the U.S. (indicated by the histogram) in comparison with ten levels in the global grid of sectoral development, indicated by the deciles in the rankings of indicators from the latest year, and the maximum number of countries, for which comparable data are available. [For sources, see (24)] might be considered costs or benefits, inputs or outputs, causes or effects, needs or resources, means or ends. The preparation of development profiles requires neither classification of the variables nor understanding of the nature and extent of their interactions—neither explicit nor implicit assumptions other than recognition of a tendency toward balance or complementarity in the development of human and natural resources. Whether progress is the inevitable result of free enterprise or the intended result of a planned economy, if and when a system or policy or fortuitous combination of factors results in development, the balance in the development of human and of natural resources is remarkable.

For different countries, paths of development are usually and essentially the same, but the path may be followed with greater or lesser speed. Harmonizing the objectives and choosing the best possible targets may accelerate the passage from traditional to modern stages of society and economy.

Since grids such as Fig. 11 have no time scale, it is not possible to schedule the achievement of individual targets within fixed periods. Rather, the profiles suggest, for example, that it might be realistic to choose as a target reductions in infant mortality from 127 to 68 per 1000 live births coincidentally with an increase in the product per capita from $89 to $185 a year.

The observed balance in the development of human and natural resources permits us to decide what is necessary or desirable and feasible at the various stages of development, even though we lack a comprehensive mathematical model of development. In effect, the open-ended nature of the grid permits approximation of a comprehensive model of development, albeit associatively rather than structurally.

The method of analysis is discussed more fully elsewhere (21).

EVOLUTION OF GOALS AND SERVICES

Integration of planning, programming, and budgeting of health services into a system for accelerating development may confirm the belief that differences between a sound economic point of view and a bona fide humanitarian point of view are more apparent than real. Of course, there are situations where the two are irreconcilable. In such situations, the deliberate political decision may be to choose a humanitarian policy rather than the most economic alternative. However, in the long run it may not be politically opportune or economically feasible to consistently ignore either humanitarian or economic considerations.

Fortunately what is necessary or desirable from the economic and the humanitarian points of view may, and usually does, turn out to be essentially the same, when analyses of the relative costs and benefits are based on targets or budgets for programs that are possible and feasible, valid

Table 1

Table 1
Evolution of environmental health problems; predominant patterns of disease, mortality, and fertility; goals, type and scope of
health services; and the state of nutrition

State of society	Environmental health problems	Predominant patterns of disease, mortality, and fertility	Goals, type and scope of health services	State of nutrition
Traditional	Largely rural environment with contamination of water and food; proliferation of insects and rodents; periodic food scarcities.	Endemic infections, parasitisms, infestations, nutritional deficiencies. High death rate and high birth rate.	Indigenous systems of medicine based on traditional practices and beliefs.	Undernutrition as a result of food scarcities in a subsistence economy with practices and preferences of food production and consumption of a traditional, but youthful, society.
Early transitional	Largely rural environment with contamination of water and food; proliferation of insects and rodents; adulteration of foods and drugs; food scarcities.	Endemic infections, parasitisms, infestations, nutritional deficiencies. Intermediate death rate and high birth rate.	Medical relief and family planning in key centers; control of endemic diseases and environmental sanitation in selected areas; nationwide extension of categorical health services (malaria and smallpox eradication) requiring only minimal cooperation from the public and only minimal judgment from auxiliary staff with stereotype duties (residual spraying and vaccination).	Potential improvements in nutrition in areas of the monetary economy through possible modification of social, economic, and agricultural policies favoring the consumption of a variety of nutritious foods; facilitation of the extension of modern practices of agriculture, food technology and marketing, nutrition education, child-feeding and school lunch programs to the minority of the population within the scope of the nutrition programs of the

tional	sembles that of traditional society, whereas the urban environment resembles that of modern society.	levels in rural areas, whereas the disease patterns of urban areas resemble those of modern society. Low death rate and intermediate birth rate.	health and medical services in key centers, with nationwide extension of medical relief, family planning, nutrition, basic sanitation, health education, and communicable disease control.	and as the result of progressive extension of nutrition programs nationwide, including the production of protein-rich foods and the fortification of staples.
Modern	Largely urban environment with pollution of air, water, and food, plus hazards from use of cigarettes, alcohol, food additives, new drugs, and narcotics.	Bronchopulmonary and cardiovascular diseases, malignant neoplasias, mental illness, accidents, obesity. Low death rate and low birth rate.	Nationwide extension of complex systems of comprehensive and integrated preventive and curative health and medical services, requiring a prosperous society and an enlightened public, as well as ample health manpower, qualified to exercise independent judgment.	Overnutrition as a result of an abundance of foods in an industrial economy of an affluent, sedentary, and aging society.

and appropriate in the context of the evolving needs and resources. And what is necessary or desirable and feasible from the economic and humanitarian point of view may, in the long run, be a safe and sound position from the political point of view as well.

Thus, the best or only way to obviate or resolve conflicts, apparent or real, between independently derived economic and health plans would be to devise and adopt a method of planning health services and investments as integral parts of a multisectoral system for accelerating the development of an economy and a society. Such planning must be based on an understanding of the quantitative and qualitative evolution of feasible goals and optimum programs in the context of evolving needs and resources at successive stages of development.

Disease and reproduction tend to occur in definable patterns that closely reflect the degree of modernization of the society (Table 1). Where the patterns are not compatible with the process of modernization, we can attempt to modify the patterns and make them compatible.

The ideal health policy would be one of short-term and long-term planning such that the manpower and organization of the health services, designed to attack the most prevalent diseases that are amenable to attack, would evolve along with the needs and resources in the complex process of economic, social, and demographic transition.

There are various alternative strategies and tactics that might be pursued by the health services. Before we try to determine the relative cost effectiveness of alternatives we must decide which of the many alternative programs are valid paths to the agreed-upon objectives; this decision, in turn, must be based on consideration of what alternatives are both possible and feasible.

This requires, first, consideration of the nature of the problem, which may call for epidemiologic study. Then the possibilities of prevention must be determined; this involves determination of the link in the chain of transmission or causation that is most readily broken by the possible means of prevention.

But what is possible may not be feasible. The feasibility of goals and services evolves with the needs and the resources (Fig. 11 and Table 1). And once we decide which alternative is feasible, we still must set tentative targets or budgets for the alternative programs before we can analyze the relative costs and benefits.

The profiles of relative development permit the setting of tentative but realistic targets, as well as tentative but realistic budgets for health services. Such empirical targeting and budgeting makes it possible to keep costs to a minimum and to achieve maximum benefits, by permitting cost-effectiveness analyses to be based on the empirically derived targets as well as budgets.

SUMMARY AND CONCLUSIONS

The feedbacks in a neo-Malthusian and in an alternative model of economic and demographic transition are compared with each other and tested against the real world. On the basis of the empirical evidence, it is postulated that the population problem is not simply a high rate of growth. Nor is its solution simply a low rate of growth, which could be the result of a balance between either high or low rates of mortality and fertility.

Reductions in the mortality rate are part of the solution, rather than the cause, of the problem. Mortality rates tend to vary inversely with levels of consumption and production. Moreover, reductions in mortality seem to be prerequisites for compensating reductions in fertility to achieve the desired family size.

Of course, the desired demographic changes are no more automatic than the desired economic changes. The systematic extension of information and of facilities favoring the use of acceptable methods of regulating family size is the appropriate response to spontaneous motivation to limit family size.

Successful development results in, and from, a balance between mortality and fertility at the lowest mortality rate attainable with the resources available. With improved health and greater longevity increasing the returns from human resources, and with decreasing fertility decreasing the burdens of dependency, the maximum improvements in the standard of living and the desired changes in mortality and fertility will result from interplay of efforts in both the demographic and the economic areas.

Strategy and tactics for national development evolve with the needs and resources. "Profiles of relative development" in the multiple sectors of national development may indicate what targets and budgets are necessary or desirable and feasible at successive stages.

Paths of development may be usually and essentially the same for different countries, but the path may be followed with greater or lesser speed. Harmonization of the objectives and wise choice of targets may accelerate the passage from traditional to modern stages of society and economy.

Health measures and family planning, as integral parts of the complex process of modernization, can accelerate and must complete the economic and demographic transition from low to high levels of production and consumption, and from high to low levels of mortality and fertility.

REFERENCES

1. "The Growth of World Population," *Nat. Acad. Sci. Nat. Res. Counc. Publ. No. 1091* (1963).

2. C. M. Cipolla, *The Economic History of World Population* (Penguin, Baltimore, 1964).
3. I. M. D. Little, *Aid to Africa* (Pergamon, London, 1964).
4. G. Winfield, quoted by N. K. Sarkar in *China: The Land and the People* (Sloane, New York, 1948).
5. S. Enke, *Quart. J. Economics* **71**, No. 1, 19 (1957).
6. C. E. Taylor, *Foreign Affairs* **43**, 475 (1965).
7. T. R. Malthus, *An Essay on the Principle of Population* (ed. 7, 1872), bk. 4, chap. 5.
8. H. Frederiksen, *Public Health Rep.* **76**, 659 (1961).
9. F. N. Notestein, D. Kirk, S. Segal, in *The Population Dilemma*, P. M. Hauser, Ed. (Prentice-Hall, Englewood Cliffs, N.J., 1963).
10. H. Frederiksen, *Public Health Rep.* **81**, 727 (1966).
11. President's Science Advisory Committee, *The World Food Problem* (Government Printing Office, Washington, D.C., 1967), vol. 2, p. 34.
12. T. Schultz, "A Family Planning Hypothesis: Some Empirical Evidence from Puerto Rico," *Agency Int. Develop. Mem. RM-5405-RC/AID* (1967).
13. G. E. Immerwahr, *Demography* **4**, 710 (1967).
14. Southeast Asia Development Advisory Groups (SEADAG) reports, Population Seminar, New York, March 1968.
15. D. M. Heer and D. O. Smith, *Demography* **5**, 104 (1968).
16. D. Kirk, "Natality in the developing countries: recent trends and prospects," paper presented at the University of Michigan Sesquicentennial Conference on Fertility and Family Planning, November 1967.
17. P. Newamn, "Malaria Eradication and Population Growth with Special Reference to Ceylon and British Guiana," *Univ. Mich. School Public Health Res. Ser. No. 10* (1965).
18. R. M. Titmuss and B. Abel-Smith, *Social Policies and Population Growth in Mauritius* (Methuen, London, 1961).
19. H. Frederiksen, *Public Health Rep.* **75**, 865 (1960).
20. ———, *Econ. Develop. Cult. Change* **14**, 316 (1966).
21. ———, *Int. Develop. Rev.* **11**, No. 4, 27 (1967).
22. *Annuaires Statistiques de la France* (Institut National de la Statistique et des Etudes Economiques, Ministère des Finances et des Affaires Economiques, Republique Française); *Demographic and Statistical Yearbooks* (United Nations, New York); J. Bourgeois-Pichat, in *Population History* (Aldine, Chicago, 1965); C. Clark, *The Conditions of Economic Progress* (Macmillan, London, 1951).
23. *Statistical Yearbooks* (Prime Minister's Office, Japan); I. B. Taeuber, *The Population of Japan* (Princeton Univ. Press, Princeton, N.J., 1958).
24. Population Reference Bureau, December 1965; *U.N. Food & Agriculture Organization Production Yearbook* (1964); *A.I.D. Economics Data Books* (1964); *U.N. Statistical Yearbook* (1964); N. Ginsburg, *Atlas of Economic Development* (Univ. of Chicago Press, Chicago, 1961); F. Harbison and C. A. Myers, *Education, Manpower and Economic Growth* (McGraw-Hill, New York, 1964); *U.N. Demographic Yearbook* (1964).

At first reading Frederiksen's confidence that each developing country can, at its own rate, make a successful "demographic transition" seems only an elaborate way to say that we should let nature take its course. But Frederiksen clearly recognizes the need to promote and manage the conditions necessary for a successful transition. Such management would include maximum health services, encouragement of industrialization, production and consumption, and promotion of the necessary birth control programs.

However convincing the argument for demographic transition may be, when the problem of population is integrated with those problems of environmental quality previously discussed, a whole new series of questions arise. Can ecologically sound (and thus self-perpetuating) methods of food production provide adequate nutrition for a population which has reached its natural upper limit as defined by the concept of demographic transition? Can the energy and goods necessary to the increased level of production and consumption be produced without exceeding the capacity of the biosphere to absorb the resulting pollution? Would the present population of the world, all consuming and producing at a rate adequate to motivate a desire to reduce family size, so alter the environment as to make it unsatisfactory for human life?

To say that the population explosion is, as its name implies, a transitory event, will be small comfort if the environment we need and desire is crippled by the blast. Finally, what will be the human, interpersonal response to the population density at the levels predicted?

The two latter questions explain the continued relevance of John Calhoun's 1952 paper, The Social Aspects of Population Dynamics. *Calhoun discusses the reciprocal problems of the impact of social behavior on the growth of populations and the impact of population density on social behavior. In the almost 20 years that have elapsed since Calhoun's review, nothing has occurred to reduce the significance of his approach or comments. The social aspects of population growth are still too frequently overshadowed by discussions of food or energy as limiting factors for man. It will be man's own response to his environment and to his fellow men which will be the measure of an optimum population. Extrinsic limiting factors can tell us only how many people are possible.*

THE SOCIAL ASPECTS
OF POPULATION DYNAMICS

John B. Calhoun

The subject of population dynamics is more commonly treated from the demographic point of view. This view stresses the fact that a population grows, remains stable, or declines, dependent upon the interrelationships of natality, mortality, and migration. Interactions of these phenomena determine density; that is, the number of organisms inhabiting a given space. Customarily, the results of such demographic studies are graphed as growth curves which pictorially show the change in density through time, or they are given as life tables from which such factors as life expectancy or age structure of the population may be derived.

In the analysis of those factors which alter the pattern of changes in density, consideration is normally given to the relative abundance of food or other prerequisites of life, to the incidence of disease and similar factors as they affect the general health of the population, and to the occurrence of favorable or unfavorable climatic conditions. Such factors are viewed as they depress or accelerate the growth and expansion of a population (Allee, *et al.*, 1949; Cole, 1948; Park, 1946). Scant attention is paid to the role of the individual or to the internal phenomena of those sub-groups of the population to which every individual of most species is normally a member, such as the family or other reproductive aggregates, feeding aggregations, harborage aggregations, and finally regional aggregations. This latter consists of individuals or groups which occasionally come in contact with each other without normally participating in the attaining of common goals. If social behavior really does alter the character of population dynamics, it is just such an understanding of the role of the individual and his group which we must seek. We might have rephrased our problem as "Does population dynamics alter the character of social behavior?" Both aspects will be examined here.

In the following discussion there is no attempt to review the literature. Rather, we shall hazard to discuss a wide variety of phenomena that are involved in a full appreciation of the interrelationship between sociality and population dynamics. Through such a "stock-taking" of relevant data from diverse fields of research, we shall endeavor to demonstrate the need for multi-discipline approaches to these complex problems. The

Reprinted with permission from the *Journal of Mammalogy*, Vol. 33, 1952, pp. 139–149. The author is with the National Institute of Mental Health, Bethesda, Md.

180

writer, as an ecologist, no doubt expresses bias in his treatment of this discussion.

We might first wonder if sociality really does have any influence at all on population dynamics. Perhaps it will be best for me to describe briefly a situation with which I have had intimate experience. This concerns the role of social behavior in limiting numbers among wild Norway rats. (This study of the Norway rat is still largely unpublished. It was a phase of the research program of the Rodent Ecology Project of the Johns Hopkins University School of Hygiene and Public Health, which was sponsored through a grant from the International Health Division of the Rockefeller Foundation.) (Calhoun, 1949a, 1949b.) For 28 months I observed a colony of rats (*Rattus norvegicus*) near Towson, Maryland, as it grew from a few individuals to the point of saturation in numbers. This colony was maintained in a 10,000-sqaure-foot pen where there was a superabundance of food at all times, and where harborage space was never completely utilized by the rats. At the time the colony was killed off there were considerably less than 200 adult rats, and all the evidence pointed to the fact that the adult population would never have exceeded 200 individuals. The number is particularly instructive when we compare it with the number of rats that might have been raised in the available space had each individual been isolated as a juvenile into two square feet of cage space, as is customarily done in the laboratory. Under such laboratory conditions 5,000 healthy rats might have been reared in 10,000 square feet of space instead of the 200 which utilized such space under free-ranging conditions. This figure of 5,000 rats is actually a conservative one in regard to representing the biotic potential expected from this free-ranging colony. The studies of Emlen and Davis (1948) and Davis (1949) supplemented by my own observations indicate the following conditions for determining the potential reproduction were other limiting factors not in operation: (1) 8 per weaned litter with equal sex ratio; (2) first litter by 5 months of age; (3) one litter every two months; (4) no breeding during the four mid-winter months; (5) all rats born the first breeding season should be dead by the end of the third; (6) it is within the potential life span of a rat for all othe.s to have been alive at the end of the experiment; (7) the study lasted from March 1947 to June 1949. With these conditions as a basis for judgment, 50,000 rats might have been alive in June 1949 as descendants from the original five females. Nevertheless, in the comparison above, it is believed that the figure 5,000 is a more realistic one in indicating the potential density of 10,000 square feet, although it is conceivable that 50,000 healthy rats could be maintained in a similar space by confining each to a cage somewhat less than eight inches on a side. What, then, was the cause of this 25-fold decrease in utilization of space under naturalistic conditions? The obvious explanation is that under free ranging conditions the rats expressed genetically determined and culturally modified behavioristic potentialities, which were impossible under caged conditions. This explanation has philosophically broad implications. Whenever the density of a population becomes increased beyond that level to which the heredity-to-environment relationship provides optimum adjustment, then the individual and the group must forfeit some of their potentials of behavior if all members are to maintain an adequate state of health.

There are three basic ways in which the social behavior of this colony of rats altered the population growth. They are as follows:

1. Development of local groups which maintain their integrity restricts the utilization of space. Local colonies or aggregates were formed primarily on the basis of continued association in the locality of birth. There was sufficient conflict existing between these local colonies that there developed intermediate buffer zones in which burrows were never constructed and across which there was a reduced incidence of locomotion. The development of these social buffer zones seems essential to the maintenance of group integrity and it is a major factor in reducing the number of animals which utilize a given amount of space.

2. Social stability favors successful reproduction. A stable group is one in which there is a well-developed dominance hierarchy, is one where there are well-established relationships between all the members of the group, and is one in which the individual members have experienced few behavioral disturbances and have exhibited favorable patterns of growth. Among such stable groups the frequency of conception is high, and most of the young born are successfully raised.

On the contrary, among socially unstable groups the frequency of conception is reduced and very few of the young born survive to weaning, and if they do the chances of their, in turn, leaving any progeny are very slim indeed. Socially unstable groups are those consisting of members who have had few associations in common, and/or who have experienced many behavioral disturbances and have exhibited retarded rates of growth. Such groups normally have an unstable or poorly defined hierarchial system.

3. Social stability favors decreased mortality. Predation from flies was the chief direct cause of death. During the immediate post-weaning period, when the young rats are making their adjustments to colony life, flies frequently lay eggs in the fur of the young. The young most likely to succumb are those which have received excessive punitive action from their associates or who, for various reasons, have no permanent home. Flies also kill adults by laying eggs in open wounds, even fresh wounds. Rats low in the social order receive more wounds and are thus more subject to being consumed "alive" by maggots.

As the population increased in numbers there was an increase in frequency, intensity, and complexity of behavioral adjustments necessitated among and between groups of rats. This forced more and more rats to be characterized by social instability with the accompanying result of lowering the biotic potential to the point where there was a balance between natality and mortality—all this in the continued presence of a superabundance of food and unused space available for harborage.

This influence of social behavior upon population growth in the Norway rat is exhibited in various degrees among other animals. However, in the time and space available here, no attempt will be made to present a critical review of the field. Rather, we shall examine the phenomena of social behavior and the condition of sociality as they relate to the broad problem of growth exhibited both on the individual and on the population level. Through this discussion we shall place sociality in perspective to other biological phenomena and suggest avenues for further research.

Various concepts of levels or types of sociality exist. According to Allee (1940) these are: 1. "Sociality includes all integrations of two or more organisms into a supra-individualistic unity on which natural selection can act"; 2. Sociality is coextensive "with the existence of an innate pattern of a certain specialized appetite" whose satisfaction demands that animals live together and engage in common activities; 3. "True sociality occurs only in the presence of abstract values of which members of the group are more or less conscious." Thus, sociality ranges from unconscious automatic co-operation (Allee, 1945) to conscious co-operation in which the members react to socially conditioned symbols (Northrop, 1948). A bridging of this range of social characteristics is begun as soon as the association between a social behavior and its consequences is modified by the learning process. For example, when a mouse who has repeatedly lost in combat makes the adjustment of running away upon sight of his opponent, values are effecting social behavior. Approaching the opponent will result in pain, while avoidance prevents pain. Not only does such a behavior illustrate the realization of values, but also that such values may be generalized. A case (Allee, 1942) in point is that of an albino mouse, who submits to other albino mice on first encounter, after having previously been conditioned from repeated defeats by the more aggressive C57 black mice. To such a mouse any other mouse, and not just the one by which it had been beaten, serves as a symbol of the dire consequences which will result, if he fails to submit or run away. Such generalizations from prior experience form the major basis for the origin of abstract values.

For our consideration of the interrelationship of sociality to growth phenomena, the most important considerations cover those conditions permitting a population to develop and express those characteristics of sociality which are possible within the limitations imposed by the genetic potentialities of the species in question.

Wherever animals live they are constantly altering the environment about them. This occurs through such diverse phenomena as release of excreta, alteration of surrounding temperature and humidity, construction of trails and burrows, and the development of habits, all of which may alter the behavior of members of their own or alter generations. These phenomena are spoken of as biological conditioning of the environment. Such activity has repeatedly been shown to alter the welfare of existing members of a population as well as the density exhibited by later generations (Allee, 1942, 1945; Allee, *et al.*, 1949). Under essentially random dispersal of individuals through the environment, any effect of biological conditioning upon the welfare of the members of a population may be assumed to be dissociated from social phenomena. However, when such effects are associated with animals which live in aggregates (as opposed to different effects occurring when the same kind of animals live dispersed) we may, with assurance, infer that sociality is a factor in affecting the welfare of the group. There is a tendency among many animals toward group activity, the result of which ameliorates the environment so that their physiology is more efficient or that survival rate is increased. Such biologically conditioning phenomena are the result of co-operative activity. Beyond a certain point the same activity may become deleterious as the participating group increases in numbers, to the point that the formerly beneficial activity lowers survival rate or physiological efficiency. *The merits of any social behavior are thus relative to the condition and history of the group within which they occur.* For example, copulation among mammals is a desirable and necessary social behavior if the species is to survive. Yet, among certain socially disturbed groups of my Towson colony of rats, which lacked a well-integrated dominance-hierarchy, copulation rarely led to conception despite, or perhaps because of, its high frequency.

As soon as animals begin to condition their environment through the elaboration of relatively permanent artifacts such as trails, nests, burrows, and the like, biological conditioning assumes a more definite cultural aspect. To be sure, such artifacts satisfy primary organic requirements; dens are a place of retreat from enemies or inclement weather; nests are places where the young are safe; trails lead to food or harborage, and food caches serve to make food more accessible. However, beyond such primary functions, dens, nests, trails and the like further serve as a physical mold in which the social matrix takes its form.

It is with reference to the construction and utilization of these animal-made structures that many patterns of behavioral relationships become established. Where more than one animal uses one of these biological artifacts either conflict, tolerance, or the acceptance of rank-oriented priority develops (Collias, 1944). When two rats, who are familiar with each other, meet along a trail, each usually steps slightly aside and passage occurs with no sign of conflict, even where difference in rank occurs.

Furthermore, young animals who develop within an artifact-conditioned environment find life much easier than did the original colonizers. They not only find previously established places of retreat and established pathways of movement between harborages, sources of food and the like, but they also encounter an artifact-oriented stabilized social structure within which their own integration during maturation is facilitated.

This alteration of the habits and social behavior of one generation by the activities of generations which precede it represents a cultural process, when culture is considered from a broad biological viewpoint. The term culture will here be used in this limited sense, without attempting to discuss the further elaborations which are expressed among human societies. If this restriction is placed upon the concept of culture, there exists the possibility of treating it comparatively in experiments with infra-human organisms. By so doing we may hope to arrive at generalizations which are useful on the human level. For such comparative purposes we can deal with effects and modifications produced by inherent behavior as well as those which are further structured through the process of learning.

There are striking similarities between the culture of man and that of some of the other vertebrates. Artifacts are constructed, learned patterns of social behavior are developed, and both are passed on to influence the life of later generations. Chance behavior or superstition may affect the pattern of learned social behavior (Skinner, 1948), and the character of vocalization may be handed down through cultural inheritance. Regarding the cultural modification of vocalization, Altmann (1950) has recently described an interesting situation among elk. In herds whose social structure has been upset by hunting, very little vocalization occurs. However, in a herd which lived far back in the Teton Mountains, where they had escaped being hunted, there was a continual calling back and forth between members of the herd.

Much in common exists between the patterns of culture among different species of veretebrates. Culture, particularly when continuity through many generations is insured, provides a stabilizing influence on the activities of the members of a population and permits them to make more effective use of their environment. Although there is as yet no experimental data to verify this postulate, it is quite likely that the genetic inheritance of many species is such that optimum adjustment by the individual or the group is made only under those conditions favoring the existence of a stabilized culture with its accompanying biologically produced artifacts. However, we must realize that cultural stability also restricts the potentialities of behavior, since other patterns of culture are automatically excluded.

It is through the alteration of the complexity and stability of culture that sociality exerts a controlling influence upon population dynamics. One of the inherent aspects of this concept concerns the relative continuity through space and time of both the population and the physical and social alterations which have been produced by the population. Discontinuities impose conditions of cultural instability as well as inhibit the maintenance of developing complexities of social organization. As mentioned previously, for the Norway rat such social control of population dynamics operates by influencing reproductive capacity, growth rate, mortality rate, incidence of disease, and behavioral adjustment. Our problem, then, resolves itself into a consideration of factors which may influence the complexity or stability of the culture of a population.

Analysis of operant factors must take into consideration the perception of the environment by the individual. The manner in which animals perceive their environment is socially important because it largely determines the rate and manner in which animals contact each other, and the manner in which they utilize the space about them. We often overlook the fact that the same physical environment, such as a mat of grass, may be differently perceived or is differently reacted to by different organisms (Schneirla, 1949). Similarly, the same environment may have different meaning to two different individuals of the same species, due to differences in heredity or experience. In this discussion we shall treat the responses (or lack of responses) of animals as resulting from their perception of the environment. However, we must realize that the physiological state of the individual may alter the response regardless of how the environment is perceive (Fuller, 1950).

There are two phenomena relative to perception of the environment which must be kept in mind upon interpreting observations. First, an animal may react to an environmental situation as if it were complete, whereas portions of it are actually missing. Second, an animal may fail to perceive or react to portions of its environment which are actually present, and which it is capable of perceiving and reacting to. In either case, unfavorable usage of the environment, with resultant density effects, may occur.

The first phenomenon of reacting to an incomplete environmental situation is a derivative of the "releaser" concept developed by Lorenz and by Tinbergen (1948). A releaser is a structure of the environment or a behavior of one animal, which elicits a sequence of behavior by another animal. It is characteristic that the releaser is only a segment of the complete goal-object or goal-situation to which the reacting animal responds. Under usual conditions the behavior of the reacting animal proves satisfactory, since the complete goal-object of goal-situation is actually present. Tinbergen showed that the red belly of male stickleback fish during the breeding season served as a releaser, which elicited the female to follow the male to the spawning ground. Females will follow objects with ventral red areas which only remotely resemble fish in appearance. Under such conditions the behavior of the female can have no effective solution. Admittedly, much research needs to be done in the field of elicitation of behavior of social implication by releasers, but the releaser concept, nevertheless, provides a useful theoretical framework for orienting research.

Harris (1950) has made some interesting studies of spatial orientation in the deermouse, *Peromyscus*, which bears on the problem of the role of "releaser phenomena" on population dynamics. *Peromyscus maniculatus bairdi* inhabits grassland, whereas *Peromyscuc maniculatus gracilis* inhabits woodlands. These two closely related subspecies may live in adjoining habitats and yet never interbreed, although they do so freely in the laboratory. Adjoining rooms with an inter-connecting passage were arranged to simulate the natural habitats. "Grassland" was made of bunches of thin strips of heavy paper, while "forests" were simply sections of small trees standing on end. When given a free choice of movement between these two rooms each of these subspecies of mice spent a significantly greater amount of time in the habitat simulating their natural one. Such orentation was just as efficient by mice born and raised in small laboratory cages as it was by mice trapped in the wild. It showed that these mice possess an innate capacity for tropistic behavior for which only a small segment of the environment is required as a *releaser*. This type of behavior is one of the keys as to why animals make differential usage of the available environment—space in particular being considered. Although extrapolating from experimental situations sometimes leads to false conclusions, one would strongly suspect that both the spacing and form of vegetation are important factors in both the occurrence of a deermouse in a habitat and the size of its home range, perhaps irrespective of the supply of food and harborage. Certainly, these ideas present a provocative subject for both observational and experimental studies. In fact, one is led to wonder how the behavior of animals is altered when they find themselves confined, as on islands, to habitats from which they cannot escape and to which their heredity does not permit their proper adjustment. Such an area of investigation might be designated as *"comparative esthetics."* Its ultimate analysis presumably would concern the manner in which the art forms of the material world about him affect man's behavior and peace of mind. Further theoretical aspects of releaser phenomena to social behavior have been pointed out by Ginsburg (1949). He says: "What interests me here is that a phylogeny of such releasers amounts to a phylogeny of symbolic behavior and indicates an innate capacity to derive meaning from abstract symbols. It is true that we do not know what this meaning is on an ideational level; nevertheless, it has its counterpart in human behavior if we accept the findings of orthodox Freudians."

The second phenomenon of failure to react to those existing portions of the environment, which potentially should contribute to the wellbeing of the organism, is one with reverberations in the dynamics of populations. The point involved here is that conditions arise which preclude the organism make the optimum use of available resources, whether they be physical, biological or social. In the field of psychology a large portion of the research in learning theory and abnormal behavior is actually involved with this problem. Likewise, it is the crux of the endeavors of psychoanalysis to reveal the origins of such situations. Field workers in ecology frequently observe animals whose reactions are out of harmony with their environment, and it is one of the aims of wildlife management to prevent their origin. In the experimental field we find such attempts to designate the problem, as in Tolman's (1949) concept of "perceptual blindness," or we find the conditions exemplified in such artificial situations as Liddell's (1942) work in producing "abnormal behavior" in his investigation of conditioned reflexes.

I would like to cite an observation of my own from my free-ranging colony of Norway rats. It exemplifies the complexities which may arise in an open society. Most rats, particularly those which have received mild degrees of punitive action from their associates, stored food in their burrows. The food might or might not be eaten immediately upon taking it to the burrow. Transportation of food in itself might satisfy a drive; however, it is to be noted that these rats deposited the transported food in locations where they themselves would have a good chance of securing it later. On the other hand, the storing behavior of rats who have experienced excessive punitive action from their associates is quite different. Repeated trips would be made from the food hopper depositing food at scattered points nearby, usually not more than 15 feet away, whereas the burrows were all further away. Once this food was left the rats which had done the transporting paid no further attention to it. Whatever the mechanism of development of this behavior may be, it is readily evident that the rats exhibiting it are no longer making a favorable use of this aspect of their environment.

An interesting aspect of this behavior, which is certainly abnormal from the individual's viewpoint, is beneficial with reference to the entire colony. (This type of behavior occurred in less than five percent of over 200 rats observed. Associated characteristics in such rats formed a syndrome which included (1) accentuated pre-weaning competition with older sibs, (2) inhibited growth during entire life span, (3) "freezing" when cornered in a trap or harborage, (4) lack of successful reproduction.) This scattering of the food made it more available and thus reduced competition at the main source of food. This observation raises the question, "how abnormal is abnormal behavior?" Though an individual rat may have its behavior so disturbed that its own effective reproduction is prevented and its own proper usage of food inhibited, it may, nevertheless, make a significant contribution to the welfare of its society through making the environment more favorable for its associates. For proper evaluation the range of variation in individual behavior needs to be viewed both as it affects the individual and the group.

Perception of spatial relationships and the manner in which animals utilize the space available to them have important social implications and exert a controlling influence on density. Territoriality, the active defense of a given tract, and home range, the occupancy of a preferred area, function as active or passive means of maintaining dispersion of individual or groups (Allee, *et al.*, 1949; page 412; Burt, 1943; Nice, 1941). Although we lack sufficient knowledge to state exactly why an animal occupies a territory or home range of a given size, one rather general characteristic is that more food exists in the occupied area than is utilized.

This restriction of the privilege of occupying space irrespective of food imposes limitations to population growth not realized by the earlier students of this subject (Davis, 1950). Social hierarchies provide an elaboration to the complexity of territory or home range. The development of rank-order systems permits the organization of group integrity and stability which in turn leads to in-group and out-group status. Attraction between members of a group and antagonism between members of different groups produce local concentrations with intervening buffer zones which are little used by the members of the adjacent groups (Keith, 1949; Scott, 1943; and author's observations on rats).

Perception of spatial relationships may have repercussions directly or indirectly on both social behavior and population dynamics, because patterns of locomotion through an environment alter the rate of contact between associates, as well as their orientation to the physical structures of the habitat.

At the Jackson Laboratory litters of dogs are raised in 20 × 70-foot pens. Snow trails reveal the manner in which the dogs utilize their confined area. Wirehaired Fox Terriers beat a single path about the periphery; Cocker Spaniels also beat a path about the periphery of the pen, but they also beat a few trails diagonally across the pen; Beagles and Basenjis form trails as do Cocker Spaniels, but in addition there are occasional to frequent wanderings away from the paths through the otherwise unbroken snow; and finally, the opposite extreme from the Wirehaired Fox Terriers is exhibited by Shetland Sheep Dogs—their tracks appear to be distributed completely at random over the pen with very little indication of a peripheral trail adjacent to the fence. Of course, we do not know what sort of natural population these breeds are capable of developing, but the snow-trail pattern exhibited indicate that these breeds would markedly differ in their utilization of their home range.

Another factor which has direct implications for population dynamics, particularly among social species, is that of *preadaptation* (Allee, *et al.*, 1949, page 642). Although natural selection may have been operating on a species with the result that this species exhibits the ability to make an optimum adjustment to some particular environment, the species may, nevertheless, make a very excellent adjustment to some new environment with which it has had no prior association. In fact, some animals prosper in the new situation, as indicated by expansion of the population into new areas or by increases in density. Such adaptation is particularly prominent among such birds as robins, chimney swifts, bluebirds, wrens, and kingbirds (Kennedy, 1915), which have utilized many man-made structures to increase their available nesting or feeding niches. This same utilization of environments, highly altered by man, is especially exhibited by such forms as the house mouse and the Norway rat. Preadaptation phenomena include the ability to engage in complex behaviors in entirely new situations. Under the artificial environment of the laboratory myriads of experiments with the derived strains of the Norway rat have amply demonstrated this ability. Under completely free-ranging conditions ground squirrels will engage and solve many intricate problems presented to them in their normal environment (Gordon, 1943).

The phenomenon of preadaptation becomes of particular importance when the opportunity for it to be exhibited occurs in a population characterized by cultural continuity. Although the original manner of exploitation of a new environmental situation may be by chance, by learning, or by reasoning, its continued contribution to the welfare of the

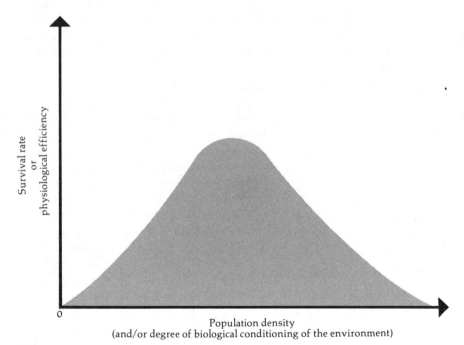

Fig. 1

The relationship of population density to biological activity (after Allee). It is through the operation of this principle that sociality influences the rate of individual growth, biotic potential of population growth, and the permutations of behavior.

population is greatly enhanced by the new patterns of behavior being passed on to later generations through cultural processes. In time, the behavior may be further elaborated, so as to further the biological conditioning of the environment and also to modify the cultural pattern. In the long run, what preadapted and culturally modified behavior does is to permit the population to make more effective use of available energy. A striking example of this is reflected in the population growth (Fig. 2) of Germany (Dewey and Daikin, 1947). One cycle of growth during an agricultural economy had just about terminated at the beginning of the industrial revolution. At that time there arose a new growth curve which has only recently approached completion. Thus, the carrying capacity of an environment must also be considered from the ability and opportunity of its inhabitants to exploit the available energy. Each new type of exploitation gives rise to a heightened level of population density. (Many similar examples could be cited utilizing infra-human animals. An outstanding one is that of the chimney-swift. Prior to the arrival of white

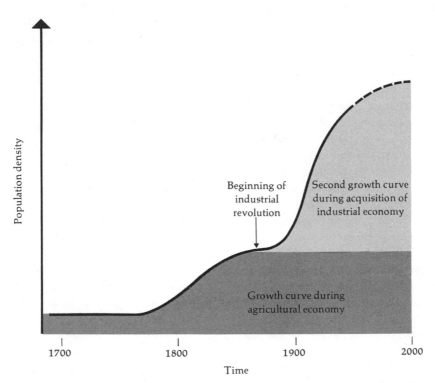

Fig. 2
Population growth in Germany (after Dewey and Daikin). This figure typifies the influence upon the resultant population growth of the ability of an organism to utilize the available energy. Such changes in ability may arise through either genetic or cultural changes within the species.

man in North America it nested in hollow trees, and during the migration seasons they aggregated in fairly large flocks which spent the night together. With the replacement of hollow trees by myriads of chimneys as a nesting niche, the abundance of this species has greatly increased. In addition to the increase in social contacts imposed by the proximity of chimneys, much larger aggregates—at times reaching many thousands —are formed in chimneys of large buildings during migration. Similar phenomena are characteristically observed in the changes of population densities during the succession of plant and animal communities (Allee, *et al.*, 1949). Animals or plants characteristic of a later stage of succession are commonly found as scarce invaders of an earlier stage. As the community structure changes and as conditions become more favorable for the invader its numbers increase. An important aspect of this situation is that the organism participates in the production of an environment more favorable to itself. From a research viewpoint the investigation of this phenomenon resolves itself into two aspects: (1) In what ways do organisms alter their environment to make them more favorable? (2) How can animals be induced to make more rapid and more efffcient alterations and yet maintain their cultural stability? The repetition of this process requires continued increase in complexity of the social organization. And as has been previously remarked, after a time there are continued restrictions to the development and expression of behavioral potentialities—a process, which we may anticipate, will terminate with the individual being only a hollow shell of his potential self. Opportunity for free expression of hereditary potentials of behavior and the drive toward increased utilization of available energy by the group are in part complimentary and in part conflicting tendencies.

Natural selection toward the survival of organizations of life which make more effective use of available energy is exhibited in the succession of plant and animal communities (Allee, *et al.*, 1949). The final stages are characterized by an increased rate of energy intake from the sun (by plants), by an increased rate of release of free energy (particularly by animals), by greater complexity of organization, and usually by a greater weight of living matter per area. In our search for guide posts for human civilization we would do well to examine more closely the dynamics of community succession whose terminal stage is self perpetuating as long as drastic changes in climate do not occur.

Nor can we consider the utilization of available energy without taking into account the growth of a population (that is, its density) with reference to the growth of the individual members of the population. Fishery research has shown that in a given body of water a relatively large number of stunted fish or a much fewer number of large fish may live. Density cannot be considered irrespective of the welfare of the individual. If the rat is at all typical, mammals behave much as do fish. In my Towson colony of Norway rats, as the population increased, more and more individuals were physically stunted despite having plenty of food available. Such stunted rats seemed healthy, as judged by the occurrence of fat—they simply failed to grow very large and attained their mature weight very slowly. These stunted rats were characterized by behavioral disturbances imposed by the increasing complexity of the social structure. Dwarfism or abnormal growth in many may also be associated with behavioral disturbances arising from unstable social environments (Binning, 1948; Fried and Mayer, 1948; Talbot, *et al.*, 1947).

Thus, we see that several growth processes are closely interrelated: (1) the rate of physical growth and skeletal maturation in the individual, (2) the level of mature growth of the individual, (3) the level of sexual and behavioral maturity in the individual, (4) the degree to which an individual or group is enabled to express genetic potentialities, (5) the growth rate of a population and its density at maturity, and (6) the social integration of a population—all these are inter-dependent variables whose expression is in turn influenced by the structure of the environment and the degree of cultural continuity possible.

The extent to which one of these growth phenomena may be enhanced through the partial suppression of the others raises the problem of value systems. Population density may be intensified at the expense of reduction in individual growth, and an increase in social tension. Maximum individual growth may be assured, through isolation with the resultant induced social sterility, irrespective of population density. A realization of the interdependence of these growth phenomena provides the viewpoint for the establishment of a truly comparative science of sociobiology.

As our human society becomes more highly technical, there arises the tendency to accentuate one of these growth phenomena without any consideration as to its effect on other aspects of life. This is particularly so as regards increasing population density, which in many quarters is accepted as a desirable objective. Bateson (1912) long ago realized the fallacy of this concept when he said: "It is not the *maximum* number but the *optimum* number, having regard to the means of distribution, that it should be the endeavor of social organization to secure. To spread a layer of human protoplasm of the greatest possible thickness over the earth—the implied ambition of many publicists—in the light of natural knowledge is seen to be reckless folly."

Yet such accentuation of a single aspect of the value systems relating to growth phenomena continue. E. G. Rochow (1949) predicts that it will be possible to feed a population of one billion persons (this is over five times the upper level indicated by the present trend) living within the boundaries of the United States. In a letter to me, Dr. Rochow made this further elaboration: "The chief difficulty arises, of course, in feeding so large a population, particularly if it is to spread over and inhabit a large part of the present farm lands. This is the part of the problem that becomes a challenge to chemists" and "I should also like to point out that the high population density in large cities is in part alleviated by purposeful isolation of many of the inhabitants." The choice before us is to develop a society whose numbers are limited, but whose members live a full life, or, as Rochow believes, to develop a society of maximum numbers whose members have had a restricted experience accompanied by an inhibition of many potentialities of expression. Maximum production of protoplasm is a valid concept and objective in the field of animal husbandry, but it is of doubtful value when applied to human society or even to game management. Current discussions of increasing agricultural production are also frequently so worded as to imply that what is possible is desirable—with little critical thought as to the consequences on the human population.

In this whole problem of the social aspects of population dynamics an important consideration is the individual's learning the nature of his physical and social environment. Although some behavior does not reach full development until an animal is quite mature, such as copulation and defense of territory, nevertheless, most contacts that an animal has with his environment begin very early in life. In fact, even where the complete behavior pattern or the full experience only occurs during adult life, the experiences of infancy and the juvenile period markedly alter later life (Hymovitch, 1949). The learning process among immature animals is qualitatively different; where the young are prevented from perceiving the environment, they, as adults, do not profit as well from similar experiences. Experiences during early life have a profound effect upon adult behavior and health. These conclusions apply to both physical and social aspects of the environment. Among dogs the latter part of the nursing period and the period just following weaning form a brief but critical one for the development of social adjustments (Scott and Marston, 1950). My own observations on wild rats were not such as to result in any clear-cut conclusions regarding the role of pre-weaning experience, but they amply demonstrated that the immediate post weaning and preadolescent periods were critical for future development. Among these rats social status, rate of growth, adult size, and stability of behavior were in large part determined during this juvenile period. In our observations of animals under natural conditions, in experimental studies of population ecology, and in laboratory studies of isolated animals or small groups, we need to give increasing attention to the manner in which the environment and experience of juvenile animals affect their behavior as adults.

In all species, regardless of their degree of sociality, natural selection operates on all levels of organic complexity from the individual to the population (Allee, 1945). *By a population we mean: any contiguously distributed grouping of a single species which is characterized by both genetic and cultural continuity through several generations.* Therefore, if we are to make real progress in understanding the interrelationships of sociality and population dynamics, our observations need to be focused upon the population as the major unit in which the lives of individuals find reality. Particular stress needs to be laid upon those factors which alter the maturation of the individual on the one hand, and, on the other, to the variations in the structure of the environment, which mold the fate of both individuals and populations. From an experimental standpoint this means that we must use populations as our experimental units; these to be allowed from their inception with a few members to the maturity and possible senescence of the population, and to be studied in environments where many of the physical factors of the environment are controlled and organized into meaningful patterns. Fuller (1950), in his Situational Analysis, has provided a framework for the experimental manipulation of the field parameters of behavior (incentive, barriers, and complexity) into meaningful patterns. This framework coupled with Calhoun's (1950) approach to the experimental manipulation of population as the unit of investigation presents the necessary background for objective investigation of the social aspects of population dynamics. Many helpful suggestions for planning experimental studies of sociality are included in the "Minutes of the Conference of Genetics and Social Behavior" (Scott, 1946).

In the planning of such experiments we may rely on the great wealth of ecological field observations and the equally great wealth of laboratory studies of the psychology and physiology of individuals and small groups. At best, experimental studies into population dynamics, even with those vertebrates characterized by high reproductive potentials, take several years for completion. They require substantial sums of money and should be pursued simultaneously by investigators trained in several diverse disciplines. To be sure, this is a large order, but small in comparison to the likely contributions to the welfare of man and the world about him. Any interpretation of results pertaining to the interrelationship between sociality and population dynamics involves judgment values. This is as it should be. However, such judgment values can only gain reliability when viewed against a background of experimentation, which enables manipulation of the variables, as well as repetition of experiments with the view of determining the variability of the end results of social equilibrium, when the accompanying static aspects of the enviroment (and heredity) are maintained constant.

Initial studies under controlled conditions of the interrelationship between sociality and population dynamics are likely to be most fruitful if we utilize some of the common experimental mammals and their wild counterparts. Of these the most useful will be: (1) the mouse, *Mus musculus*; (2) the rat, *Rattus norvegicus*; (3) the rabbit, *Oryctolagus cuniculus*, (4) the dog-wolf complex, *Canis lupus*; and (5) the rhesus monkey, *Macaca mulatta*. This arises from the fact that there is a great backlog of biological information concerning them, and that scientists in several biological disciplines are accustomed to working with these forms. Four of these forms (mouse, rat, rabbit, and dog-wolf) are particularly suitable, since for them there is available a large number of highly inbred strains or genetically divergent breeds. This variability may be used to exploit the heredity parameter of the organism-environment complex. Scott (1949) has dicussed in detail the value of inbred strains for experimental work relative to behavior, and Heston (1949) has similarly treated the usage of inbred strains in physiological studies. Inbred strains or breeds exhibit accentuation or inhibition of behavior characteristic of the wild form. It is this type of variability from the wild type which makes the use of such genetic derivatives useful. On the primate level we should have available breeds or inbred strains of a species suitable for use in the laboratory and in the field situation required by experimental population ecology. The rhesus monkey (Carpenter, 1942) is probably most suitable for such genetic work leading to further behavior studies. Although I have mainly stressed environmental influences in the present discussion, we must bear in mind that an analysis of the social aspects of population dynamics must be based upon a consideration of both heredity and environment. Sumner (1922) long ago ably pointed out that, insofar as the existence of life was concerned, neither heredity nor environment had reality in the absence of the other.

It so happens that all five of the species are characterized by rather complex social structure in comparison with many other representatives of their orders. To produce the fullest understanding of sociality and population dynamics some of those species with less complex social structures should also be thoroughly investigated.

Although present knowledge, derived from ecological studies of animals living in their native habitat, and from psychological studies of animals in the semi-isolated unsocial conditions of the laboratory, gives us a firm foothold for planning controlled studies of population ecology, much additional basic information is desirable. We particularly need many more detailed life-history studies of animals in their native habitats. These will be most effective when parallel life histories are made comparing related species known to differ in social structure. In practically all orders and many smalled taxonomic categories of mammals, there exists a wide range in the degree of sociality between different species. Table 1 presents examples of the wide range of sociality existing between related genera. In each instance the degree of sociality is judged on the basis of the size and permanence of groups, as well as the complexity of interrelationships between individuals and groups.

The existence of wide ranges of sociality among many groups of mammals, even including the primitive marsupials, makes it highly likely that determination of social structure is in large part independent of the degree of evolution of the cerebrum.

Investigation of the following topics by those making life history

Table 1
Comparative degrees of sociality between related genera[1]

Common name	Order	Slightly social	More highly social
Deer	Artiodactyla	Moose (*Alces*)	Elk (*Cervus*)
Rabbits	Lagomorpha	Cottontails (*Sylvilagus*)	European rabbit (*Oryctolagus*)
Rodents	Rodentia	Deermouse (*Peromyscus*)	Norway rat (*Rattus*)
Opossums	Marsupialia	American opossum (*Didelphis*)	Australian opossum (*Trichosurus*)

[1] Literature references: Moose (Denniston, 1949); elk (Altmann, 1950); cottontails (Trippensee, 1934); European rabbit (Southern, 1940, 1947); deermouse (Howard, 1949; Nicholson, 1941); Norway rat (Calhoun, 1949a, 1949b); American opossum (Lay, 1942); Australian opossum (Pracy and Kean, 1949).

studies will be most helpful in bringing about a better understanding of the relationship between sociality and population dynamics.

1. What are the goal-objects toward or between which animals orient?
2. How are these goal-objects distributed through space and time, particularly as they relate to the energy expenditure of the organism in re-encountering a goal-object?
3. What are the physical barriers of the environment and the complexity of their arrangement, which modify the likelihood of an animal perceiving or reaching a goal-object or of contacting other individuals?
4. What are the pain-producing barriers (both physical and social) which may occur between an animal and its goal-object?
5. How are the physical barriers or the pain-producing barriers distributed through space and time?
6. Describe each observed type of behavior in terms of:
   A. Composition of group involved (sex, age, relationship, etc.—see especially Carpenter, 1942).
   B. Type of behavior as regards its origin and function (see Scott, 1946, p. 23).
   C. Innate drives whose satisfaction depends upon the occurence and distribution of goal-objects and barriers.
7. What are the conditions of juvenile life as related to:
   A. Relative maturity at birth.
   B. Length and pattern of dependency of young upon their mother or other associates, including frequency and kind of contact.
   C. Manner in which the young are integrated into the social structure.
   D. The maturation of each goal-object oriented behavior.

8. In what ways do the animals biologically condition their environment, and how does such conditioning influence the expression of either innate or learned behavior?
9. What is the social structure of groups in terms of rank-order relationships or other inter-individual adjustments?
10. What is the pattern of relationship between different groups?
11. How is the growth of the individual, its reproductive success, and likelihood of survival associated with the above types of data?

Whereas, other types (refer to the outlines appearing from time to time in Ecology, whose publication is sponsored through the Committee for Life History Studies) of observations are useful in preparing life history studies, the systematic accumulation of data of the above type will be of great usefulness in the next step of analysis—the planning and execution of controlled experimental studies into population ecology. Such data will facilitate a systematic arrangement of environmental components. In the native habitats of most animals goal-objects, barriers, and other physical structures are so irregularly arranged as to enable us to arrive at only vague approximations of their influence. From these life history-derived approximations we may logically plan the arrangement of goal-objects, barriers, and the like so that we may derive general principles as to their influence on population dynamics, social structures, and evolution of culture.

Concepts and techniques developed in the science of psychology will also be of great usefulness in planning and conducting experiments in population ecology. In its development, psychology has relied mainly on clinical studies of man and of experimental studies of various laboratory animals, the latter under essentially unsocial conditions. Both of these approaches are atomistic in the sense that they must perforce view the individual whose past history and environment is little known, or which is living essentially out of context with its natural physical and social environment. Nevertheless, these two psychological approaches have given us great insight into the manner in which the individual perceives, learns, and adjusts, and to a more limited extent it has shown how individuals react to and with others of their kind in rather simple stereotyped environments. The time is now ripe to utilize this great host of information in planning experiments and analyzing results in which the unit of investigation is the population.

The potential contribution of psychology to the investigation of the behavioral aspects of population dynamics may not be realized by current trends in psychological research. Psychology has stressed the development of concepts at the expense of the descriptive aspects of behavior. Such comparative psychological endeavors can provide a cataloging of the range of behavior exhibited by a species and of the range of conditions which elicit such behaviors. Such data needs to be available both for the wild-type representative of each species and also for genetically similar isolated groups of the species, such as subspecies, inbred strains, or breeds. Such description studies will form the building blocks of behavior with which we can proceed with greater assurance in planning experimental studies into group dynamics and population ecology.

With each new increase in complexity of life new properties arise, and the phenomena exhibited by the less complex forms of life take on new meaning. Thus, our knowledge of the behavior of individuals and small groups will assume richer connotations and reveal new concepts when applied to the social population level of organic organization. In turn, it is inevitable that investigation at this level of organization will produce new topics for investigation under strictly laboratory conditions.

Concepts of the social aspects of population dynamics are of potential value to the three spheres of human activity. They contribute to man's management of himself through the development of a "preventive medicine" of mental hygiene, through its contribution to psychiatry by providing a better appreciation of the relationship of the total individual to his total environment (Cameron, 1948); through the provision of principles of community planning; and through the assessment of desirable population densities. They contribute, in the sphere of animal husbandry, to man's management of domestic animals, so that they will most economically provide him with sustenance. They contribute to the essential problem of man's management of the world about him in the broad fields of conservation and wildlife management; for man lives not alone, but in context with the "balance of nature," which he disrupts at his own peril. Admittedly, the concepts of the social aspect of population dynamics are as yet in an embryonic state. Their development to the point where we may safely and surely apply such knowledge presents a challenge to research. To meet this challenge we must plan long-term observational studies of the social ecology of man and other animals under their normal conditions of existence; we must plan long-term experimental studies of population ecology where conditions of the physical environment, which mold social structure, are systematically controlled, and where the history of the population is followed through the years from infancy to maturity; we must have the courage and foresight to depart from the laboratory in its customarily accepted sense, and take with us into the broader laboratory of field situations our extensive knowledge derived from analytical studies of the individual and small groups. Such procedures will lend greater insight into the dynamics of group behavior as well as provide new problems to carry back with us into the laboratory for other analytical treatment.

LITERATURE CITED

Allee, W. C. 1940. Concerning the origin of sociality in animals. Scientia, 154–160.

———— 1942. Social dominance and subordination among vertebrates. Biological Symposia, 8: 139–162:

———— 1945. Human conflict and cooperation: the biological background. Chapt. XX, pp. 321–367. In Approaches to National Unity, New York, Harper Bros.

Allee, W. C., A. E. Emerson, O. Park, T. Park, and K. P. Schmidt. 1949. Principles of animal ecology. 837 pp. W. B. Saunders, Phila.

Altmann, Margaret. 1950. Problems of social behavior in wapiti of Jackson Hole. Unpublished paper delivered at 1950 meeting of Amer. Soc. of Mammalogists.

Bateson, W. 1912. Biological fact and the structure of society. The Herbert Spencer Lecture. Delivered at the examinations Schools on Wednesday Feb. 28, 1912. 34 pp. Clarendon Press, Oxford.

Binning, Griffith. 1948. Peace can be on thy house. The effects of emotional tensions on the development and growth of children, based on a study of 800 Saskatoon School children. 4 pp. reprinted from March–April issue of Health.

Burt, Wm. H. 1943. Territoriality and home range concepts as applied to mammals. Jour. Mamm., 24: 346–352.

Calhoun, John B. 1949a. A method for self-control of population growth among mammals living in the wild. Science, 109: 333–335.

————1949b. Influence of space and time on the social behavior of the rat. (Abstract.) Anat. Record, 105: 28.

———— 1950. The study of wild animals under controlled conditions. Annals New York Academy Sci., 51: 1113–1122.

Cameron, D. Ewen. 1948. The current transition in the concept of science. Science, 107: 553–558.

Carpenter, C. R. 1942. Sexual behavior of free ranging rhesus monkeys (*Macaca mulatta*). Jour. Comp. Psychol., 33: 113–162.

Cole, Lamont C. 1948. Population phenomena and common knowledge. Scientific Monthly, 67: 338–345.

Collias, Nicholas E. 1944. Aggressive behavior among vertebrate animals. Physiological Zoology, 17: 83–123.

Davis, David E. 1949. The weight of wild brown rats at sexual maturity. Jour. Mamm., 30: 125–130.

———— 1950. Malthus—A review for game managers. Jour. Wildlife Mgt., 14: 180–183.

Denniston, R. H. 1949. Certain aspects of the development and behavior of the Wyoming moose—*Alces americana shirasi*. (Abstract.) Anatomical Record, 105: 25.

Dewey, Edward R., and Edwin F. Daikin. 1947. Cycles, the science of prediction. 255 pp., Henry Holt & Co., New York.

Emlen, John T., and David E. Davis. 1948. Determination of reproductive rates in rat population by examination of carcasses. Physiological Zoology, 21: 59–65.

Fried, Ralph, and M. F. Mayer. 1948. Socio-emotional factors accounting for growth failure in children living in an institution. Jour. Pediatrics, 33: 444–456.

Fuller, John L. 1950. Situational Analysis: a classification of organism-field interactions. Psychological Review, 57: 3–18.

Ginsburg, Benson E. 1949. Genetics and social behavior—a theoretical synthesis. pp. 101–124 in lectures on Genetics, Cancer, Growth and Social Behavior at the R. B. Jackson Memorial Laboratory Twentieth Commemoration. Bar Harbor Times.

Gordon, Kenneth. 1943. The natural history and behavior of the western chipmunk and the mantled ground squirrel. Oregon State Monographs, Studies in Zoology No. 5, 104 pp.

Harris, Van T. 1950. An experimental study of habitat selection by the deermice, *Peromyscus maniculatus*. 157 pp. Ph.D. dissertation, Univ. of Michigan.

Heston, W. E. 1949. Development of inbred strains of mice and their use in cancer research. pp. 9–31 in Lectures on Genetics, Cancer, Growth, and Social Behavior at the Roscoe B. Jackson Memorial Laboratory Twentieth Commemoration. Bar Harbor, Maine.

Howard, Walter E. 1949. Dispersal, amount of inbreeding, and longevity in a local population of prairie deermice of the George Reserve, Southern Michigan. Contributions from the Laboratory of Vertebrate Biology, Univ. of Michigan. Ann Arbor, No. 43, 52 pp.

Hymovitch, B. 1949. The effects of experimental variations on problem solving in the rat (including an Appendix review of the effect of early experience upon later behavior). 71 pp. Ph.D. Thesis, McGill University.

Keith, Sir Arthur. 1949. A new theory of human evolution. Philosophical Library, 451 pp., New York. Comments taken from a review by Dr. W. C. Allee: Concerning human evolution. Ecology, 31: 155–157.

Kennedy, Clarence H. 1915. Adaptability in the choice of nesting sites of some widely spread birds. Condor, 17: 65–70.

Lay, D. W. 1942. Ecology of the opossum in eastern Texas. Jour. Mamm., 23: 147–159.

Liddell, H. S. 1942. The alteration of instinctual processes through the influence of conditioned reflexes. Psychosomatic Medicine, 4: 390–395.

Murie, Adolph. 1944. The wolves of Mt. McKinley. Fauna of the National Parks of the United States. Fauna Series No. 5, 238 pp. U.S. Government Printing Office.

Nice, Margaret M. 1941. The role of territory in bird life. Amer. Mid. Nat., 26: 441–487.

Nicholson, A. J. 1941. The homes and social habits of the wood-mouse (*Peromyscus leucopus noveboracensis*) in southern Michigan. Amer. Mid. Nat., 25: 196–223.

Northrop, F. S. C. 1948. The neurological and behavioristic psychological basis of the ordering of society by means of ideas. Science, 107: 411–417.

Park, Thomas. 1946. Some observations on the history and scope of population ecology. Ecology Monographs, 16: 313–320.

Pracy, L. T., and R. I. Kean. 1949. The opossum (*Trichosurus vulpecula*) in New Zealand, N.Z. Dept. of Internal Affairs, Wildlife Branch Bulletin No. 1, 19 pp., Blundell Bros. Ltd., Wellington.

Rochow, Eugene G. 1949. Chemistry tomorrow. Chemical and Engineering News, 27: 1510–1514.

Schneirla, T. C. 1949. Levels in the psychological capacities of animals. pp. 243–286, in Philosophy for the Future, edited by R. W. Sellars and V. J. McGill, the MacMillan Co.

Scott, J. P. (Editor). 1946. Minutes of the conference on genetics and social behavior. 35 pp. Published by the Roscoe B. Jackson Memorial Laboratory, Bar Harbor, Maine.

Scott, J. P. 1949. Genetics as a tool in experimental research. Amer. Psychologist, 4: 526–530.

———— 1950a. The cause of fighting in mice and rats. Unpublished manuscript.

———— 1950b. The social behavior of dogs and wolves: An illustration of sociobiological systematics. Annals New York Acad. Sci., 51: 1009–1021.

Scott, J. P., and Mary-'Vesta Marston. 1950. Critical periods affecting the development of normal and mal-adjustive social behavior of puppies. Jour. Genetic Psychol., 77: 25–60.

Scott, Thos. G. 1943. Some food coactions of the northern plains red fox. Ecological Monographs, 13: 427–479.

Skinner, B. F. 1948. 'Superstition' in the pigeon. Jour. Exp. Psych., 38: 168–172.

Southern, H. N. 1940. The ecology and population dynamics of the wild rabbit (Oryctolagus cuniculus). Annals of applied Biology, 27: 509–526.

———— 1947. Sexual and aggressive behavior in the wild rabbit. Behaviour, 1: 173–194.

Sumner, Francis B. 1922. The organism and its environment. Scientific Monthly, 14: 223–233.

Talbot, Nathan B., E. H. Sobel, B. S. Burke, Erich Lindemann, and S. B. Kaufman. 1947. Dwarfism in healthy children: Its possible relation to emotional disturbances. New England Medical Journal, 236: 783–793.

Tinbergen, N. 1948. Social releasers and the experimental method required for their study. Wilson Bulletin, 60: 6–51.

Tolman, Edward C. 1949. The psychology of social learning. Jour. Social Issues, Vol. V, Supplement Series No. 3, 18 pp.

Trippensee, R. E. 1934. The biology and management of the cottontail rabbit. 217 pp., Ph.D. thesis. University of Michigan.

Young, S. P., and E. A. Goldman. 1944. The wolves of North America. Amer. Wildlife Institute, Washington, D.C. 636 pp.

PART SIX

THE REMORSELESS WORKING
OF THINGS

Ten years back, in the twilight years of the
Eisenhower Era, I served with some very distinguished
Americans on a committee called the Commission on
National Goals. . . . Our job, back in the late 1950's, was
to suggest goals for our country in the 1960's, and
two things surprised me at the time. First was the
realization that this country had no specific goals
set down on paper; and second was the realization that no
matter what goals we chose, there was practically no
mechanism in government to methodically implement
them—and there isn't now.

Thomas J. Watson, Jr.

Reprinted with permission of the author from remarks presented to the Bond Club
of New York, January 7, 1970. Mr. Watson is Chairman of the Board, International
Business Machines Corporation.

In managing population growth, Calhoun suggests, the objective should be to seek the optimum, not the maximum. If we agree with this proposition, any given population level will be below optimum, above, or just right. Thus at any given time we must decide to either increase, decrease, or stabilize the population. This may seem a simplistic statement, but it places the population problem in a much better perspective than to either "let nature take its course" or direct population policy toward providing food and resources for the largest possible number of people. Thinking in terms of optimum population forces us to face every census figure with the question "Have we already provided for too many?"—not just "How many more can we provide for?"

But what is an optimum population—for either rats or men? Calhoun's work and subsequent studies in behavioral ecology have suggested some reasonably objective answers for rats and some other well-studied species. When population densities get too high, the species experiences physiological and psychological changes which lead to disease, hormonal imbalance, and nonadaptive behavior.

It is obviously difficult to make fully equivalent studies of men, and we must face the question, "How much like man is a rat?" It is tempting to make analogies between a potential rat population of 5000 caged rats contrasted to 200 free-ranging rats, and the situation of modern urban apartment dwellers—but is such an anology fair?

Hugh Iltis in his comments on the optimum human environment will tell us that man is quite probably more like his brute brothers and cousins than he is unlike them. Darwin's great contribution to our culture was to create a functional bridge between human and nonhuman nature. We are only just beginning to engage in profitable traffic across that bridge.

Just as it seems wise to talk about populations in terms of optimum numbers, so we can ponder the properties of an optimum environment— not just an adequate environment. This again requires that we consider the possibility of planning to have less of some things and not more and more. As difficult as they are to define, man is endowed with consciousness, imagination, emotions—perhaps even a conscience. An optimum human environment will have to provide food for thought and for spirit as well as for procreation.

THE OPTIMUM HUMAN ENVIRONMENT AND ITS RELATION TO MODERN AGRICULTURAL PREOCCUPATIONS

Hugh H. Iltis

To discuss the biological bases for human existence is to try to reformulate our cultural concepts of man's ancient relationships to his natural environment. That similar dialogues are going on all over this campus and in many parts of the world is evidence for the overriding urgency of the problem. The problem is one of a single species of animal who is making the earth unfit for habitation by conquering it.

The city-dwelling American, in particular, has been so removed from an intimate relationship with nature through the spectacular advances of science, industry, and agriculture that he tends to lose sight of his very real dependence on nature (a dependence brought forcefully home by the 1966 water shortage in New York, by the famines in India, by the pollution of air in Los Angeles). The more complex science and technology become, and the more extensive their use, the more far-reaching will be their destructive effects on nature, and the more difficult it will be to assess those effects, to stop them, or reverse them. The more successful science becomes the more difficult also will it be to ask the pertinent questions and expect any sensible answers. Technological success corrupts the ability to see the human animal in proper biological perspective. Technological success has become a technological plague.

It would be blind not to acknowledge the immense debts of modern man to this technological destruction. In mastering the environment, the fabulous inventiveness of modern agriculture has allowed a cultural explosion that continues to this day. In fact, it has made our civilization possible. Agricultural technology of the 19th and 20th centuries, from Liebig and the gasoline engine to hybrid corn, weed killers and pesticides, has crashed an exploitative barrier of increased production and prosperity in favored regions of the world whose long-term effect for good (and for evil) we must now try to assess.

Because of this success, some of our chemical or agricultural leaders now firmly hold that we can feed the world, that we can do anything we wish. Because of the population explosion, we must bend nature, willy-nilly, to our human will. Today we look upon wild or even tamed

Reprinted with permission from *The Biologist*, Vol. L, No. 3–4, 1968, pp. 114–125. The author is Professor of Botany and Director of the Herbarium at the University of Wisconsin, Madison.

nature without any patience. A large proportion of our university curricula are based on the archaic presumption that it is man's God-given prerogative to conquer and destroy nature solely for his own use. "Nature is neither sacred nor is it to be venerated but is solely to be used for the benefit of man" (*Leitmotif* of a University of Wisconsin conservation course syllabus). Yet the side effects of this destruction have been enormous, and the consequences have been characterized well in the ancient saying, "Man strides across the landscape and deserts follow in his footsteps." This is more true today than ever.

Thus, the prevailing optimism of the post-World War II days in the ability of man to solve his problems—that faith in science that we of Western culture are literally born with—this optimism, this occidental technological arrogance, appears more and more unfounded. Somehow, in our struggle to cultural affluence and perfection, we have neglected to ask the proper questions of nature, a nature that will not give up her riches for nothing, that will not let us forget that life is a holistic concept of which man is but one part.

One may approach man's ecological problems in two ways:

1. Through questions pertinent to the future of man based on man's past ecological relationship to nature, his evolutionary heritage. (We will talk about these human adaptations, and the lack of adaptations, to the cultural advance and destruction of the environment).
2. Through the critical analysis of some specific problems in Wisconsin and elsewhere, viz., in use of the land connected with agricultural programs.

WHAT QUESTIONS SHOULD WE ASK?

What are the proper questions for man to ask for his continuing existence and evolution? It seems to me that, *first and foremost, any questions pertinent to the future of man must be based on his evolutionary past.* It is only within this evolutionary context that we should discuss resource management and environmental health, or whether preservationists are sentimental or exploiters stupid. Ecologies and genetic adaptations are amenable to study, whether of mice or men. Human destinies can only be planned on evolutionary platforms. To answer "What does man now need?" we need to ask "Where did he come from?" and "Where might he be going?"

Man, as has been recently overstressed by Dobzhansky (1967) and others, is indeed unique. Nevertheless, it should never be forgotten that he is a unique animal. He is the result of over a 100 million years of evolution as a mammal, of over 45 million years as a primate, of over 15 million years as an ape. His human uniqueness is, at most, 2 million years old or less. The refined human neurological and physical attributes are but a few hundred thousand years old. Knowing what we do concerning evolutionary rates, we must conclude that modern man has experienced but relatively few major genetic innovations. Thus our major chemical-physiological patterns, those basic, inner, seething, and mysterious chemical frameworks of the human animal, be they digestion, nervous system or sex, are much more similar to those of our primate relatives than they are different. They, as well as we, are nothing more or less than the result of natural selection in nature. As unique as we may think we are, we are nevertheless programmed genetically to need clean air and sunshine, a green landscape and unpolluted water, and natural animal and vegetable foods. To be healthy, which after all has nothing to do with IQ or culture, means simply allowing our bodies to react in the way that 100 millions of years of evolution in tropical or subtropical nature have equipped us to do.

Physically (fundamentally) we are adapted to wild tropical nature, but culturally to cities and towns. In our houses, of course, we try to imitate not only the climate, but the setting of our genetic geologic past with warm humid air, green plants, and even animal companions. If we are rich and can afford it, we may even build greenhouses next to our living rooms, but a place in the country, or at least take our children for a vacation on the seashore. What the specific bodily physiological reactions are to natural beauty and diversity, to the shapes and colors of nature (especially to green), to the motions and sounds of other animals such as birds, we as yet do not comprehend. It is clear from our preferences (even to the extent of plastic flowers in restaurants) on the one hand, and from the standpoint of evolutionary doctrine by natural selection on the other, that, like the need for love and loving, the need for nature, the need for its diversity and beauty, must have a genetic basis. Thus, nature in our daily life must be thought of as an indispensable biological need. I think this sound perhaps very simplistic, yet is nevertheless true. In any case, it is generally neglected in any discussions of resource policy for man. There is an overemphasis on our uniqueness, a degrading of our animal ancestry. Yet, since the quality of our sensory experience depends on it, it is of overwhelming importance.

Every basic human adaptation, be it ear, eye, skin, lungs, gut—yes, even brain and psyche—demands, for proper functioning, an environment similar to the one in which these structures evolved over the millions of years of evolution. George G. Simpson pointed out that any of our monkey ancestors with faulty vision who misjudged distances when jumping, or who didn't hear the approach of another carnivorous animal, died. Only those who were adapted to nature contributed to our gene pool and becamse our ancestors.

Take the gorilla, for example. As George Schaller (1964) points out in *The Year of the Gorilla*, if we study his behavior in a zoo he is an incomprehensible, dangerous, erratic brute; but, if we study him in his evolutionary context in the tropical forests of Africa, his native habitat, he is a shy, mild, alert, and well-coordinated animal. Only there can he be understood. Neither gorilla nor man can be evaluated out of context of the evolutionary environments that shaped him.

Thus the endless arguments as to what kind of environment man needs (short of daily intake of appropriate calories and vitamins) are unnecessary, because the answer is obvious: *The optimum human environment is one in which the human animal can have maximum contact with the natural (evolutionary) environment in which he evolved* and for which all our basic processes are genetically programmed, *yet in which at the same time the many advantages of civilization are not sacrificed.* It is a compromise— this humane human environment—between our genetic heritage, which we cannot deny except at great emotional and physical misery, and the fruits of an unbelievably varied civilization which we are loath to give up.

If the concrete and steel city, this great arena of bright lights and stimulation as well as of heartbreak, the largest, filthiest, most seductive, and most dangerous living thing in the world, turns man into an asocial, erratic, and sick animal; if urbanization degrades human society through increased emotional stress, crime, delinquency, slums, and other neuroses and psychoses, it is because the genetic flexibility of the human animal trapped in this necropolis is not great enough, because no natural selection has given us gene combinations to cope with this environment, and no natural selection ever will. Our human genetic adaptations are here simply out of evolutionary context. Man is dehumanized in the city because of his near total victory over nature. When the last tree dies in Brooklyn, dehumanization will spread like a plague. We may look upon megalopolis as a giant experiment in sensory deprivation. And, eventually, total destruction of nature will bring total destruction of man.

A recent article in the press, telling how two psychiatrists went with a team to help "unfortunate deprived children in poverty-stricken areas at Appalachia," concludes with the following remarks:

In addition, the two medical men said they found in the mountain children a developing intimacy with the soil, the land's surface and variations, its changing height, its bodies of water, its ability to produce or supply ore. . . . Children learn to care for animals, to feed them and clean up after them, to help them in sickness . . . to have them, as company, a kind of uncomplicated, nonhuman company.

They told of a white mother who recently left Appalachia for the North. She had said: "You get up here and you get a job better than back home, but whether it's worth it or not, to tell the truth, I'm not sure. The other day I told my husband that I don't think my children ever see the earth any more. There are the buildings and the sidewalks and the roads, and then there's some more buildings. . . . I'm going to be telling my little kids that someday we'll go back home and they'll see what the earth looks like, and then they'll be able to walk as they please. . . .

It may be that these so-called "deprived" have something to teach us of the privileged city middle class. Perhaps there should be a reverse "poverty program."

The reasons medicine cannot cope well with this physical and social malaise are several. First, although we may admit to needs of nature (i.e., a "good" environment) to solve the problems of the human environment, it will take nothing short of a revolutionary reappraisal of our economic and social structures to truly preserve nature and its diversity. When people make money from the ecological miseries of others, one cannot talk of environmental health. Very frankly, industrial free enterprise and long-range human needs are hardly compatible. In the larger, longer evolutionary sense, truly free industrial enterprise in the use of nature is a shortsighted and inexcusable luxury. The expanding economy, likewise, is an economic mania based on technological self-delusion. Land-use planning will have to be based on motives of continuing use and not of profit. Our current faiths cannot, and will not, exist in the evolutionarily based homeostatic human community of the future, if indeed there is a future for man.

Second, the whole area of human adaptations to such subtle and deceptive factors as beauty, diversity, need for nature, and human reactions to crowding, noise, light, darkness, pollution, etc., that are closely interlinked with cultural factors from which they cannot easily be separated, is essentially unstudied. We simply don't know! We sense a relationship to depression and aggression, to low or high blood pressure, to neuroses and psychoses, and all the other ailments of what is generally referred to as modern high-speed technological city civilization, but these prevalent, mostly degenerative, disorders are much harder to understand than are earaches.

There are some interesting studies on this that are worth following up. Ardrey's *The Territorial Imperative* (1966) explores the genetically fixed attribute of territoriality as a basic animal attribute and tries to extend it even to man. Yet we have no conception of what the thwarting of this instinct does to decrease human happiness, or, for that matter, how much territoriality we have in us. Lorenz's *On Aggression* (1966) and several recent symposia dealing with aggression explore the roots of human conflicts, roots that were hammered out on the anvils of natural selection over millions of animal generations.

Other studies have shown that a person bored with monotony will show continuously highly vacillating alpha brain waves that keep his body on alert (this again, no doubt, evolutionarily selected). In a person whose mind or body is active, due to diversity of physical activity or mental processes, the brain waves will flatten out to beta-waves, which let his system relax more. Who knows what the monotony of asphalt jungles, or of cornfields, does to the nervous system of a man? And who cares to study it? Biotic and cultural diversity, from the neurological standpoint, then, may well be an important attribute to general health, a psychiatric safety valve that is not a luxury but an indispensable human need.

Support for the therapeutic effects of nature comes not only from the commonplace negative association of ill health with cities and slums and from the positive fact that we go vacationing in the natural diversity of mountain, seashore, or forest, but also from the therapeutic effects of the out-of-doors on the mentally ill. The interesting and encouraging results of M. Weismann et al. (1965) of Maryland in taking the chronically hospitalized (for 2 to 30 years) mentally ill out camping are worth noting. Here, hiking through the woods was, next to eating, the most cherished activity, and nearly 40% of the 90 patients were released into their communities within 3 months—this as a result of only a 2 weeks' camping experience. Other studies have shown similar results. Many factors may well be involved here; but, could one not suppose that, in a person whose cultural load has twisted his normal functioning into bizarre reactions, his most basic inner drives will be functioning like a psychological gyroscope especially well in the environment where they originally evolved millions of years ago? Leaves and trees do not talk back; they are a nonaggressive, neutral element, free of danger; and, especially important, they do not represent intraspecific competition. They rest the overstrained reaction system of the sick man to the point where he can, so to speak, pick up the pieces of his later-acquired evolutionary or social adaptations and begin to function in more complex spheres.

We may then quote for nature what Weston La Barre (in his *The Human Animal*, 1954) said in different context for the physiological pleasure of love: "rooted as it now is in Man's very autonomic nervous system—that ancient and unconscious smooth-muscle nerve net where the tides of animal appetites and feelings surge, deep below thinking and far earlier than words."

Obviously, it should not be necessary to enter a mental hospital to gain access to a good recreational program (and a chance to go hiking in nature), and yet there is a grain of truth in all this. Conversely, one wonders if a sound recreational program (including a deliberate effort to get large segments of the population into contact with nature) might not reduce the number entering mental hospitals. (W. C. Gibson).

In short, we have a lot to learn. As Sigmund Freud taught us about man's psychological adaptations, we can begin to understand the true meaning of the human environment only from an evolutionary view-point, and can implement our understanding only by planning in an ecologically meaningful way.

We have shown that only by understanding our evolutionary past can we plan a fulfilling present and a promising future. Only by recognizing what we are doing today can we predict the kind of life we may wish to have tomorrow. We have shown that, to remain a sensitive, well-adjusted human in the best sense, man needs nature. Yet we also recognize today that nature cannot survive the onslaught of modern man. If both of these suppositions are shown to be true, the future of *Homo sapiens* is bleak indeed.

This paradoxical problem can be solved in one of two ways: either by changing man through manipulation of our genotypes so that he can adapt to his new, depleted environment; or by the preservation of the nature to which man is now adapted.

The current "evolutionary optimism," the rather blind faith in the ability of man to adjust genetically and thus culturally to the desrtuction of his environment, is incongruous, not because man cannot change, but because, due to his long life span and genetic limitations, he could not possibly change fast enough. Today, man is modifying his environment so rapidly that soon all his adaptations will be out of phase. But, suppose he could keep up with this environmental deterioration. Suppose Dob-zhansky (1967) and some of the geneticists are right. Man, then, would gain smaller ears and less sensitive eyes, a toleration to crowding and pollution, and, as a consequence, lose all the most precious values of the human animal. The enjoyment of life and living, enjoyment of nature, of art and music, for example, would lose all meaning. And furthermore, these genetically fixed ecological idiots of the future, like many of our culturally fixed ecological idiots of today, would then control the fate of the living landscape, doubly accelerating its destruction. A "Brave New World" would indeed be upon us! If we can gain anything from Huxley's nightmare, it is that such a life would not be worth living. Yet it may be already late in the game. Has there been, or will there soon be, sufficient selection by the polluted, metropolitan environment to remove modern man's unspoken needs for open spaces, wild mountains, flowers, clean lakes, and small towns? Let us hope not! Let us hope that we value these assets highly today because we still need them.

NATURE'S NECESSARY DIVERSITY

The second point I wish to make is a practical one. We need nature and its diversity in order to survive as human beings, as well as a techno-logical and agricultural civilization. We must, therefore, accept that *nature is the most precious of all human possessions.* Our educational system's main responsibility, therefore, is to train people, not only in the exploitation, but now also in the protection of nature—the only nature to which man is adapted, in which man can exist.

We must, I think, learn to accept that the environmental sciences (including agriculture) will have to spend as much time in correcting the ecological consequences of human activities, or in preventing them, as worrying about increased exploitation of Nature.

Yet how preoccupied we are with an expanding economy and with progress, where increased production and quantity, not quality, are the main aims. Increased economic growth was, and is, after all, largely dependent on the rape of the redwoods, the destruction of buffalo or prairie, and the exploitation of the sea. To continue all this madness our schools must train properly indoctrinated citizens, not those who love flowers and butterflies, or those who protect nature!

Now that buttercups are rare, and springs silent, why study them? The ever-increasing emphasis on technology and the (until recently) continued deletion of natural history from the curriculum have slowly but surely produced generations of children who can, at most, distinguish a dandelion from a daisy, but to whom the fields and woods are a closed book. And where are they to learn? Teacher doesn't know; the curriculum makes no provision for natural history; and the public doesn't care. And most city kids have had to cease to wonder at natural beauty for other reasons as well—the simple unavailability to city schools of woods with song birds, of prairies with lilies. There is ample money for buying expensive laboratory benches for our schools, but none whatever for buying some wild land for learning.

Yet this cultural intensification of environmental ignorance is very dangerous. What American children and adults neglect to learn about American flowers or landscapes, or Russian or Chinese children about theirs, may bear strange and disastrous fruits in their own as well as in foreign lands. It is especially dangerous in the United States, since we, as the richest country in the world, now have the power of enforcing, economically or militarily, our economic ways on foreign cultures and alien agricultures and on biotic communities totally different from ours. We have the means and ways to change the face of the earth—and we are proceeding by destroying its diversity.

I could talk a great deal about the importance of diversity in nature and in agricultural stability, but Charles Elton (1958) has explained it much better than I ever could in *The Ecology of Invasion by Plants and Animals*. Furthermore, the fate of this diversity represents the fate of life, of future, and of continuing evolution and, therefore, very probably of man himself.

We must farm, but must we do it often so blindly? Must we destroy this diversity without heed to other values, including often direct agricultural ones? By pesticides and other means we are exterminating countless species of plants and animals and whole plant associations (such as the American Prairie) with a ferocity that only the human species is capable of, tens of thousands of species whose roles in the ecology of land we cannot even guess at, whose uses to man we do not even know, and will not know for many, many years to come. And, as David Gates recently said, we are depriving future generations of a chance to *ever* properly study or understand the living communities, the ecosystems, of the earth. Once extinct, a species or a community is gone forever.

Some concrete examples from my own experiences in Wisconsin and elsewhere illustrate how man in his blind rage to exterminate all but the edible and in his compulsive desire for unreasonably high profit is undermining his own self-interest.

Modern agricultural practices bring to mind two problems:

One is that of clean fences. In the Middle West there used to be strips of land between the fields with shrubs, flowers and animals— hedgerows with a rich life. Agriculture practice for many years encouraged clean fences as a sign of progress: no weeds, no pests—yea, and no songbirds either to eat insects, no pollinators such as bumble bees, no flowers that can survive for their own sake, no living barriers to catch the nutrients after a rain and prevent "flushing," no game animals to hunt; in short, no diversity whatever. Nothing but human misery can come out of such biotic simplifications. Today we do know better, so we artificially plant hedges of multiflora roses. But the diversity is gone. The new hedges are no substitutes for the old. Yet, in many Wisconsin and Illinois counties only a few years back, countless hedges were ripped out on the advice of county agents. Now we even plow the narrow strips of virgin prairies that accidentally survived along Illinois railroads to plant more corn and still more corn.

We build dams on the big rivers even though, as Albrecht (1956, p. 922) has shown, a great deal of the fertility of the Middle West comes from the dust that was blown out of the stream beds each winter. Will centuries of dustless winters have an effect on the corn belt? Do giant dams, no matter how wonderful technologically, justify agricultural disaster?

The chemical scene in agriculture has been discussed by Rachel Carson (1962)—the terrifying problem of the pesticides, long-lived compounds that tend to concentrate in the food chains and wreak havoc with life (see *Scientific American*, March 1967).

The sterility of eagles and depletion of other birds, the tremendous fish kills in our rivers, and the disappearance of countless insects are but some of the unforeseen side-effects of pesticides. Much more than half of the 50 species of Colombian parrots have become extinct during the past decades as a result of habitat destruction and pesticides, according to Roger Tory Peterson. Can we afford to continue to use these chemicals? Nevertheless, the entomologists talk about risk-benefit evaluations and the Ribicoff committee "found no reliable evidence to suggest that the benefit-risk equation was *presently* unbalanced in any *significant* ways, (but) much more information is needed. . . ."

It has been recently shown that most pesticides are *mutagenic* in plant tissue and very probably in animal tissue as well. Human fat tissue may contain from 2 to 30 ppm of DDT. The consequences of this are unknown. Thus pesticides are an example of the application of dangerous knowledge (in the sense of Van Potter), i.e., knowledge applied before we know the consequences of the application—a blind application.

In addition, there are some very interesting and disturbing side effects, nowhere so apparent as in insect pollination. As many species of plants have specific insect pollinators, destruction of these insects will eventually result in the extermination of the interrelated plant species. In central Wisconsin, for example, spraying which results in the death of certain local bee species of the genus *Osmia*, apparently specific on the plant *Penstemon wisconsinensis*, would eventually result in the death of the latter as well. Similarly delicate converse relationships are observed in the sexual response of the *Polyphemus* sp. moth to odors of oak species.

The destruction of populations in animal and plant species becomes critical long before the species is on the verge of extinction. A certain diversity in the genetic pool, and therefore a large population, is essential. Examples where minimal size will mean imminent extinction include our now decimated and fragmented prairie flora and animal species such as the whooping crane. Our experience with insecticides is largely based on results in glaciated areas with few or no endemic species. Applied to tropical areas with thousands of unique local species, the results on plant and animal diversity are catastrophic. Other mispractices in use of chemicals include the Green River poisoning by Rotenone and the spraying of elms. A recent *Milwaukee Journal* article reports a serious fish kill in the Wisconsin River and in a northern trout stream. Should not the agricultural schools support Senator Nelson's bill to outlaw nondegradable pesticides suc has DDT?

Domestic problems resulting in the destruction of life are many. We have few natural teaching areas, especially prairies. Yet the soil bank has had destructive effects on remaining areas of prairie, as do most midwestern highway "improvements." In our sense of "wastelands," of roadsides, of rivers and dunes, our attitude is to make the whole earth livable for man and his crops at the expense of most other factors.

Foreign Aid Programs. Our agricultural schools are not, despite considerable financial support, training local ecologists in these respective countries to study ecological factors as they occur there. Yet they should! Our approach has been to send our own biologists and have them reshape foreign lands into our own image by our methods. Examples include the introduction of alfalfa instead of using, or even studying, the numerous native legume species which are not even looked at (likewise the native grasses); introduction of higher yielding hybrids of potato, replacing a diversity of disease-resistant native potato clones; and destruction by bulldozer or 2–4D of the species-rich tropical forests of the Amazon Basin.

The shortsightedness and blindness of modern land use is staggering. We know so little about the things we are destroying. It is apparent that we need a radical, new, holistic approach to land use.

The far-reaching and irrevocable destructive effects of technology on nature have to be seen to be believed, especially in the fragile tropics; thus it will not do to stop the fearless "winnowing and sifting" of the truth at our universities and colleges. To encourage hundreds of students to regard Rachel Carson's *Silent Spring* (1962) with a smirk without being required to read it (or even inducing them not to read it), or to continue to preach cornucopic doctrines of superabundance and technological solutions to hunger, is to make students instruments of a carefully perpetuated ignorance, because, when selected knowledge is regarded as sin, ignorance must be transmitted in its stead. This will not do. We must reshape our agricultural horizons to ecological facts of life. The responsibilities are awful. For this is the only biosphere that is fit for man.

REFERENCES

Albrecht, W. A. 1956. *In* W. L. Thomas (ed.), Man's role in changing the face of the earth. Univ. Chicago Press.

Ardrey, R. 1966. The territorial imperative. Atheneum, New York. 390 p.

Carson, R. 1962. The silent spring. Houghton Mifflin, Boston. 368 p.

Dobzhansky, T. 1967. Changing man. Science 155:409–415. (cf. Iltis, H. H. 1967. A plea for man and nature. Science 167: 581.)

Elton, C. S. 1958. The ecology of invasions by animals and plants. Methuen and Co., London. 181 p.

La Barre, W. 1954. The human animal. Univ. Chicago Press, Chicago. 371 p.

Lorenz, K. 1966. On aggression. Harcourt, Brace & World, New York. 306 p.

Schaller, G. G. 1964. The year of the gorilla. Univ. Chicago Press, Chicago. 260 p.

Weisman, M. N., L. Mann, and B. W. Barker. 1965. Camping: an approach to releasing human potential in chronic mental patients. Mimeo., 9 p. (Delivered at 121st Annual Meeting. American Psychiatric Assoc., 7 May 1965.)

I am easily convinced by Iltis' argument of the need for green nature to relieve the monotony of gray concrete; or that, as Thoreau said, wildness really can be the preservation of mankind. Does my conviction come so easily because the three of us share a common truth or a common taste? My colleague at Bates College, Dr. Carl Straub, feels the incredible failure of the American people to create a truly civilized urban environment is rooted in their prejudices against the city itself. However widespread this prejudice is, I confess to find it in myself. It may be possible to create a truly civilized urban environment but I can't see myself living in it. Perhaps this is no more than to say that the optimum human environment must contain a sufficient variety of habitats to satisfy a variety of human needs. Of course, I am in a position to exercise a choice of habitat, whereas an increasing number of urban residents have no real choice. That is part of Iltis' urgent message.

It may be, of course, that man's power of adjustment (physiological and psychological), if not his genetic adaptability, will be an adequate basis for life in the technological era. If so, what concerns us here is the possibility of major changes in the quality of that life.

The kind of dehumanizing monotony that Hugh Iltis decries is not restricted to the largest urban areas. It spreads out to the shopping centers, the suburban housing developments, and even to the small towns. In the small city where I teach, an urban renewal project has removed a section of buildings and opened up a short segment of river bank. Before the start of the project a series of natural rock formations and clumps of tough, adventurous plants clung below the backs of the riverside buildings. Now the riverbank is restyled in a smooth curve and uniformly dressed with evenly sized stones. That little touch of wildness that had managed to hang on by its claws in spite of the buildings, dumping, and pollution has now been urbanized. In the small town where I live, a fine new regional high school has been built. It will be, I am assured, efficient. It may turn out students as well rounded as are the products of a ball-bearing factory. Only the sign in front would tell you which kind of institution you are passing. The interior is equally undisturbed by variety.

In an attempt to define an optimum human environment we can turn to the processes of organic evolution. The slow rate of genetic adaptation as contrasted with the rate of technological change is the basis for recommendations that we slow the rate of technological change and that we stabilize populations to minimize alteration of the ancestral habitat. We must, to follow these recommendations, assume control of our future evolution. We haven't the capacity at present to manipulate the genetic basis of our adaptability. We do have the capacity to shape our environment. What are the basic assumptions of the people to whom we recommend this awesome responsibility? Scott Paradise has a radical view of our community presuppositions.

THE VANDAL IDEOLOGY

Scott Paradise

Some call it an ecological crisis; others admit only to a variety of serious environmental problems ranging from pollution to ugliness. In any case, the bombardment of articles, books and television programs in the past few years have made us aware that something is wrong. Exploding populations, advancing technology and economic development have joined to face us with a triple threat. But except for a few voices, the depth of the difficulty eludes expression.

We assume, rightly, that more science and technology, better planning, or more adequate political arrangements are needed; but we assume, wrongly, that a combination of these will save us. The argument runs, if we lack as yet the political will to solve the problems, a few local catastrophes will surely bring us to our senses and force us in due course to achieve general solutions. While admitting that stricter regulation of polluters and developers will be necessary, we talk as though the American industrial system could survive without really radical modification.

The contrary is true. Not only must our industrial system be changed; the system of beliefs about man's relationship with the natural world which underlies it must be corrected if we are to escape the jaws of the coming crisis. This system of beliefs might be described as an ideology. It is almost always assumed. In one way or another, its propositions are often asserted as self-evident truths. In fact, their influence on social policy and the allegiance they hold over the majority of Americans should make envious the proponents of the traditional religions.

American ideology of man and nature might be reduced to the following seven propositions:

(1) Man is the source of all value. This is not *anthropocentrism* for that implies only that man is the center of value. Rather it is *anthroposolipsism*, which asserts that man alone has any inherent value. Everything else is valuable only as it benefits man.

(2) The universe exists only for man's use. This proposition is a corollary of the first. If man is the single source of value, anything which men

Reprinted with permission from *The Nation*, December 22, 1969, pp. 730–732. The author is Executive Director of The Boston Industrial Mission, 56 Boylston St., Cambridge, Mass.

cannot use is useless and can be destroyed without compunction. Some of us broaden the idea of usefulness to include things of scientific, aesthetic and ecological value. But in practice this belief more often further narrows the meaning of value to that which has calculable economic value. Thus if the world's whaling fleets find profit in exterminating the last of the great whales, the whales must go. No argument about either the rights of whales or their ecological value will be admitted. The only argument that might possibly have effect contends that more profit might be made if whaling were limited so as to guarantee a perpetual harvest of blubber and meat.

Since the universe exists only for man's use, man may with a crusader's zeal war against nature and bring it to unconditional surrender.

(3) Man's primary purpose is to produce and consume. This is the heart of the good life. We sometimes define man as the tool-using animal, *homo faber.* Theologians pronounce us co-creators with God. As co-creator, man has a license also to destroy and waste. In spite of such protests as the hippies represent, the work ethic still reigns. Neither a play ethic, nor a love ethic, nor a service ethic yet challenges it. Only a consumer ethic grapples with it for supremacy.

(4) Production and consumption must increase endlessly. Since life's primary purpose is producing and consuming, abundant life blesses us through increasing material abundance. Goods equal the good, and nothing can quench our infinite thirst for them. Growth of the gross national product defines progress and makes possible a continual and simultaneous increase in population and rise in standard of living. Those concerned with social justice see evil in that some nations have enjoyed too little economic growth; they see hope in the possibility that all nations will have more.

(5) Material resources are unlimited. The thrust of this proposition lies not in the absurdity that the finite Earth has infinite resources but rather that we do not need to heed the warnings of those concerned with their depletion. New deposits of minerals and fossil fuels are found every decade. Our technology of extraction constantly improves and enables us to develop deposits unreachable or uneconomical a few years ago. For those resources genuinely scarce we can find substitutes. Ultimately our technology will be equal to extracting all the raw materials we need for millions of years from sea water and the granite on the earth's surface. When worried voices speak of overcrowding, they need only be referred to the vast empty spaces on the map of the world and the statistics that 70 per cent of Americans are needlessly crammed together on a tiny fraction of the country's land surface. Even warnings about pollutions need not cause alarm because the human genius for short-range technical improvisation is equal to any crisis that is likely to arise.

(6) Man need not adapt himself to the natural environment since he can remake it to suit his own needs.   This assumption, sometimes referred to as "the bulldozer mentality," manifests itself most clearly when American military or business personnel live overseas. There they often create an environment more like that of continental United States than of the country in which they are stationed. We see it also in the possibility, sometimes realized through central heating and air conditioning, of never needing to spend more than a few minutes at a time in temperatures below 65 or above 75 degrees Fahrenheit from one year to the next. We see it in the vacationer who sprays his seaside acreage with DDT. On the other hand, while man need not adapt himself to the natural environment, it is assumed he can and must adjust to any stress perpetrated by his own technology. Smog, noise and ugliness come with progress, and man can and must learn to live with them.

(7) A major function of the state is to make it easy for individuals and corporations to exploit the environment to increase wealth and power. Ideas concerning private property stand central in this proposition. Because it has influenced the shape of the American social structures, it is easier for a lumber company to cut down redwoods than for the government to prevent it from doing so. It is easier for a developer to destroy a beautiful old mansion to make way for new ranch houses than for the public to organize a drive and raise money to save the historic house. It is easier for strip miners to destroy a countryside than for a legislature to pass preventive legislation or the courts to enforce it. All these business initiatives increase the gross national product. The government srtucture and operation is biased to encourage such development rather than effectively to protect the natural and cultural heritage.

Although people often assert each of these beliefs, most Americans would perhaps not subscribe to them when stated this baldly. Nevertheless, our social policy, both public and private, operates as if these were our beliefs. And not only does this system of beliefs run in the mainstream of American culture but it is also spreading to infect societies all over the world. Any nation wanting to industrialize will find a certain usefulness in it. It tends to free a society from a veneration of places and things which might inhibit their being used for economic development. It directs attention away from personal and family relationships, away from tradition and ceremonial. It offers a moral alternative to leisure. These ideas seem necessary in order to blast most nations out of ancient ways and set them on the road of development.

But in the long run the consequences of this ideology must be disastrous—first, because no organism can endlessly multiply and exploit its environment; second, because it betrays life's meaning to elevate the economic, technical and procreative processes to absolutes. In America where this ideology has long been dominant, people tend to forget that it is not self-evident and has not always been universally accepted. It contradicts assumptions around which most cultures have organized life throughout history. Even today in the developing nations many governments are struggling with wrongheaded persistence to win the unwilling and recalcitrant people of the villages to this ideology.

The profound challenge facing America today is whether we can discover a new orientation which will preserve the necessary values and the truths in the current ideology, and yet redirect our goals so as to preserve our environment and our humanity itself.

To correct the seven propositions just stated is a good place to begin. They might be restated thus:

(1) Man is to be valued more highly than other creatures. Such a proposition is truly anthropocentric. It puts man at the pinnacle of creation but does not isolate him as the only thing of value. Other creatures have beauty and splendor of their own.

That this kind of assertion perplexes many in the culture is hardly surprising. A nation that coined the phrase, "The only good Indian is a dead Indian," is not likely to defend the cause of wildlife. But moral progress follows a widening awareness of the circle of fellowship. If we see it as ethical advance to discover Indians as our brothers, it is a move in the same direction to recognize animals as our cousins. Some of the most eloquent spokesmen for this perception speak out of the scientific community. Men like Loren Eiseley and Konrad Lorenz, who have spent lifetimes sensitively observing nonhuman life, can tell us without sentimentality that many animals are capable of relationship with us. Unfortunately, they cannot say with like confidence that we are interested in relating to them.

But many cannot believe that anything has value not bestowed on it by men. Those so invincibly anthroposolipsists might just understand that the human race is not an island but a part of the whole community of life. If any species disappears, man and all the rest are diminished. The extermination of animal species attendant on the growth of human population reduces the variety, fascination and stability of the biosphere. And therefore it erodes the quality of human life.

(2) Man has become the guardian of the earth. His prerogatives to use the earth's resources are balanced by his responsibility to cherish them, protect them and use them carefully. Man does evil when he exterminates species of animals or does irreversible damage to the environment. When he does destroy life he needs to calculate the benefits he receives against the impoverishment of the living community. Man also is able to improve the environment. These changes entail disadvantages as well as benefits. Here, too, costs as well as benefits need to be carefully calculated before the project which will effect the change is undertaken.

(3) Man is far more than a producer and consumer.   Without production and consumption, of course, life cannot continue. But without singing, dancing or poetry, without loving, discovering or learning, without art, music or drama, life is hardly worth continuing. By participating in these pursuits in concert we lay hold of our humanity. The model of life as mass production and massive consumption is only one of many possible models. Most cultures throughout most of the human experience have been decidedly less obsessed than we with getting and spending. A recent study of the Kung Bushmen in the Kalihari Desert reports that on the average these people spend only three days a week food gathering and hunting. During the remaining four days they vigorously pursue noneconomic activities. Such a record, while perhaps arousing the wrath of their work-oriented fathers, would fill many of today's youth with envy and admiration. Our massive affluence should make it possible to emulate the Bushmen to some degree and so recover new dimensions of our humanity.

(4) Improvement in the quality of life takes precedence over increasing the quantity of material production.   The growth of the gross national product does not necessarily lead to an enlargement of human well-being. It may in some instances lead to the opposite. Our social goal should be to achieve a zero rate of population increase and a state of increasing human well-being with a minimum increase in material production and consumption. Herein lies a new understanding of efficiency. In the long run this policy should lead to a state of relative equilibrium between the human race and the natural environment. But within this relative equilibrium men could make great progress in the arts, literature, sciences and human relationships.

(5) Material resources are to be used carefully and cherished.   The assumption of limitless resources breeds indifference to waste and to the likely needs of our descendants. This indifference drains us of joy and appreciation for things in the intoxication of consumption. Russell Baker observed in *The New York Times* that to transform goods into trash as quickly and efficiently as possible has become America's major pastime. On the other hand, human fulfillment comes not through an ascetic denial of the value of material things but by passionately and sensitively embracing them. Using and loving a few things long and carefully leads to a different kind of experience, a more profoundly fulfilling one, than does the careless use and abandonment of many things in rapid succession. We need a new materialism to replace the consumerism which now goes by that name.

(6) Man is to relate himself to the natural environment, remaking it according to its nature as well as for the sake of his short-term economic advantage.   Such considerations in many instances might deter us from covering superb farm land with parking lots, shopping centers and sub-

urban subdivisions, or from carelessly filling or polluting intensely rich protein-producing wetlands and estuaries. It might save us from building expressways on some or our urban shore lines or trying to farm areas whose soil will predictably respond by becoming wasteland. Man's power to improve the world for his own use is not unlimited. His actions on it result in ecological reactions. He is part of a living web which responds when he acts and forces him to respond when it acts. Such a pattern of mutual action and reaction may be described as a relationship. In most instances man rightly claims the initiative and determines the quality of the relationship. But to make war on nature and force it to an unconditional surrender will lead to unexpected and disconcerting counterattacks. To win final victory requires that we make a desert and call it peace.

(7) A major function of the state is to supervise a planning process which will prevent the impairment of the quality of the environment. This proposition implies a different conception of the rights of property. Land and resources cannot be seen as ours in the sense that we can abuse or destroy them for profit or pleasure. Instead, the right to hold and develop them depends on these actions contributing to the public good and preserving the quality of the environment. Of course, this principle can be applied only with complicated calculations of costs and benefits, but too often the calculations are still being made on the assumption that measures for private gain usually lead to public benefit and that short-run, measurable economic advantage is an adequate criterion for determining action. The burden of proof must be shifted from those who would preserve the environment to those who would exploit it, and from those who would limit property rights in the interest of public and environment to those who would defend such rights for private advantage.

These suggested modifications of our beliefs about man's relationship with nature are perhaps so radical as to be almost incomprehensible to many. Nevertheless, such thoughts are increasingly in the air. Conservationists, ecologists, hippies and certain groups of the New Left have created a climate in which such ideas have become more plausible than they were only a few years ago. [See "Man in Nature: Model for a New Radicalism" by Catherine Riegger Harris, *The Nation*, November 10.] Most of us, however, still doggedly embrace the hope that we can continue in the present course and save our society by tinkering. We still prefer to hope that if we reduce the military budget, develop better urban planning and pollution-control techniques, and enlarge the war against poverty, all will be well.

Technological forecasters and other futurists are still debating whether such a hope is realistic. The supposition that "something will turn up" to retrieve the situation can keep the hope alive and the argument continuing beyond the point of no return.

And, of course, it is just possible that the present system can continue on approximately its present path. But even if it can, argument can be made that it shouldn't. The perceptions and commitments suggested in the modified statement of belief serve as a far more satisfying basis for human fulfillment than does the current ideology. A society that would emerge from this new vision might have powerful appeal. Rebellious youth and growing interest in conservation may be straws in the wind to suggest that it would. In this appeal may lie seeds of revolution.

In the final paper of this collection, Beryl Crowe takes us back to our starting point. In The Tragedy of the Commons Revisited, *the problems that Hardin sees as having no technical solutions are given little chance of a political solution. In the course of the argument (see page 232), the life history of a typical regulatory commission is presented. You may feel that this description of the method by which both our political parties attempt to regulate the commons is too cynical. To anticipate such a reaction I present, in lieu of editorial comment, the following excerpt from the May 15, 1970,* Conservation News, *published by the National Wildlife Federation, Washington, D.C. (pp. 14–15).*

A Bad Year for Cabbage

As of April 9 the biggest industrialists of them all are advising the President and his fledgling Council on Environmental Quality on how to fight pollution. In a little-noticed executive order the President appointed 53 industrial magnates to be members of the National Industrial Pollution Control Council. . . .

The creation of the council probably would have passed unnoticed if Montana Senator Lee Metcalf hadn't called attention to it shortly thereafter on the floor of the Senate. The Council members, Metcalf observed, "are the leaders of the industries which contribute most to environmental pollution. . . ." Where, asks Metcalf, is a council of "the hitherto silent majority which is now becoming aroused by industrial pollution?" And he points out, "There is not even for window-dressing, a council composed of those ecologists, students, earthlovers and plain old-fashioned conservationists who have forced the administration and big industries to take some action regarding environmental protection."

Rather, says Metcalf, "Let us tell it like it is: The purpose of industry advisory committees to Government is to enhance corporate image, to create an illusion of action and to impede Government officials who are attempting to enforce law and order and gather the data upon which enforcement is based. . . ." Or as Colman McCarthy of *The Washington Post* concluded, "Until the President appoints an advisory pollution council composed of independent citizens with nothing at stake but their lungs and the balance of nature, the goats will continue to guard the cabbage patch."

THE TRAGEDY
OF THE COMMONS REVISITED

Beryl Crowe

There has developed in the contemporary natural sciences a recognition that there is a subset of problems, such as population, atomic war, and environmental corruption, for which there are no technical solutions (1, 2). There is also an increasing recognition among contemporary social scientists that there is a subset of problems, such as population, atomic war, environmental corruption, and the recovery of a livable urban environment, for which there are no current political solution (3). The thesis of this article is that the common area shared by these two subsets contains most of the critical problems that threaten the very existence of contemporary man.

The importance of this area has not been raised previously because of the very structure of modern society. This society, with its emphasis on differentiation and specialization, has led to the development of two insular scientific communities—the natural and the social—between which there is very little communication and a great deal of envy, suspicion, disdain, and competition for scarce resources. Indeed, these two communities more closely resemble tribes living in close geographic proximity on university campuses than they resemble the "scientific culture" that C. P. Snow placed in contrast to and opposition to the "humanistic culture" (4).

Perhaps the major problems of modern society have, in large part, been allowed to develop and intensify through this structure of insularity and specialization because it serves both psychological and professional functions for both scientific communities. Under such conditions, the natural sciences can recognize that some problems are not technically soluble and relegate them to the nether land of politics, while the social sciences recognize that some problems have no current political solutions and then postpone a search for solutions while they wait for new technologies with which to attack the problem. Both sciences can thus avoid responsibility and protect their respective myths of competence and relevance, while they avoid having to face the awesome and awful possibilty that each has independently isolated the same subset of problems and given them different names. Thus, both never have to face the conse-

Reprinted with permission from *Science*, Vol. 166, 1969, pp. 1103–1107. Copyright © 1969 by the American Association for the Advancement of Science. The author is Assistant Professor of Political Science at Evergreen State College, Olympia, Wash.

quences of their respective findings. Meanwhile, due to the specialization and insularity of modern society, man's most critical problems lie in limbo, while the specialists in problem-solving go on to less critical problems for which they can find technical or political solutions.

In this circumstance, one psychologically brave, but professionally foolhardy soul, Garrett Hardin, has dared to cross the tribal boundaries in his article "The tragedy of the commons" (1). In it, he gives vivid proof of the insularity of the two scientific tribes in at least two respects: first, his "rediscovery" of the tragedy was in part wasted effort, for the knowledge of this tragedy is so common in the social sciences that it has generated some fairly sophisticated mathematical models (5); second, the recognition of the existence of a subset of problems for which science neither offers nor aspires to offer technical solutions is not likely, under the contemporary conditions of insularity, to gain wide currency in the social sciences. Like Hardin, I will attempt to avoid the psychological and professional benefits of this insularity by tracing some of the political and social implications of his proposed solution to the tragedy of the commons.

The commons is a fundamental social institution that has a history going back through our own colonial experience to a body of English common law which antidates the Roman conquest. That law recognized that in societies there are some environmental objects which have never been, and should never be, exclusively appropriated to any individual or group of individuals. In England the classic example of the commons is the pasturage set aside for public use, and the "tragedy of the commons" to which Hardin refers was a tragedy of overgrazing and lack of care and fertilization which resulted in erosion and underproduction so destructive that there developed in the late 19th century an enclosure movement. Hardin applies this social institution to other environmental objects such as water, atmosphere, and living space.

The cause of this tragedy is exposed by a very simple mathematical model, utilizing the concept of utility drawn from economics. Allowing the utilities to range between a positive value of 1 and a negative value of 1, we may ask, as did the individual English herdsman, what is the utility to me of adding one more animal to my herd that grazes on the commons? His answer is that the positive utility is near 1 and the negative utility is only a fraction of minus 1. Adding together the component partial utilities, the herdsman concludes that it is rational for him to add another animal to his herd; then another, and so on. The tragedy to which Hardin refers develops because the same rational conclusion is reached by each and every herdsman sharing the commons.

ASSUMPTIONS NECESSARY TO AVOID THE TRAGEDY

In passing the technically insoluble, problems over to the political and social realm for solution, Hardin has made three critical assumptions: (i) that there exists, or can be developed, a "criterion of judgment and a system of weighting . . ." that will "render the incommensurables . . . commensurable . . ." in real life; (ii) that, possessing this criterion of judgment, "coercion can be mutually agreed upon," and that the application of coercion to effect a solution to problems will be effective in modern society; and (iii) that the administrative system, supported by the criterion of judgment and access to coercion, can and will protect the commons from further desecration.

If all three of these assumptions were correct, the tragedy which Hardin has recognized would dissolve into a rather facile melodrama of setting up administrative agencies. I believe these three assumptions are so questionable in contemporary society that a tragedy remains in the full sense in which Hardin used the term. *Under contemporary conditions, the subset of technically insoluble problems is also politically insoluble, and thus we witness a full-blown tragedy wherein "the essence of dramatic tragedy is not unhappiness. It resides in the remorseless working of things."* [My italics.]

The remorseless working of things in modern society is the erosion of three social myths which form the basis for Hardin's assumptions, and this erosion is proceeding at such a swift rate that perhaps the myths can neither revitalize nor reformulate in time to prevent the "population bomb" from going off, or before an accelerating "pollution immersion," or perhaps even an "atomic fallout."

ERODING MYTH OF THE COMMON VALUE SYSTEM

Hardin is theoretically correct, from the point of view of the behavioral sciences, in his argument that "in real life incommensurables *are* commensurable." He is, moreover, on firm ground in his assertion that to fulfill this condition in real life one needs only "a criterion of judgment and a system of weighting." In real life, however, values are the criteria of judgment, and the system of weighting is dependent upon the ranging of a number of conflicting values in a hierarchy. That such a system of values exists beyond the confines of the nation-state is hardly tenable. At this point in time one is more likely to find such a system of values within the boundaries of the nation-state. Moreover, the nation-state is the only political unit of sufficient dimension to find and enforce political solutions to Hardin's subset of "technically insoluble problems." It is on this political unit that we will fix our attention.

In America there existed, until very recently, a set of conditions which perhaps made the solution to Hardin's problem subset possible: we lived with the myth that we were "one people, indivisible. . . ." This myth postulated that we were the great "melting pot" of the world wherein the diverse cultural ores of Europe were poured into the crucible of the frontier experience to produce a new alloy—an American civilization. This new civilization was presumably united by a common value system that was democratic, equalitarian, and existing under universally enforceable rules contained in the Constitution and the Bill of Rights.

In the United States today, however, there is emerging a new set of behavior patterns which suggest that the myth is either dead or dying. Instead of believing and behaving in accordance with the myth, large sectors of the population are developing life-styles and value hierarchies that give contemporary Americans an appearance more closely analogous to the particularistic, primitive forms of "tribal" organizations living in geographic proximity than to that shining new alloy, the American civilization.

With respect to American politics, for example, it is increasingly evident that the 1960 election was the last election in the United States to be played out according to the rules of pluralistic politics in a two-party system. Certainly 1964 was, even in terms of voting behavior, a contest between the larger tribe that was still committed to the pluralistic model of compromise and accommodation within a winning coalition, and an emerging tribe that is best seen as a millennial revitalization movement directed against mass society—a movement so committed to the revitalization of old values that it would rather lose the election than compromise its values. Under such circumstances former real-life commensurables within the Republican Party suddenly became incommensurable.

In 1968 it was the Democratic Party's turn to suffer the degeneration of commensurables into incommensurables as both the Wallace tribe and the McCarthy tribe refused to play by the old rules of compromise, accommodation, and exchange of interests. Indeed, as one looks back on the 1968 election, there seems to be a common theme in both these camps— a theme of return to more simple and direct participation in decision-making that is only possible in the tribal setting. Yet, despite this similarity, both the Wallaceites and the McCarthyites responded with a value perspective that ruled out compromise and they both demanded a drastic change in the dimension in which politics is played. So firm were the value commitments in both of these tribes that neither (as was the case with the Goldwater forces in 1964) was willing to settled for a modicum of power that could accrue through the processes of compromise with the national party leadership.

Still another dimension of this radical change in behavior is to be seen in the black community where the main trend of the argument seems to be, not in the direction of accommodation, compromise, and integration, but rather in the direction of fragmentation from the larger community, intransigence in the areas where black values and black culture are concerned, and the structuring of a new community of like-minded and like-colored people. But to all appearances even the concept of color is not enough to sustain commensurables in their emerging community as it fragments into religious nationalism, seculiar nationalism, integrationists, separationists, and so forth. Thus those problems which were commensurable, both interracial and intraracial, in the era of integration become incommensurable in the era of Black Nationalism.

Nor can the growth of commensurable views be seen in the contemporary youth movements. On most of the American campuses today there are at least ten tribes involved in "tribal wars" among themselves and against the "imperialistic" powers of those "over 30." Just to tick them off, without any attempt to be comprehensive, there are: the up-tight protectors of the status quo who are looking for middle-class union cards, the revitalization movements of the Young Americans for Freedom, the reformists of pluralism represented by the Young Democrats and the Young Republicans, those committed to New Politics, the Students for a Democratic Society, the Yippies, the Flower Children, the Black Students Union, and the Third World Liberation Front. The critical change in this instance is not the rise of new groups; this is expected within the pluralistic model of politics. What is new are value positions assumed by these groups which lead them to make demands, not as points for bargaining and compromise with the opposition, but rather as points which are "not negotiable." Hence, they consciously set the stage for either confrontation or surrender, but not for rendering incommensurables commensurable.

Moving out of formalized politics and off the campus, we see the remnants of the "hippie" movement which show clear-cut tribal overtones in their commune movements. This movement has, moreover, already fragmented into an urban tribe which can talk of guerrilla warfare against the city fathers, while another tribe finds accommodation to urban life untenable without sacrificing its values and therefore moves out to the "Hog Farm," "Morning Star," or "Big Sur." Both hippie tribes have reduced the commensurables with the dominant WASP tribe to the point at which one of the cities of the Monterey Peninsula felt sufficiently threatened to pass a city ordinance against sleeping in trees, and the city of San Francisco passed a law against sitting on sidewalks.

Even among those who still adhere to the pluralistic middle-class American image, we can observe an increasing demand for a change in the dimension of life and politics that has disrupted the elementary social processes: the demand for neighborhood (tribal?) schools, control over redevelopment projects, and autonomy in the setting and payment of rents to slumlords. All of these trends are more suggestive of tribalism than of the growth of the range of commensurables with respect to the commons.

We are, moreover, rediscovering other kinds of tribes in some very odd ways. For example, in the educational process, we have found that one of our first and best empirical measures in terms both of validity and reproducibility—the I. Q. test—is a much better measure of the existence of different linguistic tribes than it is a measure of "native intellect" (6). In the elementary school, the different languages and different values of these diverse tribal children have even rendered the commensurables that obtained in the educational system suddenly incommensurable.

Nor are the empirical contradictions of the common value myth as new as one might suspect. For example, with respect to the urban environment, at least 7 years ago Scott Greer was arguing that the core city was sick and would remain sick until a basic sociological movement took place in our urban environment that would move all the middle classes to the suburbs and surrender the core city to the ". . . segregated, the insulted, and the injured" (7). This argument by Greer came at a time when most of us were still talking about compromise and accommodation of interests, and was based upon a perception that the life styles, values, and needs of these two groups were to disparate that a healthy, creative restructuring of life in the core city could not take place until pluralism had been replaced by what amounted to geographic or territorial tribalism; only when this occurred would urban incommensurables become commensurable.

Looking at a more recent analysis of the sickness of the core city, Wallace F. Smith has argued that the productive model of the city is no longer viable for the purposes of economic analysis (8). Instead, he develops a model of the city as a site for leisure consumption, and then seems to suggest that the nature of this model is such that the city cannot regain its health because it cannot make decisions, and that it cannot make decisions because the leisure demands are value-based and, hence, do not admit of compromise and accommodation; consequently there is no way of deciding among these various value-oriented demands that are being made on the core city.

In looking for the cause of erosion of the myth of a common value system, it seems to me that so long as our perceptions and knowledge of other groups were formed largely through the written media of communication, the American myth that we were a giant melting pot of equalitarians could be sustained. In such a perceptual field it is tenable, if not obvious, that men are motivated by interests. Interests can always be compromised and accommodated without undermining our very being by sacrificing values. Under the impact of the electronic media, however, this psychological distance has broken down and we now discover that these people with whom we could formerly compromise on interests are not, after all, really motivated by interests but by values. Their behavior in our very living room betrays a set of values, moreover, that are incompatible with our own, and consequently the compromises that we make are not those of contract but of culture. While the former are acceptable, any form of compromise on the latter is not a form of rational behavior but is rather a clear case of either apostasy or heresy. Thus, we have arrived not at an age of accommodation but one of confrontation. In such an age "incommensurables" remain "incommensurable" in real life.

EROSION OF THE MYTH OF THE MONOPOLY OF COERCIVE FORCE

In the past, those who no longer subscribed to the values of the dominant culture were held in check by the myth that the state possessed a monopoly on coercive force. This myth has undergone continual erosion since the end of World War II owing to the success of the strategy of guerrilla warfare, as first revealed to the French in Indochina, and later conclusively demonstrated in Algeria. Suffering as we do from what Senator Fulbright has called "the arrogance of power," we have been extremely slow to learn the lesson in Vietnam, although we now realize that war is political and cannot be won by military means. It is apparent that the myth of the monopoly of coercive force as it was first qualified in the civil rights conflict in the South, then in our urban ghettos, next on the streets of Chicago, and now on our college campuses has lost its hold over the minds of Americans. The technology of guerrilla warfare has made it evident that, while the state can win battles, it cannot win wars of values. Coercive force which is centered in the modern state cannot be sustained in the face of the active resistance of some 10 percent of its population unless the state is willing to embark on a deliberate policy of genocide directed against the value dissident groups. The factor that sustained the myth of coercive force in the past was the acceptance of a common value system. Whether the latter exists is questionable in the modern nation-state. But, even if most members of the nation-state remain united around a common value system which makes incommensurables for the majority commensurable, that majority is incapable of enforcing its decisions upon the minority in the face of the diminished coercive power of the governing body of the nation-state.

EROSION OF THE MYTH OF ADMINISTRATORS OF THE COMMONS

Hardin's thesis that the administrative arm of the state is capable of legislating temperance accords with current administrative theory in political science and touches on one of the concerns of that body of theory when he suggests that the ". . . great challenge facing us now is to invent the corrective feedbacks that are needed to keep the custodians honest."

Our best empirical answers to the question—*Quis custodiet ipsos custodes?*—"Who shall watch the watchers themselves?"—have shown fairly conclusively (9) that the decisions, orders, hearings, and press releases of the custodians of the commons, such as the Federal Communications Commission, the Interstate Commerce Commission, the Federal Trade Commission, and even the Bureau of Internal Revenue, give the large but unroganized groups in American society symbolic satisfaction and assurances. Yet, the actual day-to-day decisions and operations of these administrative agencies contribute, foster, aid, and indeed legitimate the special claims of small but highly organized groups to differential access to tangible resources which are extracted from the commons. This has been so well documented in the social sciences that the best answer to the question of who watches over the custodians of the commons is the regulated interests that make incursions on the commons.

Indeed, the process has been so widely commented upon that one writer has postulated a common life cycle for all of the attempts to develop regulatory policies (10). This life cycle is launched by an outcry so widespread and demanding that it generates enough political force to bring about the establishment of a regulatory agency to insure the equitable, just, and rational distribution of the advantages among all holders of interest in the commons. This phase is followed by the symbolic reassurance of the offended as the agency goes into operation, developing a period of political quiescence among the great majority of those who hold a general but unorganized interest in the commons. Once this political quiescence has developed, the highly organized and specifically interested groups who wish to make incursions into the commons bring sufficient pressure to bear through other political processes to convert the agency to the protection and furthering of their interests. In the last phase even staffing of the regulating agency is accomplished by drawing the agency administrators from the ranks of the regulated.

Thus, it would seem that, even with the existence of a common value system accompanied by a viable myth of the monopoly of coercive force, the prospects are very dim for saving the commons from differential exploitation or spoliation by the administrative devices in which Hardin places his hope. This being the case, the natural sciences may absolve themselves of responsibility for meeting the environmental challenges of the contemporary world by relegating those problems for which there are no technical solutions to the political or social realm. This action will, however, make little contribution to the solution of the problem.

ARE THE CRITICAL PROBLEMS OF MODERN SOCIETY INSOLUBLE?

Earlier in this article I agreed that perhaps until very recently, there existed a set of conditions which made the solution of Hardin's problem subset possible; now I suggest that the concession is questionable. There is evidence of structural as well as value problems which make comprehensive solutions impossible and these conditions have been present for some time.

For example, Aaron Wildavsky, in a comprehensive study of the budgetary process, has found that in the absence of a calculus for resolving "intrapersonal comparison of utilities," the governmental budgetary process proceeds by a calculus that is sequential and incremental rather than comprehensive. This being the case ". . . if one looks at politics as a process by which the government mobilizes resources to meet pressing problems" (*11*) the budget is the focus of these problem responses and the responses to problems in contemporary America are not the sort of comprehensive responses required to bring order to a disordered environment. Another example of the operation of this type of rationality is the American involvement in Vietnam; for, what is the policy of escalation but the policy of sequential incrementalism given a new Madison Avenue euphemism? The question facing us all is the question of whether incremental rationality is sufficient to deal with 20th-century problems.

The operational requirements of modern institutions makes incremental rationality the only viable form of decision-making, but this only raises the prior question of whether there are solutions to any of the major problems raised in modern society. It may well be that the emerging forms of tribal behavior noted in this article are the last hope of reducing political and social institutions to a level where incommensurables become commensurable in terms of values *and* in terms of comprehensive responses to problems. After all, in the history of man on earth we might well assume that the departure from the tribal experience is a short-run deviant experiment that failed. As we stand "on the eve of destruction," it may well be that the return to the face-to-face life in the small community unmediated by the electronic media is a very functional response in terms of the perpetuation of the species.

There is, I believe, a significant sense in which the human environment is directly in conflict with the source of man's ascendancy among the other species of the earth. *Man's evolutionary position hinges, not on specialization, but rather on generalized adaptability.* [My italics.] Modern social and political institutions, however, hinge on specialized, sequential, incremental decision-making and not on generalized adaptability. This being the case, life in the nation-state will continue to require a singleness of purpose for success but in a very critical sense this singleness of purpose becomes a straightjacket that makes generalized adaptation impossible. Nowhere is this conflict more evident than in our urban centers where there has been a decline in the livability of the total environment that is almost directly proportionate to the rise of special purpose districts. Nowhere is this conflict between institutional singleness of purpose and the human dimension of the modern environment more evident than in the recent warning of S. Goran Lofroth, chairman of a committee studying pesticides for the Swedish National Research Council, that many breast-fed children ingest from their mother's milk "more than the recommended daily intake of DDT" (12) and should perhaps be switched to cow's milk because cows secrete only 2 to 10 percent of the DDT they ingest.

HOW CAN SCIENCE CONTRIBUTE
TO THE SAVING OF THE COMMONS?

It would seem that, despite the nearly remorseless working of things, science has some interim contributions to make to the alleviation of those problems of the commons which Hardin has pointed out.

The contributions can come at two levels:

1) Science can concentrate more of its attention on the development of technological responses which at once alleviate those problems and reward those people who no longer desecrate the commons. This approach would seem more likely to be successful than the ". . . fundamental extension in morality . . ." by administrative law; the engagement of interest seems to be a more reliable and consistent motivator of advantage-seeking groups than does administrative wrist-slapping or constituency pressure from the general public.

2) Science can perhaps, by using the widely proposed environmental monitoring systems, use them in such a way as to sustain a high level of "symbolic disassurance" among the holders of generalized interests in the commons—thus sustaining their political interest to a point where they would provide a constituency for the administrator other than those bent on denuding the commons. This latter approach would seem to be a first step toward the ". . . invention of the corrective feedbacks that are needed to keep custodians honest." This would require a major change in the behavior of science, however, for it could no longer rest content with development of the technology of monitoring and with turning the technology over to some new agency. Past administrative experience suggests that the use of technology to sustain a high level of "dis-assurance" among the general population would also require science to take up the role and the responsibility for maintaining, controlling, and disseminating the information.

Neither of these contributions to maintaining a habitable environment will be made by science unless there is a significant break in the insularity of the two scientific tribes. For, if science must, in its own insularity, embark on the independent discovery of "the tragedy of the commons," along with the parameters that produce the tragedy, it may be too slow a process to save us from the total destruction of the planet. Just as important, however, science will, by pursuing such a course, divert its attention from the production of technical tools, information, and solutions which will contribute to the political and social solutions for the problems of the commons.

Because I remain very suspicious of the success of either demands or pleas for fundamental extensions in morality, I would suggest that such a conscious turning by both the social and the natural sciences is, at this time, in their immediate self-interest. As Michael Polanyi has pointed out, ". . . encircled today between the crude utilitarianism of the philistine and the ideological utilitarianism of the modern revolutionary movement, the love of pure science may falter and die" (*13*). The sciences, both social and natural, can function only in a very special intellectual environment that is neither universal or unchanging, and that environment is in jeopardy. The questions of humanistic relevance raised by the students at M.I.T., Stanford Research Institute, Berkeley, and wherever the headlines may carry us tomorrow, pose serious threats to the maintenance of that intellectual environment. However ill-founded *some* of the questions raised by the new generation may be, it behooves us to be ready with at least some collective, tentative answers—if only to maintain an environment in which both sciences will be allowed and fostered. This will not be accomplished so long as the social sciences continue to defer the most criticial problems that face mankind to future technical advances, while the natural sciences continue to defer those same problems which are about to overwhelm all mankind to false expectations in the political realm.

REFERENCES AND NOTES

1. G. Hardin, *Science* **162**, 1243 (1968).
2. J. B. Wiesner and H. F. York, *Sci. Amer.* **211** (No. 4), 27 (1964).
3. C. Woodbury, *Amer. J. Public Health* **45**, 1 (1955); S. Marquis, *Amer. Behav. Sci.* **11**, 11 (1968); W. H. Ferry, *Center Mag.* **2**, 2 (1969).
4. C. P. Snow, *The Two Cultures and the Scientific Revolution* (Cambridge Univ. Press, New York, 1959).
5. M. Olson, Jr., *The Logic of Collective Action* (Harvard Univ. Press, Cambridge, Mass., 1965).
6. G. A. Harrison *et al.*, *Human Biology* (Oxford Univ. Press, New York, 1964), p. 292; W. W. Charters, Jr. in *School Children in the Urban Slum* (Free Press, New York, 1967).
7. S. Greer, *Governing the Metropolis* (Wiley, New York, 1962), p. 148.
8. W. F. Smith, "The Class Struggle and the Disquieted City," a paper pre-

sented at the 1969 annual meeting of the Western Economic Association, Oregon State University, Corvallis.

9. M. Bernstein, *Regulating Business by Independent Commissions* (Princeton Univ. Press, Princeton, N.J., 1955); E. P. Herring, *Public Administration and the Public Interest* (McGraw-Hill, New York, 1936); E. M. Redford, *Administration of National Economic Control* (Macmillan, New York, 1952).

10. M. Edelman, *The Symbolic Uses of Politics* (Univ. of Illinois Press, Urbana, 1964).

11. A. Wildavsky, *The Politics of the Budgetary Process* (Little Brown, Boston, Boston, Mass., 1964).

12. Corvallis *Gazette-Times*, 6 May 1969, p. 6.

13. M. Polanyi, *Personal Knowledge* (Harper & Row, New York, 1964), p. 182.

IN CONCLUSION

If our major problems have no technical solutions, and no political solutions—where do we go from here? Beryl Crowe argues that extensions of morality are unlikely. Garrett Hardin argues that appeals to conscience are not only useless but dangerous. Scott Paradise suggests that only truly revolutionary changes in our attitudes will help. Where do we go from here? Do we know enough about our own biology and ecology to be sure our future actions will not disrupt or cause irreversible changes in our environment? Are we wise enough to create an environment with a sufficient variety of habitats as well as sufficient energy, food, and shelter?

We cannot read Hardin's, Crowe's, or Paradise's paper as a rejection of traditional values. The thinking of all three is deeply enmeshed in those values. What their various treatments do reveal is the subjugation of those values to short-range expediency and the application of those values to a circle of concern so limited as to exclude the true self-interest of society. The circle of concern radiating out from our ego toward the ecosystem has not yet fully closed around the members of our own species, much less nonhuman species or our nonliving environment.

Beryl Crowe asks the academic community to deal with current demands for campus reform in order that the opportunity for continued study and research can be preserved—so that science can at least provide some short-term relief for our major problems. Such relief is unlikely, she says, as long as the natural sciences and the social sciences mutually defer to each other for solutions. Any relief is unlikely unless we all cease to defer the questions of value to others.

The basic problem of value cannot be delegated by natural sciences to the social sciences or by the social sciences to the humanities. There is no escape from the responsibility for each individual to admit to and to deal with the primary problem of value which arises as a necessary consequence of living and working. A prudent society would do all it could to slow the onrush of "progress" to allow time for a thoughtful, integrated search, not just for knowledge, but also for solutions.

In conclusion I offer a series of quotations from the articles in this collection. They may serve as kind of summary, as topics for discussion, or as stimuli for further study.

Natural selection commensurates the incommensurables. (Hardin)

Men join in a chain of decisions which facilitate the emergence of a new symbiotic relationship to nature—that is, we create civilization and culture. (Means)

Some consume beauty for gain; but all of us must consume it to live. (Tuan)

The laws of Nature apply to man as they do to animals. There are no exceptions. (Kendeigh)

Life on our planet is dependent upon the cycle of elements in the biosphere. (Bormann and Likens)

Pesticides are the greatest single tool for simplifying the habitat ever conceived by the simple mind of man, who may yet prove too simple to grasp the fact that he is but a blind strand of an ecosystem web, dependent not upon himself, but upon the total web, which nevertheless he has the power to destroy. (Niering)

We are too affluent to be able to afford the use of our "night soil." (Hasler)

. . . they [radioactive waste storage tanks] will require maintenance, cooling and replacement of corroded tank-walls when the obliteration of Hiroshima is as remote as the fall of Constantinople. (Patterson)

We know that as far as our interests in the next decades are concerned, pollution operates on the time scale of succession, not of evolution, and we cannot look to evolution to cure this set of problems. (Woodwell)

If there is a population problem . . . reductions in the mortality rate are part of the solution, rather than the cause, of the problem. (Frederiksen)

Whenever the density of a population becomes increased beyond that level to which the heredity-to-environment relationship provides optimum adjustment, then the individual and the group must forfeit some of their potentials of behavior . . . (Calhoun)

Very frankly, industrial free enterprise and long-range human needs are hardly compatible. (Iltis)

A major function of the state is to supervise a planning process which will prevent the impairment of the quality of the environment. (Paradise)

. . . due to the specialization and insularity of modern society, man's most critical problems lie in limbo, while the specialists in problem-solving go on to less critical problems for which they can find technical or political solutions. (Crowe)

INDEX